Resurrection

FAITH AND SCHOLARSHIP COLLOQUIES SERIES

The Dead Sea Scrolls and Christian Faith
Light in a Spotless Mirror
Resurrection

Resurrection

The Origin and Future of a Biblical Doctrine

James H. Charlesworth
with C. D. Elledge, J. L. Crenshaw,
H. Boers, and W. W. Willis Jr.

Faith and Scholarship Colloquies

t&t clark

NEW YORK • LONDON

T & T Clark International,
80 Maiden Lane, Suite 704, New York, NY 10038

T & T Clark International,
The Tower Building, 11 York Road, London SE1 7NX

T & T Clark International is a Continuum imprint.

Unless otherwise indicated, all translations are by the authors.

Cover art: Balassi, Mario. Transfiguration.
Scala / Art Resource, New York

Cover design: Wesley Hoke

Library of Congress Cataloging-in-Publication Data

Charlesworth, James H.
    Resurrection : the origin and future of a Biblical doctrine / James H.
Charlesworth; with C. D. Elledge ... [et al.].
        p.   cm. – (Faith and scholarship colloquies series)
    Includes bibliographical references and indexes.
    ISBN 0-567-02871-2 (hardcover : alk. paper)
    ISBN-10 0-567-02748-1 (paperback)
    ISBN-13 978-0-567-02748-1 (paperback)
    1. Resurrection. 2. Resurrection – Biblical teaching.   I. Elledge, C. D.
(Casey Deryl) II. Title.   III. Faith and scholarship colloquies.
BT482.C43 2006
236′8. – dc22
                                                                    2005025341

Printed in the United States of America

06   07   08   09   10   9   8   7   6   5   4   3   2   1

Dedicated to
Fuad and Terry Ashkar
Tom and Ann Cousins

And in memory of
Donald Juel

Contents

Preface

This book has taken many years to reach the present form. I am grateful to each of those who spoke at the symposium on resurrection at Florida Southern College in 1999. They have helped me improve and edit their own chapters. As many readers of this preface will know, moving a lecture to a publishable form takes time and concerted effort. I am pleased by the teamwork evident as this book took shape.

I am full of thanks, again, to those who made our stay in Lakeland so enjoyable and memorable, with special dinners and the final luncheon in the Lakeland Yacht Club. The saunters through the walkways and the sessions in the elegant buildings designed by Frank Lloyd Wright are now shrouded in fond memories of being accompanied by stunning art and pleasing vistas of Lake Hollingsworth. Descendants of the original orange trees that Wright replaced with architectural masterpieces still frame the white sculptured edifices. I am grateful to many who made our days in Lakeland, Florida, so relaxing and profitable, namely, Tom and Dottie Reuschling (former President and "first lady" of Florida Southern College), Frank and Daphne Johnson, Waite and Susan Willis, Alan and Dee Smith, Sarah and Rob Harding, Dan Silber, and Beverly Johnson (secretary of the department of religion and philosophy). I am also appreciative of the many interested ministers and laity who faithfully frequent the annual FSC, many coming from as far away as Canada. I do hope they will appreciate the present volume as they did the previous one, *Light in a Spotless Mirror: Reflections on Wisdom Traditions in Judaism and Early Christianity.*

I am indebted to Professor Casey Elledge for spending the summer of 2004 helping me edit these chapters. I am also pleased to work again with Henry Carrigan, who has served us all by helping move this book through T & T Clark.

JHC
Princeton
2004

Contributors

HENDRIKUS BOERS is Professor of New Testament Emeritus at Candler School of Theology, Emory University, Atlanta, Georgia.

JAMES H. CHARLESWORTH is the George L. Collord Professor of New Testament Languages and Literature at Princeton Theological Seminary in Princeton, New Jersey.

JAMES L. CRENSHAW is the Robert L. Flowers Professor of Old Testament at Duke University in Durham, North Carolina.

C. D. ELLEDGE is Assistant Professor of Religion at Gustavus Adolphus College in Saint Peter, Minnesota.

W. WAITE WILLIS JR. is Edward J. Pendergrass Professor of Religion and Chair of the Humanities Department at Florida Southern College, Lakeland, Florida.

Faith and Scholarship Colloquies

The Faith and Scholarship Colloquies (FSC) bring together explorers of ancient scriptures and cultures. An assessment of what has been seen in the past helps us better perceive our own time and even contemplate future vistas. We are not merely handling archaic artifacts; we are attempting to enliven by ancient truths.

The goal is to explore and open the boundaries where faith and academic study — the church and the academy — intersect. At these borders, the sharp edge of current biblical scholarship is allowed to cut theologically and pose its often challenging questions for traditional faith. In the process Christian theology is enlightened by bygone geniuses so that Christian living is grounded in reality and truth.

The series includes contributions from leading scholars in contemporary biblical studies. As we Christians seek to send a word on target in our day as powerful as those in the past, we may learn from those who did so previously in ancient Palestine (Jesus, Paul, and Origen), in North Africa (Augustine), in Germany (Luther), in Switzerland and Scotland (Calvin and Knox), in England and America (the Wesleys), and more recently in all lands by many men and women.

In this endeavor Christians need to sharpen their perceptions and proclamations, while moving from honest and truthful insights into human knowing, and from first-century archaeology to twenty-first century astronomy. Those who have endeavored to establish these symposia with me would concur that Christian faith must not be recast so that it is acceptable to the canons of logic and reason; but it also cannot degenerate into mindless myths. In the process our sacred traditions, confessions, and theological reflections may become purified, and indeed more real and deep to each of us.

The FSC contain the proceedings of the annual sessions at Florida Southern College. The series in this idyllic location, made famous by Frank Lloyd Wright's college campus above Lake Hollingsworth, is sponsored and endorsed by the president of the college and the members of the department of religion and philosophy. The FSC originated under the initiative of Hugh Anderson, Jack Cook (both now deceased), Walter Weaver, and myself.

JHC
Princeton

List of Abbreviations

General

ch./chs.	chapter/chapters
esp.	especially
ET	English translation
lit.	literally
NS	new series
olim	formerly
v./vv.	verse/verses

Ancient Writings

1 En.	*1 Enoch*
2 En.	*2 Enoch*
1QH^a	*Thanksgiving Hymns = Hodayot*
1QpHab	*Commentary on Habakkuk = Pesher Habakkuk*
1QS	*Rule of the Community*
1QS^b	*Rule of Blessings*
2 Bar.	*2 Baruch*
2 Esd.	2 Esdras (= *4 Ezra*)

4Q385–88, 391	*Pseudo-Ezekiel* [a–e]
4Q416	*Sapiential Work A*
4Q521	*On Resurrection,* or *Messianic Apocalypse*
4QMMT	*Some of the Works of the Torah = Miqsat Ma'aśe Ha-Torah*
11QPs[a]	*Psalms Scroll* from Qumran Cave 11, manuscript A
Ant.	Josephus, *Jewish Antiquities*
Antr. nymph.	Porphyry, *De antro nympharum*
Apoc. Ab.	*Apocalypse of Abraham*
Apoc. Mos.	*Apocalypse of Moses*
b. Sanhedrin	Babylonian Talmud *Sanhedrin*
Cels.	Origen, *Against Celsus*
Comm. Matt.	Origen, *Commentary on Matthew*
Dial.	Justin, *Dialogue with Trypho*
Gen. Rab.	*Genesis Rabbah*
Haer.	Hippolytus of Rome, *Refutation of All Heresies*
In remp.	Proclus, *In Platonis rem publicam commentarii,* 2 vols.
In Somn. Scip.	Macrobius, *Commentarii in Somnium Scipionis*
Lev. Rab.	*Leviticus Rabbah*
m. Sanh.	Mishnah *Sanhedrin*
Marc.	Seneca, *Ad Marciam de consolatione*
Od.	Homer, *Odyssey*
Op.	Hesiod, *Works and Days*
Pss. Sol.	*Psalms of Solomon*
Rep.	Cicero, *De republica*
Res.	Tertullian, *On the Resurrection of the Flesh*
	Athenagoras of Athens, *On the Resurrection*
Sacr.	Philo of Alexandria, *Sacrifices*
Testaments of the Twelve Patriarchs	
T. Ash.	*Testament of Asher*
T. Ben.	*Testament of Benjamin*
T. Dan	*Testament of Dan*
T. Gad	*Testament of Gad*

T. Iss.	*Testament of Issachar*
T. Jos.	*Testament of Joseph*
T. Jud.	*Testament of Judah*
T. Lev.	*Testament of Levi*
T. Naph.	*Testament of Naphtali*
T. Reu.	*Testament of Reuben*
T. Sim.	*Testament of Simeon*
T. Zeb.	*Testament of Zebulon*
War	Josephus, *Jewish War*

Contemporary Publications

AB	Anchor Bible
ABD	*Anchor Bible Dictionary.* Edited by D. N. Freedman. 6 vols. New York, 1992
ABRL	Anchor Bible Reference Library
AnBib	Analecta biblica
ANET	*Ancient Near Eastern Texts Relating to the Old Testament.* Edited by J. B. Pritchard. 3d ed. Princeton, 1969
ANRW	*Aufstieg und Niedergang der römischen Welt: Geschichte und Kultur Roms im Spiegel der neuer Forschung.* Edited by H. Temporini and W. Haase. Berlin, 1972–
BBB	*Bonner biblische Beiträge*
BibOr	Biblica et orientalia
BO	Bibliotheca orientalis
BZNW	Beihefte zur Zeitschrift für die neutestamentliche Wissenschaft
CBET	Contributions to Biblical Exegesis and Theology
CBQ	*Catholic Biblical Quarterly*
CBQMS	Catholic Biblical Quarterly Monograph Series
CRINT	Compendia rerum iudaicarum ad Novum Testamentum
CTM	*Concordia Theological Monthly*

DBSup	*Dictionnaire de la Bible: Supplément.* Edited by L. Pirot and A. Robert. Paris, 1928–
DJD	Discoveries in the Judaean Desert
ÉBib	*Études bibliques*
HAT	Handbuch zum Alten Testament
HibJ	*Hibbert Journal*
HNT	Handbuch zum Neuen Testament
HTR	*Harvard Theological Review*
HTS	Harvard Theological Studies
JAL	Jewish Apocryphal Literature
JANESCU	*Journal of the Ancient Near Eastern Society of Columbia University*
JBL	*Journal of Biblical Literature*
JJS	*Journal of Jewish Studies*
JPS	Jewish Publication Society
JQR	*Jewish Quarterly Review*
JSHRZ	Jüdische Schriften aus hellenistisch-römischer Zeit
JSOTSup	Journal for the Study of the Old Testament Supplement
JSS	*Journal of Semitic Studies*
NIB	*The New Interpreter's Bible*
NovT	*Novum Testamentum*
NRSV	New Revised Standard Version of the Bible
NTS	*New Testament Studies*
NTT	*Norsk Teologisk Tidsskrift*
OTP	*Old Testament Pseudepigrapha.* Edited by J. H. Charlesworth. 2 vols. New York, 1983–85
PTSDSSP	Princeton Theological Seminary Dead Sea Scrolls Project
PVTG	Pseudepigrapha Veteris Testamenti Graece
RevQ	*Revue de Qumran*
RSV	Revised Standard Version of the Bible
SBLDS	Society of Biblical Literature Dissertation Series

SBLMS	Society of Biblical Literature Monograph Series
SUNT	Studien zur Umwelt des Neuen Testament
SVTP	Studia in Veteris Testamenti Pseudepigraphica
TZ	*Theologische Zeitschrift*
VC	*Vigiliae christianae*
VT	*Vetus Testamentum*
VTSup	Supplements to Vetus Testamentum
WUNT	Wissenschaftliche Untersuchungen zum Neuen Testament
WZKM	*Wiener Zeitschrift für die Kunde des Morgenlandes*
ZAW	*Zeitschrift für die alttestamentliche Wissenschaft*

Chapter 1

Where Does the Concept of Resurrection Appear and How Do We Know That?

James H. Charlesworth

Scholars have disagreed on the places where the concept of resurrection appears in the Old Testament, the Dead Sea Scrolls, and the Jewish apocryphal literature. It is important, at the beginning of this book, to clarify the various meanings of "resurrection" in biblical and parabiblical literature. The biblical and apocryphal documents contain passages that are often ambiguous. How do we know that a passage contains the belief in the resurrection?[1]

How should we proceed to answer this question? We should not look for the concept of resurrection by isolating a word or a number of words, thinking that ideas can be conveyed by one word in isolation.[2] Such a concept does not reside in one word, as some scholars have assumed. Instead, we can detect the concept of resurrection only by exegetically examining a cluster of words in a particular context. It is startling to observe that few of the experts in Second

Temple Judaism who claim the Jewish documents contain a belief in the resurrection have presented a detailed exegesis of each passage purported to contain such a belief. This point leads us to clarify what concept is represented by the noun "resurrection."

Resurrection denotes the concept of God's raising the body and soul after death (meant literally) to a new and eternal life (not a return to mortal existence). This belief should not be confused with the Hellenistic concept of the immortality of the soul, which seems to be espoused in the Wisdom of Solomon (3:1–4:16). The concept of immortality is also what Josephus mistakenly thought the Essenes believed (*War* 2.154–158), perhaps because he was modifying their concept so that Romans could comprehend it.[3]

As we seek to discern the intention of a text, it is also good to contemplate the following main questions: (1) Is the text presenting us with an allegory or thinking allegorically?[4] (2) Are words like "dead" to be taken literally, or are they metaphors for physically or spiritually "weak" people?[5]

A preliminary attempt at a classification of the many dimensions of resurrection, and naming of the various categories of "resurrection," should include at least the following categories.[6]

Categories of "Resurrection"

1. Resurrection of the Nation

The raising of the nation Israel from disgrace or defeat has too often been confused as "resurrection" of mortals who have died. The locus classicus for the concept of the resurrection of the nation is found in Ezekiel's description of the dry bones. Recall these words from Ezek 37:

> The hand of the Lord came upon me. He took me out by the spirit of the Lord and set me down in the valley. It was full of bones. He led me all around them; there were very many

of them spread over the valley, and they were very dry. He said to me, "O mortal, can these bones live again?" I replied, "O Lord God, only You know." And He said to me, "Prophesy over these bones and say to them: O dry bones, hear the word of the Lord! Thus said the Lord God to these bones: I will cause breath to enter you and you shall live again. . . . " And He said to me, "O mortal, these bones are the whole House of Israel. They say, 'Our bones are dried up, our hope is gone; we are doomed.' Prophesy, therefore, and say to them: Thus said the Lord God: I am going to open your graves and lift you out of the graves, O My people, and bring you to the land of Israel."

(Ezek 37:1–12; JPS *Tanakh*)

For centuries, this passage was, and in many synagogues and churches today is, misinterpreted as referring to the resurrection of individuals to eternal life. Biblical scholars once concurred in assuming that this chapter presented evidence of a belief in the resurrection of the individual after death. Now, most scholars are convinced that the reference is to the rising of the nation Israel — "the whole House of Israel" — from its defeated status in world history. The same concept appears in Isa 26:19 and elsewhere (probably in the *Testaments of the Twelve Patriarchs, T. Jud.* 25:3–5; cf. also *T. Mos.* 10:7–10).

Some later readers of Ezek 37 interpreted the stunning imagery to refer to the resurrection of individuals after their deaths. This possible exegesis is proved by the discovery of a scroll found in Qumran Cave 4. Many centuries after the composition of Ezek 37, when more attention became focused on the individual as opposed to the nation, Jews interpreted this biblical text differently than the author had intended. The author of *Pseudo-Ezekiel* (4Q385 frg. 2) perceives "the bones" as belonging to "a large crowd of men" who "will rise and bless the Lord of Hosts who causes them to live."

2. Raising of a Group from Disenfranchisement

The Jews who lived at Qumran, on the northwestern shores of the Dead Sea, had been banished from the Temple (even though they claim to have left; cf. 4QMMT = 4Q394–399);

hence, some of the passages in the *Thanksgiving Hymns* (or *Hodayot* = 1QH) allude to this disenfranchisement and establishment at Qumran, to prepare the way of the Lord (interpreting Isa 40:3). It is possible that the Qumranites, or some of them, envisioned the day when they would be resurrected from this disenfranchisement and would again be in charge of the temple cult. Sometimes at Qumran it is evident that the *Yaḥad* (the Community) will arise out of its disenfranchisement because it is the "eternal planting." In particular, see this section of the *Thanksgiving Hymns:*

> You [have plant]ed a planting of cyprus, and elm,
>   with cedar together for your glory;
>   (these are) the trees of life hidden
>   among all the trees of the water
>   beside the mysterious water source.
> And they caused to sprout the shoot [*nēṣer*]
>   for the eternal planting.
>
> (1QHª 16.5–6)

The Qumranites are depicted, metaphorically, as "the trees of life" that are indeed God's "eternal planting."[7] Thus, they will rise up out of their present place of preparation in the wilderness.

3. Raising of the Individual from Social Disenfranchisement

Several passages in the *Thanksgiving Hymns* spring to mind to illustrate this category. An example is the autobiographical poem by the Righteous Teacher in 1QHª 16 (= olim 8), just cited. In this hymn the Righteous Teacher refers to himself as "the irrigator of the garden" and as the one "who causes to sprout the hol[y] shoot for the planting of truth."[8] He is "concealed" and without esteem, yet he praises the Lord for placing him in the desert "as an overflowing fountain," and as "a spring of water in a land of dryness."

   The Righteous Teacher had been one of the leading priests in Jerusalem; he may have served as the high priest. He was disenfranchised, but God chose him to prepare the eternal planting, and he will be vindicated (and perhaps some lines indicate reenfranchised in the Temple).[9] The Righteous Teacher appears to refer not to resurrection from the dead; he seems to imagine his disciples rising up out of disenfranchisement.

4. Raising of the Individual from Personal Embarrassment

This category is found in 1QH[a] 10 (= olim 2). The author is most likely the Righteous Teacher because of the claim that he is the one "to whom God made known all the mysteries of the words of his servants, the prophets" (1QpHab 7.4–5).[10] He states that he has been embarrassed, but God has removed him from such disgrace. Here are the major lines:

> And you made me an object of shame and derision for traitors. . . .
> But (then) you made me a banner for the elect of righteousness,
> And the interpreter of knowledge concerning marvelous mysteries,
>   to test [the men of] truth
>   and to try those who love instruction.
>
> (1QH[a] 10 [= olim 2].9–14)

The author celebrates how he has been elevated (resurrected) from an object of shame to the interpreter of knowledge. Though he adds subsequently that his enemies cast him down toward the pit, he has not died. He has been appointed — and in that sense elevated to — the incomparable interpreter by God. This category does not demand public or social "resurrection" to a place of honor.

5. Raising of the Individual from the Sickbed to Health

According to Mark 5:21–43 Jesus heals or "resurrects" from the dead Jairus's little daughter. The girl is clearly sick (5:23), and later the boisterous throng is convinced she is dead (5:40). Jesus announces she is not dead but "sleeping" (5:39).

Hence, according to this text, Jesus raises from near death someone who had been ill. Jesus commands her, " '*Talitha koum*,' which means, 'Little girl, I say to you, arise [*egeire*]' " (5:41). This category covers texts that contain the concept of one who is sick but is said to rise up from the sickbed (real or metaphorical). The implied author is not referring to one who is raised from the dead.

In the *Thanksgiving Hymns* are numerous expressions of similar meaning. Here, for example, is 1QH^a 17 (= olim 9).4–12:

> The breaking-waves of death [engulfed me],
> And on the couch of my bed Sheol uttered a mourning....
> But... you have not rejected me....
> In the face of the blows you have made my spirit stand up
> (or arise).

In Ps 132:3 "the couch of my bed" denotes the sickbed, and it is apparent that the poet who composed the lines just quoted from the *Thanksgiving Hymns* knew this psalm and employed the selfsame phrase with a similar meaning.

6. Raising of the Individual from Inactivity to Do God's Will

In *Qumran Studies*, Rabin argued that 1QH^a 14 (= olim 6).29–30 "definitely" spoke "about the rising of the dead."[11] More recently Puech, in a detailed and insightful study, claimed that this very passage is difficult to understand, especially because of the lacunae, which prohibit a study of the passage in a meaningful context.[12]

The passage probably does not portray a resurrection of the righteous from the dead. Here is my translation of the passage:

> And at the time of judgment God's sword shall hasten,
> And all his sons of tr[ut]h shall be awakened to [destroy]
> the sons of ungodliness.
> And all the sons of transgression shall be no more.
>   (1QH^a 14 [= olim 6].29–30)

In the following lines of the hymn is a reference to those "who lie in the dust" (14.34) — but surely, as L. R. Bailey points out, "dust" in Biblical Hebrew is often a euphemism for humility (cf. 1 Sam 2:8; Ps 44:25).[13] The passage in the *Thanksgiving Hymns* seems to predict the raising up of the righteous ones, probably the Holy Ones of the Community who are aligned with the Holy Ones in heaven (cf. the *Angelic Liturgy*), at the time of judgment, the end of time. The Qumranites have entered into the Community of the end time and are preparing for the final eschatological battle. As the *War Scroll* clarifies, this time is not postmortem. It inaugurates the final days and the judgment, after which comes the time of bliss, when there is no more evil and Belial (Satan) is defeated.

7. Raising of the Individual from Despondency Due to Consciousness of Sin

The following passage seems to be an example of this category:

> Near death was I for my sins,
> And my iniquities had sold me to Sheol:
> But you delivered me, O Lord.
> According to your great compassions,
> And according to your many righteous (deeds).
>
> (11QPsa 19.10–11)

The individual confesses he is near death due to his "sins." Using metaphorical language often employed in texts that depict life after death, the author is despondent on earth but praises the Lord for being delivered from death and out of Sheol. The author is probably not then referring to a postmortem resurrection. He is using metaphors to express his appreciation to the Lord for delivering him from going to Sheol because of his sins.

8. Raising of the Individual from Ignorance to Divinely Revealed Knowledge

In the *Thanksgiving Hymns* 19 is another passage that has been interpreted to refer to the resurrection of the dead. Rabin was convinced it was one of the passages that "definitely speak of the rising of the dead."[14] Here is the passage:

> that (you, O God) may raise up (*lĕhārîm*) the worms of the dead
>   from the dust to the secret [of your understanding],
>   and from a perverse spirit to [your] discernment;
>   and that he may be stationed before you,...
>   that he may be renewed with all that will be,
>   and with those who know in a joyful Community.
>   (1QHa 19 [= olim 11].12–14)

The poet has composed these lines according to *parallelismus membrorum*, which is synonymous. Thus "dust" is a euphemism for "perverse spirit," and the Qumranite is praising God for having been raised not to eternal life but to *divine knowledge*.[15]

9. Raising of the Individual from Meaninglessness in This World to a Realizing Eschatology (= Experiencing the End Time in the Present)

At Qumran, angels were present among humans during worship services, the future was breaking into the present, and heaven was not far off, but touching earth in the Community. When one became a full member of the Community, he moved into a new world full of meaning. He entered into an eternal Community. Thus, the dualism so explicit in the *Rule of the Community* (3.13–4.26) was breaking down, and "eternal life" was experienced in the present.[16] Thus, what was scripturally and traditionally preserved for resurrected Jews in a postmortem existence was now transferred to the Qumranites within the Community (the *Yaḥad*). Two examples of this category are 1QHa 11 (= olim 3).20 and the *Rule of Blessings* (1QSb) 5.23. In the *Thanksgiving Hymns* we find a praise to God for being raised up in life:

> I thank you, O God, for you have redeemed my soul from
> the pit;
> And from the Sheol of Abaddon.
> You have raised me up to an eternal height,
> So that I may walk about in uprightness without limit.
> And I know that there is hope for the one whom you have
> fashioned
> from dust for the eternal council.
>
> (1QH[a] 11 [= olim 3].19–21)[17]

After a careful study of the poetic form of this passage, it becomes clear that a doctrine of resurrection from the dead is not present.[18]

The issue in interpretation pertains to the meaning of "from the pit" and "from the Sheol of Abaddon." Do these prepositional phrases function as metaphors, or do they refer to the resurrection from the pit or Sheol of one who has died? We can be certain that the passage is not a metaphor only if there is a clear reference to death or to postmortem existence. There is none. Hence, I am convinced that 1QH[a] 11 (olim 3) does not present the idea of a resurrection from the dead, and that the author had no reason to need such a view, since he was living in the *Yaḥad*, in which "the eternal council" is an aspect of the Qumran organization of this Community. The Qumranite was thus already participating as one of the Holy Ones in the fruits of the end time (which were traditionally reserved for the postmortem righteous ones).

10. Both-And: The Author May Intentionally Collapse Any Distinction between the Present Age and the Future Age

This category is especially evident within two communities: the Qumran Community and the Johannine Community. This meaning may be found in the *Rule of the Community* (1QS 4.6–8). The "Sons of Truth" will receive (when is not specified) "healing and great peace in a long life, multiplication of progeny together with all everlasting blessings" (presumably in the present life), as well as "endless joy in everlasting

life [or 'perpetual life'], and a crown of glory together with
a resplendent attire in eternal light" (in the present and the
future, but not necessarily after death).

11. Raising of Christ from Sheol (*descensus ad inferos*)

Obviously, the belief that Christ descended and then as-
cended from Sheol should not be confused with a belief in
the resurrection from the dead. A belief in the *descensus ad
inferos* seems to be found in the *Odes of Solomon:*

> Sheol saw me and was shattered,
> And Death ejected me and many with me.
> (Ode 42:11)

As I understand this passage, the Odist constructed his
poetry *ex ore Christi* so that the words are Christ's. The Odist
then is referring to Christ's descent into and *ascent* out of
Hades (*descensus ad inferos*). The speaker is Christ, who did
not die ("I did not perish," 42:10). He is the one who frees
those captured in Sheol ("And I made a congregation of living among his dead," 42:14). Hence, the Ode does not refer
to postmortem resurrection; it is a resurrection out of Hades
by the living Christ.

12. Raising an Apocalyptist into Heaven

It should now be abundantly clear that the expression "the
raising up of the righteous ones" may not represent a belief
in resurrection from the dead. The expression and concept
is frequently used in antiquity to articulate the raising of an
apocalyptist from earth into one of the heavens.

Sometimes this "raising up" is in a dream, and sometimes
the expression denotes the physical ascent of an individual.
According to the author of *1 En.* 14, Enoch states in first-
person discourse that "they were calling me in a vision"
(14:8). According to the author of *2 Enoch,* in contrast, Enoch
awakes from his sleep and is taken by two huge men who

had stood by his bed. The men inform Enoch that he "will ascend with us to heaven today" (*2 En.* 1:8). Paul, as is well known, could not discern whether his ascent into the third heaven and into Paradise (cf. *2 En.* 8) was in the body or out of the body, as in a dream (2 Cor 12:1–3).

A well-known passage of raising up into the heavens is found in Rev 4:1. The Seer John sees "in heaven an open door." He is told, "Come up hither." He then ascends into heaven and sees God's throne room. Such references to raising up should not be confused with the raising of one who has died, to eternal life.

13. A Spiritual Rising Up or Awakening of an Individual

The concept of "resurrection" was applied in antiquity to one who was asleep, as if dead, and arose spiritually. The classic example of this category is found in Ephesians, as in this exhortation:

> Arise [*egeire*], O sleeper, and rise up [*anasta*]
> from those who are dead,
> And Christ shall give you light. (Eph 5:14)

Such enlightened, "resurrected," persons then live an upright life in which they are "imitators of God" (5:1). The awakened person becomes one of the "children of light" (5:8) and disassociates from the "sons of disobedience" (5:7): "those who are dead."

14. Raising of the Individual from Death to Mortal Life

We now come to examples of the concept of resurrection from apparent postmortem existence to life again on earth. Numerous examples of this category are found in the Bible. Resurrection stories are associated with both Elijah and Elisha (1 Kgs 17:17–24; 2 Kgs 4:31–37; 13:20–21). The person raised from the dead returns to the earth, presumably to die again. These passages are not only "resurrection stories";

they are also accounts of healing miracles, probably circulated to substantiate the belief that Yahweh, and not Baal, controls human destiny. There is no defeat of death in these pericopes.[19]

According to the evangelists, Jesus raised people from the dead. The most detailed and stunning example is the raising of Lazarus after several days (John 11). These individuals were not raised to eternal life. Resurrection from the dead (or perhaps a catatonic trance) to mortal life should not be confused with the following category, resurrection from the dead to immortality.

15. Raising of the Individual from Death to Eternal Life

We finally come to the concept that is the classic resurrection belief. In its full form, the implied author presents the belief in the resurrection of the person, in the body (though maybe in a spiritual body, but nevertheless in a body), at some future day (perhaps the age to come), with some continuity between the person who lived, died, and was raised again by God (perhaps through some mediator, like the Messiah), to everlasting life. Sometimes this resurrection is to life again *on the earth* (as in the *Testaments of the Twelve Patriarchs*) or perhaps in one of the heavens, as an angel (which is a conceivable interpretation of Dan 12:2); usually, the Jew and "Christian" did not specify the place (cf. *History of the Rechabites*).

The only undisputed passage in the Old Testament of category 15 (though not in the "full form") is found in Daniel, a document that reached its present form sometime before 164 BCE. Here is the key verse: "Many of those who sleep in the dust of the earth shall awake [*yāqîṣû*], some to everlasting life, and some to shame and everlasting contempt" (12:2 NRSV).[20] This verse presents what is necessary for an undisputed reference to resurrection from the dead: a clarification that those to be raised are literally dead ("those who sleep in the dust of the earth"), a mention of resurrection ("they shall awake"), and a resurrection of these people not to mortality but to "everlasting life."

Dan 12:2–3 may denote a resurrection of the righteous into heaven. Those who are raised to "eternal life" are the *Maśkilîm* (the wise), who will be radiant "like the bright expanse of the sky." These seem to be identical to "those who lead the many to righteousness" who "will be like the stars forever." Does each "like" specify "where" or "how" those raised will have postmortem eternal life? The author of Daniel seems to indicate the "how," but some of his later readers may have thought about an existence in the heavens, since in some apocalypses the stars are angels (cf. esp. *1 En.* 90:21; cf. 18:15: "And the stars . . . are the ones which have transgressed the commandments of God").

The earliest evidence of this category in Early Judaism is found in *1 En.* 22–27, which antedates 200 BCE.[21] Note especially that according to 1 En 22:13–14 the "souls" of the unrighteous "on the day of judgment . . . will not rise from there" (*OTP* 1.25). The author of the *Epistle of Enoch* (= *1 En.* 92–105), which dates from the early decades of the second century BCE, seems to portray the wicked and righteous at a future time of judgment, perhaps after a (or the) resurrection. The text seems to imply the eschatological rewards of the righteous; for example, in the future judgment day "all the righteous," which seems to include those who are dead, "shall rejoice" (104:13).[22]

The concept of a postmortem resurrection of the body is abundantly evident in the books of the Maccabees. According to the author of 2 Macc 14, Razis tore out his entrails, hurled them at his tormentors, Nicanor's soldiers, and called on the Lord of life and spirit to give them again back to him (14:46). The *Testament of Judah* promises that "after these things,[23] Abraham, Isaac, and Jacob will arise to life" (25.1). Not only the patriarchs but also *some* of the righteous shall arise: "And those who died in grief shall arise in joy. . . . And those who died on account of the Lord shall be aroused to life" (25:4).[24]

Thanks to the recent publication of fragments of scrolls available since the 1950s, it is now clear that a hope and belief in an afterlife and postmortem resurrection is explicit in some scrolls found in the Qumran caves. The claim that no passage in the Dead Sea Scrolls refers to the belief in a resurrection after death is now disproved by the publication of some fragments that clearly refer to this belief.

Resurrection beliefs should be expected at Qumran since the Qumranites knew Daniel and the books of *Enoch;* and these documents clearly contain the belief in a resurrection of the individual after death. Thus, disproved is the claim that the sectarian Dead Sea Scrolls — those scrolls composed or significantly edited at Qumran — cannot be Essene documents because they do not preserve the belief in such a resurrection.[25]

A scroll called *On Resurrection* was found in Qumran Cave 4 (4Q521). This text is so important for our study of resurrection beliefs in early Judaism that it is imperative for readers to have handy a translation of lines 1–12:[26]

1 [For the hea]vens and the earth shall obey his Messiah

2 [th]at (is) in them. He will not turn back from the commandments of the Holy Ones.

3 Persist, (all)[27] you who seek the Lord, in his service.

4 Will you not find the Lord in this, all who wait (for him with hope) in their hearts?

5 Surely the Lord shall seek the pious ones, and shall call the righteous ones by name.

6 And over the Poor Ones his spirit will hover. And (to) those believing in his might he will renew (their strength).

7 [. . .] he will glorify the pious ones with the crown of the eternal kingdom.

8 He shall liberate the captives, open the eyes of the blind ones, (and) straighten those be[nt over].

9 And for[ev]er I will hold fast . . .

10 . . . The Holy One will not linger [to come].

11 And the glorious things which are not the work of the Lord,
     when he shall [come].

12 [For] he shall heal the slain ones, and bring life (*yĕḥayeh*) (to)
     the dead ones (*ûmētîm*), (and) bear joyful news (to) the
     Poor Ones.

This is an obvious reference to the resurrection of the dead. What is clear in *On Resurrection* is the presence of a belief in the resurrection of the dead; what has been disputed is the means and actor. It seems clear, though, that God, either directly or through his Messiah, will raise up, "bring life," to those who are dead.

According to rabbinic traditions, the early rabbis taught belief in the resurrection of the dead. In the *Amidah* (*Eighteen Benedictions*), the first benediction celebrates the awesomeness of the God of Abraham, Isaac, and Jacob; then comes the second benediction. Twice in this second benediction, following with repetition the affirmation of God's power, the congregation in the synagogue liturgically utters the shared belief that God, because he is mighty, will raise up the dead:

> Mighty Thou art — humbling the haughty,
> Powerful — calling to judgment the arrogant,
> Eternal — preserving the dead;
> Causing the wind to blow and the dew to fall,
> Sustaining the living, resurrecting the dead (*mĕḥayeh hamētîm*),
> O, cause our salvation to sprout in the twinkling of an eye!
> Blessed art thou, O Lord, who resurrects the dead (*mĕḥayeh hamētîm*).[28]

This liturgical formula most likely antedates 70 CE, since the *Amidah* in basic content, order, and number, though not in wording, was set before the fall of Jerusalem in 70 CE.[29] Most likely, in synagogues and the temple, Pharisees and other Jews chanted the second benediction, perhaps in a form similar to the old Palestinian rite quoted above. It is also likely that Paul was familiar with a similar form of the *Amidah*.

According to the compilers of the Mishnah, anyone who claims there is no resurrection of the dead, like the one who denies the Torah is from heaven, is to be counted among

those who have no place in the age to come. The Hebrew for
"resurrection from the dead" is *tĕḥîyat hamētîm* (*m. Sanh.* 10).
According to Rabbi Phineas ben Jair, saintliness leads to the
reception of the Holy Spirit, and then "to the resurrection of
the dead" ([bis] *tĕḥîyat hamētîm*), which shall come "through
Elijah" (*m. Soṭah* 15). In the three instances of "resurrection of
the dead" in the Mishnah, the verbal root chosen is the same
as that in the *Amidah: ḥyh* (or *ḥyy*), "live."

The passages in the Mishnah are too late (post-second century CE) to be quoted as examples of Jewish beliefs prior to
70 CE. In addition, *Sanhedrin* is polemical — directed against
those who deny the belief in the resurrection of the dead.
Mishnah *Sanhedrin*, therefore, cannot be quoted as typical of
pre-70 Jewish belief. It is conceivable, nevertheless, that the
tradition in Mishnah *Sanhedrin* defined the belief of some pre-
70 Pharisees who believed in the resurrection of the dead and
rejected the Sadducees, who allegedly denied this belief (cf.
Acts 23:8).

Category 15 frequently defines the New Testament documents. For example, we find the belief attributed to Peter at
Pentecost:

> "Men of Israel, hear these words, Jesus of Nazareth . . . delivered
> up according to the definite plan and foreknowledge of God
> . . . God raised him up [*anestēsen*], having loosed the pangs of
> death, because it was not possible for him to be held by it."
> (Acts 2:22–24 RSV)

Obviously, Paul's theology should be mentioned under category 15. Paul stressed that the resurrection of Jesus Christ
guaranteed that those who believed in Jesus as the Christ and
Son of God would also be raised (cf. esp. 1 Cor 15). One of the
most memorable and earliest passages of this belief in Paul's
letters is 1 Thess 4:15–17:

> For this we say to you by the word of the Lord, that we who are
> alive, who are left until the coming of the Lord, shall not precede
> those who have fallen asleep. For the Lord himself shall descend
> from heaven with a cry of command, with the archangel's call,
> and with the sound of the trumpet of God. And the dead in

Christ shall rise [*anastēsontai*] first; then we who are alive, who are left, shall be caught up together with them in the clouds to meet the Lord in the air; and so we shall always be with the Lord.

This passage introduces us to another possible category: resurrection to immortal life from life on earth, without any need for any death. It is clear that when Paul wrote these words, he assumed he would still be alive when the risen Christ returned to earth.

16. Intentional Ambiguity

This category denotes passages in which the author seems to tend toward intentional ambiguity. The implied author obviously does not know what will occur in the future in this life and after death. The author then seems to have intentionally couched his belief in considerable ambiguity.

This final category is required by early Jewish theology. For example, only God knows what will happen in the future, and only God knows and will announce who is the Messiah. The sixteenth category also helps us grasp the reason for such disparity in exegetical opinions. The examples are abundant and may even apply to some of the passages previously interpreted otherwise. It is unwise to portray texts that are ambiguous as if they are clear.

Summary

Some of the sixteen categories overlap. Yet, while double entendre was an aspect of poetry in antiquity, especially in Semitics, some of the above categories are mutually exclusive.

Caveats and Conclusion

Sometimes it is impossible to be certain which of these categories was intended by a text. Thus, it is imperative to perceive the wide range of meanings of "a resurrection" an author may have meant to communicate to his readers — especially a Jewish author prior to Bar Kokhba in the early second century CE (including especially the Jewish authors of Daniel and 1 Corinthians). Previous research on the concept of "resurrection" and an exegesis of the passages mentioned previously, and others, were not sufficiently nuanced by a perception of the sixteen categories that we have seen should be considered for discussion. In past discussions of resurrection in Early Judaism and in Christian origins, the full range of options was seldom considered, and one biased opinion was often forced on complex passages.

The varieties and differing taxonomies of resurrection beliefs represent not a system but an expression of the common human hope that God has the last word, and the future of the righteous will be blessed. One articulation of this hope is the differing beliefs that death is not the end, that the faithful will enjoy a resurrection by God into an eternal and blessed existence.

What an implied author meant to communicate to a particular person or group did not restrict what a reader might interpret a passage to denote. For example, Psalm 30 may not originally have included resurrection belief, but after the middle of the second century BCE and the use of Daniel and *1 Enoch,* some Jews clearly would have seen resurrection belief in the following verses:

> I extol You, O Lord,
>> For You have lifted me up [דליתני],
>> And not let my enemies rejoice over me.
> O Lord, my God,
>> I cried out to You,
>> And You healed me.
> O Lord, You brought me up from Sheol,
>> Preserved me from going down into the Pit.
>> (Ps 30:2–4 *Tanakh*)

>> O LORD my God, I cried to you for help,
>> and you have healed me.

O LORD, you brought up my soul from Sheol,
restored me to life from among those gone down to the Pit.

(Ps 30:2–3 NRSV)

Thus, while an Israelite composed a psalm to thank God most likely for healing from a grave illness, a Jew, centuries later, might have understood the metaphorical words literally. The praise then would reflect a belief in resurrection from Sheol to a postmortem existence, not on earth as experienced now, but in the age to come. We cannot ever be certain, since there is no pesher on Psalm 30, and we have no way to interview Jews chanting Psalm 30 in the Temple.

Notes

1. The present chapter is a popular and abbreviated version of "Prolegomenous Reflections Towards a Taxonomy of Resurrection Texts," in *The Changing Face of Judaism, Christianity, and Other Grec-Roman Religions in Antiquity* (ed. I. Henderson and G. Oegema; Gütersloh: Gütersloher Verlagshaus GmbH, 2006). See also the studies in P. Benoit and R. Murphy, eds., *Immortality and Resurrection* (New York: Herder & Herder, 1970). Also, see J. H. Charlesworth, "Résurrection individuelle et immortalité de l'âme," in *Histoire du Christianisme: Des origines à nos jours* (ed. J.-M. Mayeur et al.; Paris: Desclée, 2001), 14:505–51.

2. One word almost never appears in isolation in oral speech. It is usually accompanied by a context: inflexion and bodily gesture as well as mood, all of which are accompanied by setting, time, and previous and following words or actions. In short, ostensibly isolated words enter our lives and have meaning because of our history (previous, contextual, and anticipated sounds and actions).

3. See the recent and insightful discussion by N. T. Wright, *The Resurrection of the Son of God* (Minneapolis: Fortress, 2003), 175–81. Also see Elledge's contribution to the present volume (ch. 2).

4. Vermes rightly suggests that 1QH^a 6.34–35 (= now col. 14) and 11.10–14 (now col. 19) "may connote bodily resurrection," but they also "may just be allegorical." *The Complete Dead Sea Scrolls in English* (4th ed; New York: Penguin, 1988), 88–89.

5. Ringgren thinks that the dead in 1QH^a 19 (= olim 11).12 denote "weak insignificant men." *The Faith of Qumran: Theology of the Dead Sea Scrolls* (ed. J. H. Charlesworth; New York: Crossroad, 1995), 148.

6. For a succinct discussion of resurrection beliefs in the Bible and some early Jewish texts, see the two consecutive articles by R. T. Prendergast (trans. R. Martin-Achard) and Nickelsburg, "Resurrection," *ABD* 5:680–91.

7. See J. H. Charlesworth, "An Allegorical and Autobiographical Poem by the *Moreh haṣ-Ṣedeq* (1QH 8:4–11), in *"Sha'arei Talmon": Studies in the Bible, Qumran, and the Ancient Near East Presented to Shemaryahu Talmon* (ed. M. Fishbane, E. Tov, with W. W. Fields; Winona Lake, IN: Eisenbrauns, 1992), 295–307.

8. See esp. G. Jeremias, *Der Lehrer der Gerechtigkeit* (SUNT 2; Göttingen: Vandenhoeck & Ruprecht, 1963), 249–64.

9. See Charlesworth, "An Allegorical and Autobiographical Poem," 295–307.

10. For the Hebrew and translation of the pesharim, see M. P. Horgan in *Pesharim, Other Commentaries, and Related Documents* (ed. J. H. Charlesworth; PTSDSSP 6B; Tübingen: Mohr Siebeck, 2002). Also, see A. Dupont-Sommer, *Les écrits esséniens découverts près de la mer Morte* (8th ed.; Paris: Payot, 1980), 221n1; and G. Jeremias, *Der Lehrer Gerechtigkeit,* 192–201.

11. C. Rabin, *Qumran Studies* (London: Oxford University Press, 1957), 73.

12. This comment seems odd. Lines 29 and following of this column in 1QHª are in a section of the *Hymns* that is better preserved than most. I have benefited from the photographs in the Princeton Theological Seminary Dead Sea Scrolls Laboratory.

13. L. R. Bailey, *Biblical Perspectives on Death* (Overtures to Biblical Theology; Philadelphia: Fortress, 1979), 85.

14. Rabin, *Qumran Studies,* 73.

15. Nickelsburg rightly states that, according to 1QHª 20 (=olim 12) "man is raised not to eternal life as such, but to divine knowledge." *Resurrection, Immortality, and Eternal Life in Intertestamental Judaism* (HTS 26; Cambridge: Harvard University Press, 1972), 155.

16. H.-W. Kuhn, *Enderwartung und gegenwärtiges Heil: Untersuchungen zu den Gemeindeliedern von Qumran mit einem Anhang über Eschatologie und Gegenwart in der Verkündigung Jesu* (Göttingen: Vandenhoeck & Ruprecht, 1966).

17. Translation mine.

18. B. P. Kittel, *The Hymns of Qumran: Translation and Commentary* (SBLDS 50; Chico, CA: Scholars Press, 1975), 80.

19. See the insights of Prendergast in *ABD* 5:681.

20. See the judicious insights of Prendergast in *ABD* 5:682–83.

21. See the comments by Nickelsburg in *ABD* 5:685.

22. M. A. Knibb thinks that the Aramaic of Qumran's "שמחון] ap-
pears to belong here" in the text; see Knibb, *The Ethiopic Book of Enoch:
A New Edition in the Light of the Aramaic Dead Sea Fragments* (Oxford:
Clarendon, 1978), 2:243, first note.

23. For the Greek see M. de Jonge, ed., *The Testaments of the Twelve
Patriarchs: A Critical Edition of the Greek Text* (PVTG 1.2; Leiden: Brill,
1978), 77–78.

24. Translations mine. For the full translation, see H. C. Kee, "Tes-
taments of the Twelve Patriarchs," in *OTP* 1:775–828; and M. J. de
Jonge, "The Testaments of the Twelve Patriarchs," in *The Apocryphal
Old Testament* (ed. H. F. D. Sparks; Oxford: Clarendon, 1984), 505–600.

25. R. B. Laurin claimed that the *Hodayot* cannot be attributed to
the Essenes because they do not contain a belief in the immortality
of the soul or the body. Laurin, "The Question of Immortality in the
Qumran Hodayot," *JSS* 3 (1958): 344–55.

26. I wish to thank the Israel Antiquities Authority for allowing
me to study 4Q521 and for clear photographs of all fragments.

27. The verbs are plural, so I have added "all." This reconstruction
is supported by the *kôl* (e.g., "all") in line 4.

28. For Hebrew text, see S. Schechter, "Geniza Fragments," *JQR* Old
Series 10 (1898): 656–57. My rendering is based on the translation
of J. Heinemann, *Prayer in the Talmud* (Studia Judaica 9; Berlin: de
Gruyter, 1977), 26–27.

29. See Heinemann, *Prayer in the Talmud,* 26.

Chapter 2

Resurrection of the Dead: Exploring Our Earliest Evidence Today

C. D. Elledge

Scholars now have more information than ever before about the origins and development of one of the most shocking claims in the history of religions: God supernaturally raises dead bodies from the grave and restores them to life again. At least two factors have contributed to our recent increase in knowledge on this important topic. First, increased study of the Old Testament Apocrypha and Pseudepigrapha over the last thirty years has gradually broadened our understanding of what writings like 2 Maccabees, *1 Enoch,* the *Psalms of Solomon,* and other writings can teach us about ancient resurrection hope.[1] Second, exciting new documents mentioning the resurrection have also been dramatically revealed among the Dead Sea Scrolls and fully published only within the last decade.[2] Furthermore, epigraphy and archaeology have also broadened our understandings of ancient burial practices and the various epitaphs with which Jews living in Hellenistic and Roman times inscribed the graves of the deceased.[3]

The promise of academic study in these fields is an unprecedented knowledge of early Jewish resurrection hope, prior to the origins of the Jesus movement and Christianity. This knowledge gives us greater sensitivity and meaning for appreciating the early Christian proclamation that God had raised the Messiah from the dead and would soon awaken all the dead to new life at the culmination of history. Understanding our earliest evidence for the resurrection hope also allows us a much broader range of vision into a belief that currently remains shared among the three great world faiths in the West. Throughout this book, we return to our earliest evidence for ancient belief in the resurrection and explore what the resurrection hope originally meant to those who held steadfastly to it, amid the tumultuous historical crises of Hellenistic and Roman times. The present chapter provides an introductory survey of some of our most interesting evidence for early beliefs about the resurrection and concludes with some reflections on how these materials help us better appreciate the resurrection theology of the apostle Paul and his successors.

Definitions and Clarifications

Before discussing our earliest evidence for the resurrection, a few qualifications and caveats are necessary. As a brief survey of popular literature on "life after death" will reveal, ideas about what happens to us after we die can range far and wide.[4] This was so in ancient times, just as it is today. In the present study, however, we are concerned only with ancient beliefs about resurrection of the dead. For this reason, we must exclude a number of related concerns that might otherwise distract us from our true goal.

First, the term "resurrection" as used in this survey will not refer to "dying and rising deities," like Adonis or Osiris,

well known from a number of mythological systems and
made forever popular in Sir James George Frazer's classic *The
Golden Bough: A Study in Magic and Religion*.[5] Such mythological traditions have undoubtedly influenced the history and
theology of Early Christianity.[6] Our earliest traditions about
the resurrection, however, are concerned with the deaths of
real human beings, not deities.

Second, the term "resurrection" implies more than simply
belief in immortality of the soul or life in paradise. These
ways of describing the afterlife, abundantly common in
early Judaism and Christianity, may accompany resurrection
hope. To qualify as a resurrection, however, something must
happen to the lifeless body of one who has died.

Finally, in order to appreciate our earliest expressions of
resurrection hope, we must not expect that these beliefs
always conform to a systematic and complete vision of theology. The sayings of the Jewish poet Pseudo-Phocylides,
for example, contain references to resurrection, immortality,
and divinization, without a full explanation of how these all
fit together.[7] Our earliest evidence for the resurrection hope
is often fragmentary, incomplete, occasionally inconsistent.
Nevertheless, our evidence displays the fervor and dynamism
of an emerging hope that has not yet fossilized into more
static systems of theology.

Such conservative definitions will keep our feet on the
ground; otherwise, we might float aimlessly into forbidden
realms of the afterlife and never return to the current topic.
The taxonomy proposed by James H. Charlesworth in the
current volume (ch. 1) helps us appreciate with greater precision how the resurrection hope was distinctive from other
available visions of the afterlife in ancient times.

Our Earliest Biblical Evidence?

Scholars today remain divided as to our earliest biblical evidence for resurrection of the dead. If there is a consensus

on this question, it is that Dan 12:1–3, composed sometime during the Maccabean Revolt (167 — 164 BCE), provides our earliest definitive literary evidence for resurrection in the Old Testament (Hebrew Bible).[8] Others, however, have suggested that certain passages that antedate Daniel already preserve evidence for belief in the resurrection.[9]

One intriguing passage originates from a section of the book of Isaiah often called the "Isaianic Apocalypse," chapters 24–27. Although its precise date remains unknown, most proposals situate its origins before the composition of Daniel. At least two passages of this work have been cited as evidence of the resurrection hope:

> Your dead shall live, their [or "my"] corpses shall rise.
> O dwellers in the dust, awake and sing for joy!
> For your dew is a dew of lights,
> And the earth shall bring forth the shades. (26:19)

Elsewhere in these chapters we read that God "will swallow up death forever" (25:8) — a passage that the apostle Paul understood in terms of the resurrection (1 Cor 15:54). The highly poetic and mythological language of these chapters, however, raises questions about whether or not their author is really describing a resurrection of the dead here. We may simply be reading an exultant piece of poetic literature, which hails the future glory of the people of Israel.

Another pre-Danielic text that has often been cited as a resurrection prophecy is Ezekiel's vision of the valley of dry bones (Ezek 37). This prophetic vision graphically describes an army of human bodies being reconstituted, bone by bone, and sinew by sinew; it was widely regarded in antiquity as a portrayal of the future resurrection of the dead. At least one Dead Sea Scroll was of this opinion, as we shall see. Even the perennially opposed houses of Hillel and Shammai could agree that this was a resurrection prophecy (*Gen. Rab.* 14.5; *Lev. Rab.* 14.9), as did the *Lives of the Prophets* (3.11–12), a biographical work of the late first century CE. Tertullian provides an excellent example of similar readings from an early Christian apologist (*Res.* 29–30). Ezekiel's point in this remarkable chapter, however, is not that there will be a future resurrection of the dead — but rather, that God will restore the exiles to political nationhood in their own land. They will pass, not literally from death to life, but from the national extinction of the exile to a glorious political restoration. Both Isa 24–27 and Ezek 37, thus, resemble Charlesworth's type 1, rather than 15 (see ch. 1).

We are, therefore, more judicious to turn to Dan 12:1–3 as our earliest definitive literary evidence for the resurrection hope in the Bible. As James Crenshaw suggests in his own contribution to this volume (ch. 3), these texts from Isaiah and Ezekiel clearly illustrate the Hebrew Scriptures' claim that Yahweh possesses supreme power over life and death, including the life and death of the political nation of Israel. We have also indicated that future generations of ancient readers would often look back to these texts as resurrection prophecies. When searching the Scriptures for our earliest definitive evidence for belief in a literal resurrection of the dead, however, we are on surer ground when we turn to the book of Daniel.

Daniel

The concluding chapters of the book of Daniel (Dan 7–12) recount the sage's apocalyptic dream visions about the rise and fall of the great world empires. These visions were probably composed during the violent political and religious upheavals of the Maccabean Revolt (167–164 BCE), when Antiochus IV Epiphanes and his supporters within Judaism attempted to Hellenize Jewish life with unprecedented aggression.[10] In chapters 11 and 12, Daniel reports what an angelic messenger discloses to him about the future (10:9–11:1). After a period of cosmic unrest inspired by the notorious Greek king Antiochus (11:21–45), this evil enemy of the Jewish people will finally come to his end; and Michael, the archangelic prince, will arise and spare all the righteous whose names are found written in the heavenly book (12:1). At this point the prophecy of a future resurrection emerges:

> And many of those who sleep in the land of dust[11] shall awaken:
> Some to everlasting life,
> and others to everlasting reproach and derision.
> But those who instruct in wisdom shall shine
>   like the shining of the firmament.
> And those who turn the multitudes to righteousness,
>   like the stars forever and ever. (Dan 12:2–3)

This brief passage is by no means a treatise on the resurrection. Nevertheless, its basic assumptions clearly imply that dead bodies sleeping in the dust of the earth shall be awakened in the future by divine power.

Who will be raised in this passage? It may surprise us to find that a partial, not a universal, resurrection seems to be envisioned.[12] "Many" but not all who sleep shall awaken.[13] This partial resurrection addresses, specifically, those who have fallen in the recent tumults of the Maccabean crisis.[14] Two groups are directly mentioned as those who will be raised to "everlasting life": first, "those who instruct in wisdom"; and second, "those who turn the multitudes to righteousness." The two groups are the same people who have recently fallen while trying to resist the rule of Antiochus and his supporters, as an earlier prophecy describes (11:31–35).[15] These wise teachers probably represent the same groups of conservative sages and scribes who resisted Antiochus's Hellenizing program in Judea and who shaped the book of Daniel itself. For the author of Daniel, God would not allow the enemies of these righteous sages to have the final word over their lives; they would, instead, awaken from the dust into resurrection life.

To what shall the dead be raised? An almost formulaic statement declares the divided fates of those who awaken: some to everlasting life, others to everlasting reproach. The formulaic nature of this expression implies that it declares

in abbreviated form a belief that had already enjoyed an extended prehistory in the author's historical context.[16] The
author of Daniel, therefore, did not invent the resurrection
hope. Perhaps, as Charlesworth suggests in the current volume, the author of *1 En.* 22–27 (c. 200 BCE) may already have
believed in some form of resurrection prior to Daniel; yet it
should be recognized that Daniel is far clearer on this matter
than its Enochic predecessor. For the righteous, Daniel envisions the future life as a resurrection into everlasting life;
but for the wicked, the resurrection will lead to everlasting
"reproach and derision." It is likely that this last expression
stands for some unnamed punishment or retribution beyond
the grave. By including the fate of the wicked, the author reveals his concern that justice be secured for both the just and
the unjust in the world to come.

What shall the resurrected existence be like? Our author
does not provide a treatise on the resurrection body. Nevertheless, a few details of the apocalyptist's visionary imagery
may suggest that he viewed the resurrected existence as
a transformation of the deceased body. The righteous will
"shine forth" like the heavenly bodies of the firmament in
an existence that has been supernaturally transformed into
a new state. Where will the resurrection life exist? Although
a transformed existence upon the earth cannot be ruled out
completely, our author probably understood the resurrection
as an exaltation into the heavenly world, where the righteous
would literally be immortalized "like the stars." This "astral
immortalization," for the author of Daniel, may also have implied a transformation into angelic existence, since elsewhere
in the book he understands angelic beings dwelling among
the stars (8:10). Immortalization into astral beings was a popular belief in Greek and Roman philosophy and mythology;[17]
and Daniel may well have understood the resurrection of the
dead in similar terms — as a supernatural transformation of
the deceased body into a new and starlike existence in the
heavenly world. Other early Jewish traditions that envision
life after death as a translation into astral existence include

the *Similitudes of Enoch* (=*1 En.*) 58.2–3; the *Pss. of Sol.* 3.12; 2 Esd. 7.97; and *2 Baruch*. Nowhere does Daniel suggest that the resurrection is simply a restoration of the same old, tired body one had before death.

2 Maccabees

A second group of writings that emerged from the Maccabean crisis is presented in the histories of 1, 2, and 4 *Maccabees*. These writings, though quite different from one another, commonly heroize the exploits of those who remained faithful to the laws during the rampages of Antiochus IV and his Hellenizing supporters within Judaism. Among these histories, 2 Maccabees goes out of its way to accentuate its pious adherence to the resurrection hope.[18] Apocalyptic writers, like the author of Daniel, were thus not alone in their hope in the resurrection; historiographers, too, could appeal to this hope as they tried to make meaning of the tumultuous course of Jewish history. Although there have been multiple proposals for its date,[19] reasonable consensus suggests that 2 Maccabees was composed before the Romans took Palestine in 63 BCE.

The author of this work tells us the story of seven brothers who were martyred by the Greeks during the Maccabean revolt, because of their refusal to eat foods prohibited by the Torah. Six times in 2 Maccabees 7, which Collins has called "the centerpiece" of the entire book,[20] the martyrs openly proclaim their faith in a future resurrection of the righteous (7:9, 11, 14, 23, 29, 36).[21] The brothers are all killed in a series of grotesque physical mutilations:

> The king fell into a rage, and gave orders to have pans and caldrons heated. These were heated immediately, and he commanded that the tongue of their spokesman be cut out and that they cut off his scalp and cut off his hands and feet.... The king [then] ordered them to take him to the fire, still alive, and to

fry him in a pan. The vapor from the pan spread far and wide.
(2 Macc 7:3–5 NRSV)

The graphic nature of these deaths is central to this author's understanding of the resurrection. Before their deaths,
the brothers make a number of stirring speeches, which accentuate their faith in a future resurrection. Repeatedly, the
brothers claim that their own dismantled body parts will be
reunited in a future resurrection:

> When it was demanded, he quickly put out his tongue and
> courageously stretched forth his hands, and said nobly, "I have
> received these things from heaven, . . . and from heaven I hope
> to receive them back again." (7:10–11)

Later in the work, an older martyr named Razis prays, *even
as his entrails are falling out of his physical body,* that God will
restore them (!) to him again in the resurrection (14:37–46).

The result of such grotesque death scenes is the most
graphically physical portrayal of the resurrection that we have
in all of ancient literature. The author insists that the resurrection will literally be a supernatural reunification of the
very members of the physical body lost in death. This apparently even includes the bodies of those who are vaporized,
as one of our previous citations suggests. Nowhere does the
author suggest that the resurrection will be a transformation
of the old body into a new kind of physical existence. This
distances his understanding of the resurrection from that of
Daniel, who envisions the resurrection state as an exaltation
to a new heavenly existence in the stars. One thus senses early
on in the history of resurrection hope a difference of opinion as to whether the resurrection body will be a restoration
of the same old body lost in death (e.g., like 2 Maccabees)
or a radically new transformed existence (e.g., like Daniel).
The dramatic death scenes of 2 Maccabees may seem a bit
melodramatic to the contemporary reader, and at points its
author's vision of the resurrection almost reminds us of a
Frankenstein movie. Yet the author does reveal at least two

assumptions about the resurrection that warrant more serious theological consideration.

First, our author understands the resurrection as a re-creation of the physical body and relies directly upon creation theology to support his understanding of the resurrection. In one of the speeches given by the mother of the seven martyrs, this becomes strikingly clear as she affirms the resurrection hope in terms that foreshadow the later Christian doctrine of *creatio ex nihilo* (creation out of nothing).[22] She says to her sons:

> "I know not how you came into being within my womb. It was not I who gave you life and breath, nor I who ordered the elements within each of you. Therefore the Creator of the world, who shaped the origin of humankind and devised the genesis of all things, will in his mercy give life and breath back to you again, since you now forget yourselves for the sake of his laws. . . . I beg you, my child, look at the heavens and the earth and see everything that is in them, and recognize that God did not make them out of things that previously existed. . . . Accept death, so that in God's mercy I may receive you back again along with your brothers." (7.22–23, 28–29)

As Creator, God is fully capable of raising the dead, even under the most extreme circumstances of mutilation and dismemberment. The author's creation faith is, in fact, so strong that he can even claim that God created the world out of no preexisting thing. Reconstituting the bodies of the martyrs is, thus, not beyond the divine power. Centuries after the composition of 2 Maccabees, later Christian apologists have repeatedly turned to creation in order to demonstrate how it is possible for God to raise the dead (e.g., Athenagoras of Athens, *Res.* 3). Such arguments were not exclusively used by Jewish and Christian thinkers: Centuries later, Muhammad would make a similar argument affirming the resurrection, based upon the precedent of God's power in creation (Koran 22:5–10; 23:12–22).

Second, our author reveals that he is especially concerned with how the resurrection allows him to address the pressing question of theodicy: How can God be benevolent and almighty, yet allow evil and suffering in the world?[23] In a passing comment, the author reveals his concern with this urgent theological problem:

> Now I urge those who read this book not to be depressed by such calamities, but to recognize that these punishments were designed not to destroy but to discipline our people.... [God] never withdraws his mercy from us. Although he disciplines us with calamities, he does not forsake his own people. Let what we have said serve as a reminder. (2 Macc. 6:12–17 NRSV)

The author relies upon his resurrection faith to help him come to terms with the pressing theological problem that the martyrdoms of the Maccabean age have left behind: Why do the righteous suffer, and what is God going to do about it? Thus, underlying the grotesque melodrama of 2 Maccabees, we find the hand of an ambitious theologian at work.

The Dead Sea Scrolls

In the last decade, two manuscripts from among the Dead Sea Scrolls have dramatically expanded our range of ancient texts mentioning the resurrection. The earlier of these manuscripts, *On Resurrection,* also known as the *Messianic Apocalypse* (4Q521), dates palaeographically to the early first century BCE; the later *Pseudo-Ezekiel[a–e]* (4Q385–388, 391), dates from the middle of the same century. Since both manuscripts are copies of preexisting works, there is reason to set the context of their original composition in the latter half of the second century BCE. Thus, they provide us with important insights into how the resurrection continued to enjoy a broad variety of development in the generation just after the composition of Daniel.

On Resurrection is one portion of a previously unknown exhortation that is heavily fashioned by apocalyptic themes. This work presents the resurrection of the dead as one among many coincident signs that will inaugurate the future eschatological time of salvation and deliverance for Israel. In chapter 1 of the present volume, Charlesworth has provided a translation of fragments 2 + 4. In this striking passage, God will "revive the dead" as one among a number of great reversals that will inaugurate the eschatological age. Later in the same writing, God is also described as the one who "revives the dead of his people" (frgs. 7 + 5). One can immediately sense the significance of this writing for understanding the Palestinian Jewish backgrounds of earliest Christianity: It is the only manuscript we have, dating prior to the origins of Christianity, that mentions both Messiah and resurrection within the same immediate context (cf. *1 En.* 37–71).

Although this writing is fragmentary, it reveals a number of important assumptions about the resurrection. First, the resurrection will be part of a grand reversal that will turn the fortunes of the righteous from suffering into glory. This reversal will be so radical that even the righteous dead will be revived into newness of life. Second, the resurrection is envisioned as an act of divine justice for the righteous. In the future, the fruit of a good work will no longer be delayed, but even the righteous dead will receive the reward that is their due. God is, therefore, just, even to those who have not lived to see the full reward of their goodness. Third, this document presents the resurrection for the rhetorical purpose of consolation. It calls upon its readers to strengthen themselves in pursuing God, by remembering the future rewards that await the righteous. Finally, the author tells us only of a resurrection of the dead of God's people. This may suggest that the author envisioned only a partial resurrection of the righteous, as opposed to a general resurrection of all the dead. Later, a fragmentary portion of this writing refers to "the heavens welcoming the righteous, and the presence of angels." Thus, *On Resurrection* may well have envisioned the resurrection as heavenly existence, not unlike Daniel. Other references to "the valley of death" and "the bridge of the Abyss" also suggest that our author envisioned cosmic realms of punishment for the wicked, who seem to perish without a resurrection.

In the writing known as *Pseudo-Ezekiel*, we find a clever interpreter of Scripture at work. This document provides a rewritten version of many of Ezekiel's visions, including the valley of dry bones (Ezek 37). We have already mentioned that for Ezekiel this vision was a prophecy of national restoration, not a portrayal of the resurrection of the dead. Our scroll's author, however, does not care what we have to say about this point. He has his own interpretation of Ezek 37, one that makes it clear that he understands this chapter in terms of a future resurrection that will reward the righteous for their faithfulness.[24] This is the earliest example we have of someone interpreting Ezekiel in this way. Reminiscent of *On Resurrection*, the author of *Pseudo-Ezekiel* was concerned with the reward of the righteous and the timing of their eschatological destiny (cf. 4Q521 frg. 3); and he has the biblical prophet Ezekiel inquire directly of God regarding these questions:

> I have seen many in Israel who love your name and walk on the paths of righteousness. When will these things happen? And how will they be rewarded for their loyalty?

Such striking and aggressive questioning of the Deity is found nowhere in Ezekiel; yet like the author of the later apocalypse of 2 Esdras (=4 *Ezra*), our author burns to know the answers to these great questions.

He finds an answer in Ezek 37, which describes the physical reconstitution of human bodies out of scattered bones that lie in the grave.

> And he said, "Son of man, prophesy over the bones and say, 'May a bone connect with its bone and a joint with its joint.' " And so it happened. And he said a second time, "Prophesy, and sinews will grow on them and they will be covered with skin all over." And so it happened. And again he said, "Prophesy over the four winds of the sky and the winds of the sky will blow upon them and they will live and *a large crowd of men will rise and bless the LORD of Hosts who causes them to live....*" And I said, "O Lord, when will these things be?" (4Q385 frg. 2)

If our author is reading Ezek 37 as a prophecy about the resurrection, then he likely understood the resurrection as a physical reconstitution of the same body that had been lost in death. Nowhere does this writing refer to a transformation of the deceased body into a new state of existence. It thus is possible that our author may have shared a graphically physical understanding of the resurrection comparable to that of 2 Maccabees. In answer to Ezekiel's questions about the timing of the resurrection, God finally promises, "I will not disappoint you, Ezekiel; I will shorten the days and years of the world, that the children of Israel may inherit their land" (4Q385 frg. 3). Like *On Resurrection* and 2 Maccabees, our author is especially concerned with theodicy; and the resurrection is his answer to the question of how God will reward the faithful for their righteousness.

The Origins of Resurrection Hope

Pseudo-Ezekiel illustrates an important point about the origins of resurrection hope. A long-standing theory about the origins of the resurrection hope is that it emerged from early Zoroastrian influences in Iran, as did a number of other Jewish apocalyptic beliefs. This theory gained prominence during the great generation of the history of religions school (*Religionsgeschichtlicheschule*) in the early twentieth century, especially through the work of epoch-making scholars such as R. Reitzenstein.[25] Today many scholars continue to affirm it in various ways.[26] Although this theory of Persian origins cannot be completely explained away, our literary evidence for Zoroastrian religion is notoriously late, dating from the fifth to the ninth centuries CE. It thus is precarious to attribute the origins of the resurrection hope solely to Zoroastrian influences.

Another theory for understanding the origins of apocalypticism takes a different approach. P. D. Hanson has argued that the origins of apocalyptic beliefs emerged through

a radical intensification of beliefs already present in prophetic literature.[27] This intensification involved a literaliza-
tion of certain mythical and poetic notions found in the
prophetic writings. The newly discovered *Pseudo-Ezekiel* document lends strong support to Hanson's theory. Here, we find
a biblical interpreter of the prophet Ezekiel literalizing and
intensifying the visionary imagery of Ezekiel into a literal
belief in the supernatural resurrection of the dead.

Other texts we have surveyed may also provide independent corroboration of this tendency. Several expressions in
the Hebrew of Daniel's resurrection prophecy, for example,
can be traced together only to Isa 26:19, as Nickelsburg has
shown.[28] This may indicate that Daniel's own resurrection
prophecy was shaped by a literalizing reading of this portion of Isaiah. The prophecies of *On Resurrection* also bear the
clear influence of Isa 61 and other texts. Writing in the first
century CE, the apostle Paul would anchor his own theology of the future resurrection in the promises of Isa 25–26
and Hos 13:14 (in 1 Cor 15:54). One may also compare the
manner in which the Synoptic Gospels defend the resurrection hope through a radicalized reading of Exod 3:6 (Matt
22:23–33; Mark 12:18–27; Luke 20:27–40). *Pseudo-Ezekiel*, together with these other writings, invites us to understand
the origins of the resurrection hope as a later intensification
of the promises and prophecies of earlier prophetic writings.
Crenshaw's contribution to the present volume (ch. 3) lends
further support to the possibility that the origins of the resurrection hope are to be found within Israel's own sense of "a
profound sense of community with Yahweh that could withstand any obstacle and the conviction that there was no limit
to this object of devotion's power."

How Widespread Was Ancient Resurrection Hope?

Our survey thus far has illustrated the passion and imagination with which some of our earliest evidence envisions

the resurrection of the dead. One may ask, however, How widespread was early belief in the resurrection?

A survey of texts dating from the Maccabean Revolt to the end of the first century CE yields at least thirteen literary specimens of resurrection hope (see the table on p. 47). The New Testament and Josephus broaden this number considerably. In comparison with the entire corpus of early Jewish and Christian literature, this is substantial — but not overwhelming. To these texts, we may also add other kinds of evidence, such as epigraphy. We find, for example, this playful inscription upon a tomb of the period: "Have a good resurrection."[29] Such inscriptions provide important incidental details in our study, but they do not prove that virtually every Palestinian Jew believed in the resurrection.

Furthermore, within the Old Testament and other sources we can identify traditions that explicitly deny the resurrection or at least severely call it into question. The book of Job, for instance, contains one grim meditation that explicitly denies life after death (14:7–12). One may also cite the perspective of Ecclesiastes: "A living dog is better than a dead lion. The living know they will die; but the dead know nothing" (9:4–5).[30]

We must also account for differing attitudes toward the afterlife among the three great philosophical traditions of early Judaism — the Pharisees, Sadducees, and Essenes. According to Josephus and the New Testament, Pharisees, Sadducees, and Essenes held differing views on the afterlife. These sources allege that both Pharisees and Essenes held strong support for the afterlife, while Sadducees refused to acknowledge any form of life after death. Josephus's reports about the beliefs of these early Jewish religious movements are informative and yet problematic. To cite only one example among many others, Josephus claims that Pharisees believe the following about life after death:

> Every soul is immortal, but only the soul of the good transmigrates into another body; but the souls of the wicked suffer everlasting punishment. (*War* 2.163)

> They believe that souls have power to survive death and that
> there are rewards and punishments under the earth for those
> who have led lives of virtue or vice; eternal imprisonment is
> the lot of wicked souls, while the souls of the good receive an
> easy passage toward revivification. (*Ant.* 18.14)

A close reading of Josephus's reports suggests that Pharisees
believed in something like *metempsychosis,* the transmigration
of the soul out of one body at death and into a *different* body
in the future (cf. Plato, *Phaedo* 70c–d, 72a).

The New Testament, however, states that Pharisees believed in the resurrection of the dead. A similar report is
found in Hippolytus of Rome (*Haer.* 28): "They also confess
to a resurrection of the flesh." Josephus's account confirms
the mere fact that Pharisees believed in some form of life
after death; however, it seems clear that he has distorted
the actual nature of that belief through a Hellenizing portrayal that provides apologetical praise for Judaism in the
eyes of Greek and Roman audiences. This apologetical tendency suggests that Josephus felt at least a little embarrassed
about portraying the resurrection in stark terms. Despite the
Hellenistic cast that Josephus has given this report, at least
one feature of his description is interesting in light of other
ancient evidence: Pharisees seem to believe only in a partial restoration of life, just to the righteous. This feature of
Pharisaic belief is consistent in both the reports of the *Jewish War* and the *Jewish Antiquities.* According to these reports,
not everyone will be restored to bodily existence, only the
righteous.

Josephus's reports on the Essenes are similarly corrupted
by his apologetical tendencies (*War* 2.153–58; *Ant.* 18.18). He
claims that the Essene movement perished during the Great
Jewish Revolt of 66–70 C.E., but not without the comfort of
the afterlife:

> Smiling in their sufferings and making sport of their torturers,
> they cheerfully released their souls, supposing that they will
> receive them again.

> For, indeed, this teaching has strength among them: while bodies are corruptible and their matter not enduring, souls persevere, forever immortal; and emanating to and fro from the finest *Aether,* they become entangled in bodies as in prisons, so to speak, having been pulled down by a kind of natural spell; but when they are sent back from the bonds of the flesh, then, as though set free from their long slavery, they rejoice and are borne high into the air.
>
> Now as for the good, they propound that an abode beyond the sea is set apart (for them), agreeing together with the sons of Greece — a region weighed down neither by rain nor snow nor heat; but which refreshes (itself) from the eternally gentle west wind, as it blows in from the ocean. But for the wicked, they set apart a dark and wintery chamber, filled with never ceasing punishments.
>
> It seems to me that according to the same conception the Greeks set apart the Isles of the Blessed for their own courageous (men), whom they call heroes and demigods, and the region of the wicked down in Hades for the souls of the impious, where, their mythologists relate, some are punished, such as Sisyphus, Tantalus, Ixion, and Tityus, affirming first that souls are everlasting, and then the pursuit of virtue and the deterrence of vice. For the good become better through life by the hope of reward even after death; but the passions of the wicked are hindered, since they expect to undergo immortal punishment after death, even if they should escape it in this life. These, then, are the things that the Essenes believe regarding the theology of the soul, whereby they irresistibly attract all who have tasted of their philosophy. (*War* 2.153–158)
>
> They regard souls to be immortal. (*Ant.* 18.18)

Josephus reports that Essenes, like the Pharisees, believed in some form of life beyond death; but his description of their beliefs is clearly Hellenized, with blatant poetic allusions to the Homeric "Isles of the Blessed" (see *Od.* 4.561–569; and Hesiod, *Op.* 170–172; cf. *History of the Rechabites*). It is unlikely that the Essenes themselves read Homer very often.

Recent research on the Dead Sea Scrolls preserved by the Qumran Essenes has yielded conflicting results regarding how the authors of the Dead Sea Scrolls envisioned the future life. The most comprehensive study is by É. Puech, who argues that the Qumran Essenes accepted a variety of notions regarding the future life, including the resurrection of the dead; and that Hippolytus's ancient description of the Essenes as believing in the resurrection is thus essentially in accord with Qumran writings (*Haer.* 27.1–3).[31] Other scholars have argued that one must distinguish between (1) the documents composed by the Qumran Community, such as the *Rule of the Community,* the *Thanksgiving Hymns* (or *Hodayot*), and the *War Scroll;* and (2) other works of uncertain origin, such as *On Resurrection* and *Pseudo-Ezekiel,* which may originally have been composed outside of Qumran and were only later copied and studied by the sect.[32]

The debate between these two positions continues; and Josephus's problematic description of the Essenes has not helped to resolve it. Amid the uncertainty, it seems safe to offer the provisional assessment that the Qumran Essenes probably envisioned a variety of notions about the future life, and they may not always have been consistent in doing so. Whether they were authored by the Qumran Community or not, *On Resurrection* and *Pseudo-Ezekiel* strongly suggest that some members of the Community could accept the resurrection hope and were not opposed to it. In addition to these two documents, the Community also adopted other writings, like Daniel and *1 Enoch,* which contain references to the resurrection.[33] Furthermore, the men of Qumran may well have read biblical passages of the Psalms or even Ezek 37 as containing references to resurrection. Nowhere do we find any evidence that members of the Community denied the resurrection hope, as the universally maligned Sadducees are reported to have done (Matt 22:23; Mark 12:18; Luke 20:27; Acts 23:6–10; cf. Josephus, *War* 2.165; *Ant.* 18.16).

Apart from the three great religious movements within early Judaism, a number of other texts and traditions seem to have been content to enjoy immortality without explicitly subscribing to the resurrection hope. The book of *Jubilees* provides a good example of this, as it claims, "Their bones shall rest in the earth, but their spirits shall have much joy"

(23.31). Several inscriptions from Jewish tombs encourage a more Epicurean approach to death: "Be of good cheer, no one is immortal."[34] During the period of Christian origins, we find that even some believers saw no need for a future hope in the resurrection. The apostle Paul, for example, writes to some at Corinth who said there is no resurrection from the dead (1 Cor 15:12), and to others who had serious questions about what form of body believers would inherit in the world to come (15:35).

In examining this evidence, two conclusions seem to be necessary when assessing how widespread the resurrection hope was. First, we now have a substantial amount of evidence that many ancient authors from different sectors of Judaism needed the resurrection hope to make sense of the reality of their world. Second, we also have evidence that many other groups ignored, opposed, or were generally confused by the resurrection hope. In light of these conflicting tendencies, it seems safe to conclude that, during the period of its origins, hope in the resurrection of the dead was a popular, yet insurgent, and even controversial belief. What is most surprising about the resurrection hope is that in spite of the controversies and misunderstandings it has provoked over time, Jewish, Christian, and Islamic orthodoxies have consistently aligned themselves with the resurrection hope. Perhaps this is due to the fact that no other vision of the future life combines God's care for the physical body, theodicy, and the value of personal existence in the same way that the resurrection hope does.

Pauline Hope in the Resurrection: An Appreciation in Light of Earlier Texts

In reflection upon the texts and traditions considered thus far, I would like to conclude with a few personal observations on how these materials help us better appreciate the original context of St. Paul's teachings on the resurrection.

Paul explicitly addresses the issue of a future resurrection in two of his letters: 1 Thessalonians 4, and 1 Corinthians 15 — although one recognizes that resurrection implicitly pervades the assumptions of his theology as a whole. For the sake of economy, I will confine my comments to 1 Corinthians 15. In the present volume (ch. 5), Hendrikus Boers provides a more thorough exegesis of key passages in Paul's theology of the resurrection.

Throughout the entire epistle of 1 Corinthians, we find Paul dealing with a community of believers that he perceives as having largely misunderstood the gospel. In page after page of this letter, the apostle patiently, and sometimes impatiently, attempts to correct a number of Corinthian beliefs and practices. Paul's problems with the Corinthians ultimately culminate in an eschatological controversy over the resurrection.

At Corinth, two issues about the resurrection seem to have been the focus of Paul's concern: First, some Corinthians claimed, "There is no resurrection of the dead" (15:12); second, others were confused about what manner of body would exist in the resurrection (15:35). Paul deals with each of these issues in turn. In his defense of the resurrection, he reveals a number of tendencies reminiscent of the evidence surveyed in the present chapter.

First, one senses the controversial nature of the resurrection hope in this episode. Apparently, some Corinthians were perfectly willing to subscribe to an interpretation of the good news that saw no need for hope in a future resurrection of the dead. After all, why should a predominantly Gentile group of believers living in the progressive cultural environment of Corinth weigh themselves down with an outdated and superstitious apocalyptic belief, simply to please Paul? And why was it necessary to have a future resurrection, when the living Lord was already experienced as present with believers in worship?

Paul could simply have ignored this problem. Elsewhere in his letters, he is abundantly willing to accommodate the good news to the varied settings and needs of the Gentile believers. But on the question of the resurrection, he will not budge. Nor will he even be content with afterlife traditions that accentuate immortality without accepting resurrection. For Paul, the legitimacy of his gospel rests upon God's power to raise the dead — not only in the past resurrection of the Messiah, but also in the future resurrection of the dead. Paul's conscientious stubbornness on this point illustrates in a distinctive way how powerfully his own background in Pharisaic Judaism could continue to live on in his interpretation of the gospel. Strikingly, this former Pharisee was glad to preach to the Gentiles a law-free gospel; he refused, however, to preach to them a resurrection-less one. We should not forget this when assessing the complex relationships between Paul's theology and his own background in apocalyptic Judaism. In this sense, the classic approach to Paul's theology by W. D. Davies remains fruitful even today and may be further updated by the new evidence for resurrection from Qumran.[35]

Second, Paul may well have taught only a partial resurrection of those who are dead "in Christ." Though a firm believer in God's wrath (Rom 1:18), Paul nowhere refers to a general resurrection of all the dead for divine judgment. Consistently, he interprets the resurrection in the context of the believer's unbreakable unity "with Christ." The believer's unity with Christ is one that embraces both the death and the resurrection of the Messiah. Thus, Paul may well have agreed with traditions like Daniel and *On Resurrection,* which seem to feature only a partial resurrection. Furthermore, Josephus's reports, as we have seen, suggest that Pharisees believed only in a partial resurrection, just for the righteous dead — and after all, Paul had once been a proud Pharisee. This may only be a coincidence; nevertheless, it is a striking one.

Third, the resurrection was a matter of theodicy for Paul, even as it was for 2 Maccabees, *On Resurrection,* and *Pseudo-Ezekiel.* If there is no resurrection, then death would have the final word over all believers and over the created order as a whole. The believer's unity "in Christ" would ultimately be broken by the power of death. God's work in Christ would fail to defeat the cosmic powers of sin and death; and evil would have triumphed. If this is the case, then Paul suggests believers should all just give up and go have a drink: "If the dead are not raised, 'Let us eat and drink, for tomorrow we die' " (15:32 NRSV). However, God has determined that the Messiah must reign even over the last enemy — death. Believers must therefore continue vigilant in faith, until God's triumph over death culminates in resurrection. Through the resurrection, their "labor in the Lord is not in vain" (15:58).

Fourth, Paul's treatment of the resurrection body gravitates more toward those earlier traditions that envision the resurrection as a transformation into a new state of existence. For Paul, the resurrection was not simply the restoration of the same old physical body lost in death. He would probably have disagreed with the author of 2 Maccabees on this point. One might even find him disagreeing with Luke's portrayal of Jesus' resurrection body, in which the risen Jesus eats a meal together with his disciples (Luke 24:42–43; cf. Acts 2:31).[36] Paul insists that in the resurrection the old physical body will be radically transformed into a new and exalted state of existence. Hence, "flesh and blood cannot inherit the kingdom of God" (1 Cor 15:50 NRSV).

Paul refers to this new state of existence, paradoxically, as a "spiritual body" (15:44). This problematic term is laced with both brilliance and mischief. It stands as a brilliant balance of both continuity and discontinuity in the portrayal of the future life. On one hand, it is we who will live, and we will continue to live in an embodied existence that is continuous with our present bodily life. On the other, we shall all be changed, since our present mortal bodies are not fully able to receive the glory of the world to come. One senses, however, that Paul's paradoxical cleverness probably confused the Corinthians even more than they already had been.

Our earliest traditions about the resurrection prior to Paul, however, help shed some light on what he was at least trying to do. We find the apostle more closely aligned with earlier traditions like Daniel, which describe the resurrection as a transformation of the deceased body into a radically new mode of existence (cf. *2 Bar.* 50–51; 2 Esd 7). Yet Paul's "spiritual body" does not consist in astral immortalization, as in Daniel and other apocalyptic visions of the resurrection. Instead, the "spiritual body" was already represented by the resurrected Messiah himself, into whose glorious image God had predestined that all believers would ultimately be conformed. Thus, our appreciation of Paul's own theological instincts is expanded through the study of our earliest traditions about the resurrection.

Paul's theology of the resurrection has left behind a fascinating heritage in the later history of Christian doctrine that continues into the present. In the centuries following Paul, some creedal formulations would actually bypass Paul's language of "body" and specify the more materialist language of "resurrection of the flesh." Tertullian ranks among the most important apostolic fathers to have favored such language; Athenagoras's apology on the resurrection presses a materialist understanding of the resurrection hope to its farthest possible bounds. Other thinkers, like Origen, would take Paul's paradox in a more immaterial direction. Thus, if Paul was trying to solve an important problem at Corinth, he was simultaneously creating new ones for the entire later history of Christian thought. The work of an apostle was not easy.

In defense of the apostle, however, one may say that most problems that have arisen in the later history of Christian doctrine have been the result of affirming either too little or too much about Paul's original paradox. Theologies of the resurrection that have overemphasized the spiritual nature of the resurrection at the expense of material existence have often found themselves on the wrong end of ecclesiastical councils. To the contrary, theologies that have been overzealous in their affirmation of material existence have often found themselves in the center of a hopelessly puzzling snafu of philosophical anthropology that is even more difficult to cope with than Paul's "spiritual body." Perhaps the apostle would have reminded his successors, "I had it right the first time."

In recent theological inquiry, the resurrection of the dead continues to be a topic of stimulating discussion. In the present volume (ch. 7), W. Waite Willis Jr. traces the history of theological discussion regarding the resurrection in the modern era. To cite only one provocative example of the latest reflection on the resurrection, Sir John Polkinghorne, physicist and theologian, illustrates the usefulness of Paul's concept of the resurrection in the contemporary discussion of science and theology.[37] Faced with the very real and inevitable possibilities of meteor impacts, supernova explosions, and red giants, Polkinghorne must admit that our universe is condemned to ultimate futility. Reasoning within the shadows of such inevitable doom, responsible theology must be able to reconcile two opposing claims: (1) Our material universe will change, and that change will inevitably result in the end of all we currently know. (2) The Creator remains faithful to human life and to the goodness of the creation.

Polkinghorne identifies Paul's notion of the "spiritual body" as a starting point for negotiating these two realities. On the one hand, we shall all be changed. Our world cannot always remain what it is, nor can human life. The only viable hope for the future is, therefore, a transformative one, one in which we can continue to exist only in a new reality discontinuous from the old. On the other hand, God has not forsaken the material reality of the creation and of our bodies. In the world to come, it is we who shall be changed, and when we are changed, our existence will remain a bodily one. Polkinghorne illustrates the fact that Paul's resurrection theology remains a flexible hope, one that continues to guide Christian theology even in the face of cosmic annihilation. Our earliest traditions about the resurrection, thus, continue to make an important contribution to the history of ideas, as we consider the ways of God in a changing and frequently hostile universe. I think the apostle would be pleased.

Texts Mentioning the Resurrection
(c. 200 BCE–c. CE 100)

Hebrew Bible	Pseudepigrapha
Daniel	*1 Enoch*
	Testaments of the Twelve
Apocrypha	*Psalms of Solomon*
2 Maccabees	*Biblical Antiquities*
	4 Ezra
Dead Sea Scrolls	*2 Baruch*
On Resurrection (4Q521)	*Pseudo-Phocylides*
Pseudo-Ezekiel (4Q385–88, 391)	*Life of Adam and Eve*
[possibly others]	*Lives of the Prophets*

Notes

1. To the original, classic study by R. H. Charles (*A Critical History of the Doctrine of a Future Life in Israel, in Judaism, and in Christianity* [London: Black, 1913]), we may now add a number of more recent studies: E.g., W. Bousset, *Die Religion des Judentums im Späthellenistischen Zeitalter* (ed. H. Gressmann; 4th ed.; HNT 21; Tübingen: Mohr [Siebeck], 1966), 269–74; G. Stemberger, *Der Leib der Auferstehung: Studien zur Anthropologie und Eschatologie des palästinischen Judentums im neutestamentlichen Zeitalter (ca. 170 v. Chr.–100 n. Chr.)* (AnBib 56; Rome: Biblical Institute Press, 1972); M. Hengel, *Judaism and Hellenism: Studies in Their Encounter in Palestine during the Early Hellenistic Period* (German, 2d ed., 1973; trans. J. Bowden; 2 vols.; London: SCM, 1974), 1:196ff.; G. W. E. Nickelsburg, *Resurrection, Immortality, and Eternal Life in Intertestamental Judaism* (HTS 26; Cambridge: Harvard University Press, 1972); H. C. C. Cavallin, *Life after Death: Paul's Argument for the Resurrection of the Dead in 1 Cor 15* (Lund: Gleerup, 1974); Émil Schürer, *The History of the Jewish People in the Age of Jesus Christ (175 B.C.–A.D. 135)* (German, 1885–1924; trans. T. Burkill et al.; ed. M. Black et al.; rev. ed.; 3 vols.; London: T & T Clark, 1979), 2:539–44; R. Martin-Achard, "Résurrection dans l'Ancien Testament et le Judaïsme," *DBSup* 10:438–87; idem, *From Death to Life: A Study of the Development of the Doctrine of the Resurrection in the Old Testament* (trans. J. Smith; Edinburgh: Oliver & Boyd, 1960); E. P. Sanders, *Judaism: Practice and Belief (63 BCE — 66 CE)* (London: SCM, 1994), 298–303; É. Puech, *La croyance des esséniens en la vie future: Immortalité, résurrection,*

vie éternelle? Histoire d'une croyance dans le Judaïsme ancien (2 vols.; ÉBib, NS, 21; Paris: Gabalda, 1993); H. Lichtenberger, "La résurrection dans la littérature intertestamentaire et la théologie rabbinique," *Concilium* 249 (1993): 35–44; P. Sacchi, *The History of the Second Temple Period* (JSOTSup 285; Sheffield: Academic Press, 2000), 426–38; J. H. Charlesworth, "Résurrection individuelle et immortalité de l'âme," in *Histoire du Christianisme (Des origines à nos jours)* (ed. J.-M. Mayeur et al.; tome 14; Paris: Desclée, 2001), 14:505–51; N. T. Wright, *Resurrection of the Son of God* (Christian Origins and the Question of God 3; Minneapolis: Fortress, 2003).

2. See the treatment of *On Resurrection* and *Pseudo-Ezekiel* below. The critical edition of these works may be found as follows: É. Puech, ed. *Resurrection*, in *Qumran Cave 4.XVIII: Textes Hebreux (4Q521–4Q528, 4Q576–4Q579)* (DJD 25; Oxford: Clarendon, 1997), 1–36; D. Dimant, ed., *Pseudo-Ezekiel*, in *Qumran Cave 4.XXI: Parabiblical Texts, Part 4: Pseudo-Prophetic Texts* (DJD 30; Oxford: Clarendon, 2001), 7–88.

3. H. Kant, "Jewish Inscriptions in Greek and Latin," *ANRW* II.20.2 (1987): 677–80; Pieter W. van der Horst, *Ancient Jewish Epitaphs: An Introductory Survey of a Millennium of Jewish Funerary Epigraphy (300 BCE–700 CE)* (CBET 2; Kampen: Pharos, 1991), 114–26; and J. S. Park, *Conceptions of Afterlife in Jewish Inscriptions: With Special Reference to Pauline Literature* (WUNT 121; Mohr [Siebeck], 2000); Puech, *La croyance*, 1:182–99; Cavallin, *Life after Death*, 99–101, 166–70.

4. Among innumerable works, one may note H. Coward, ed., *Life after Death in World Religions* (Faith Meets Faith; Maryknoll, NY: Orbis, 1997); E. Kübler-Ross, *On Life after Death* (Berkeley, CA: Celestial Arts, 1991); R. Moody, *Life after Life: The Investigation of a Phenomenon — Survival of Bodily Death* (Atlanta: Mockingbird Books, 1975); F. Tipler, *The Physics of Immortality: Modern Cosmology, God, and the Resurrection of the Dead* (New York: Doubleday, 1994); A. Goswami, *The Physics of the Soul: The Quantum Book of Living, Dying, Reincarnation, and Immortality* (Charlottesville, VA: Hampton Roads, 2001); G. Gallup Jr. with W. Proctor, *Adventures in Immortality* (New York: McGraw-Hill, 1982).

5. J. G. Frazer, *The Golden Bough: A Study in Magic and Religion* (3d ed.; 12 vols.; New York: Macmillan, 1935).

6. See, for example, H. Koester, *History, Culture, and Religion of the Hellenistic Age* (2d ed.; 2 vols.; Introduction to the New Testament 1; New York: de Gruyter, 1995), 1:176–84.

7. See Pseudo-Phocylides, *Sentences* 99–117. His statements on the afterlife occur in the context of ethical instructions regarding the bodies of the dead. Resurrection from the dead (103–104), immortality of the soul (105–108, 111, 115), and divinization (104) are all represented within the compass of about twenty lines. On these passages, see P. W.

van der Horst, *The Sentences of Pseudo-Phocylides: With Introduction and Commentary* (SVTP 4; Leiden: Brill, 1978), 185–95; Cavallin, *Life after Death*, 151–55; Puech, *La croyance*, 1:158–62; F. Christ, "Das Leben nach dem Tode bei Pseudo-Phokylides," *TZ* 31 (1975): 140–49.

8. Those limiting the biblical evidence for the emergence of literal resurrection to Daniel include J. Collins, *Daniel: A Commentary* (Hermeneia; Minneapolis: Fortress, 1993), 390ff.; idem, "Apocalyptic Eschatology as the Transcendence of Death," *CBQ* 36 (1974): 21–43; Nickelsburg, *Resurrection, Immortality, and Eternal Life*, 11–27; Cavallin, *Life after Death*, 23–31. Collins concedes that in Hos 6:1–3 and Ezek 37:1–14 "resurrection language is certainly used metaphorically"; *Daniel*, 391. Both authors suggest that portions of *1 Enoch* probably antedate Daniel as specimens of resurrection hope; see especially *1 En.* 22–27. John Day has proposed that Daniel is literalizing originally ancient Near Eastern mythological language that Hosea (and Isa 24–27) had used only metaphorically; "Resurrection Imagery from Baal to the Book of Daniel," in *Congress Volume: Cambridge 1995* (ed. J. Emerton; VTSup 66; Leiden: Brill, 1997), 125–33.

9. The following critical works represent more "maximalist" approaches to the resurrection in the Hebrew Bible. They take into account texts prior to Dan 12:1–3. L. Greenspoon, "The Origin of the Idea of Resurrection," in *Traditions in Transformation: Turning Points in Biblical Faith* (ed. B. Halpern and J. Levenson; Winona Lake, IL: Eisenbrauns, 1981), 189–240; G. Hasel, "Resurrection in the Theology of Old Testament Apocalyptic," *ZAW* 92 (1980): 267–84; Martin-Achard, *From Death to Life*; idem, "Résurrection dans l'Ancien Testament et le Judaïsme," 443–52; J. Sawyer, "Hebrew Words for the Resurrection of the Dead," *VT* 23 (1973): 18–34; Puech, *La croyance*, 1:33–98; A. Chester, "Resurrection and Transformation," in *Auferstehung-Resurrection: The Fourth Durham-Tübingen Research Symposium, Resurrection, Transfiguration and Exaltation in Old Testament, Ancient Judaism and Early Christianity (Tübingen, September 1999)* (ed. F. Avemarie und H. Lichtenberger; WUNT 135; Tübingen: Mohr [Siebeck], 2001), 65–67. On the Psalms, see especially M. Dahood, *Psalms* (3 vols.; AB; New York: Doubleday, 1965–70), 3:xlii–xliii.

10. On the dating of the work, see Collins, *Daniel*, 29, 61–66. R. H. Charles preferred 167–165 BCE; *A Critical and Exegetical Commentary on the Book of Daniel* (Oxford: Clarendon, 1929), lxx–lxxv.

11. Lit., "land of dust," or "dust of the earth." Cf. Charles, *Book of Daniel*, 327, "a land of dust"; Puech, *La croyance*, 1:81, "au pays de la pouissière"; G. Stemberger, "Das Problem der Auferstehung im Alten Testament," *Kairos*, NS, 14 (1972): 273–90, esp. 275: "Land des Staubes." For the expression, see Isa 26:19 and Akkadian *bît ipri*.

12. Contra Schürer, *History of the Jewish People,* 3:543; Stemberger, "Das Problem der Auferstehung," 274.

13. Martin-Achard, "Résurrection dans l'Ancien Testament et le Judaïsme," 453.

14. Others argue that the phrase refers to "the rest of Israel"; E. Haag, "Daniel 12 und die Auferstehung der Toten," in *The Book of Daniel: Composition and Reception* (ed. J. Collins and P. Flint; 2 vols.; VTSup 83; Leiden: Brill, 2001), 138.

15. Collins, *Daniel,* 66; Stemberger, "Das Problem der Auferstehung," 275. Others argue that the phrase refers to "the rest of Israel"; see Haag, "Daniel 12," 138.

16. Stemberger, "Das Problem der Auferstehung," 278.

17. Among the available primary sources for such beliefs, see Cicero, *Rep.* 6.13–17; Seneca, *Marc.* 24.3–5. Such beliefs remained especially popular among later (second–fifth centuries CE) Neoplatonists such as Porphyry, *Antr. nymph.* 28; Proclus, *In remp.,* vol. 2; Macrobius, *In Somn. Scip.* 1.12.3.

For critical comment and history, see F. Cumont, *Astrology and Religion among the Greeks and Romans* (New York: Dover, 1960); idem, *The Afterlife in Roman Paganism* (Silliman Memorial Lectures; New Haven: Yale University Press, 1922); W. Burkert, *Greek Religion: Archaic and Classical* (Oxford: Blackwell, 1985); W. Jaeger, "The Greek Ideas of Immortality," *HTR* 52 (1959): 135–47; M. Nilsson, "Die astrale Unsterblichkeit und die kosmische Mystik," *Numen* 1 (1954): 106–19; idem, *Geschichte der griechischen Religion* (2 vols.; Handbuch der Altertumswissenschaft 5.2.2; Munich: Beck'sche, 1974), 1:185ff.; idem, *Greek Popular Religion* (Lectures on the History of Religions 1; New York: Columbia University Press, 1940).

18. In addition to the passages treated below, note that even Judas himself believes in a future resurrection of the dead (2 Macc 12:38–45), an attribution attested nowhere else in the Maccabean traditions, nor in Josephus.

19. Zeitlin, for example, proposes a late date in the 40s CE, during the reign of King Agrippa II; S. Zeitlin, ed., *The Second Book of Maccabees* (JAL; New York: Harper & Brothers, 1954), 27–30. Most interpreters, however, prefer a date before 63 BCE; see R. Doran, *Temple Propaganda: The Purpose and Character of 2 Maccabees* (CBQMS 12; Washington: Catholic Biblical Association of America, 1981), 110–13.

20. J. Collins, *Daniel, First Maccabees, Second Maccabees with an Excursus on the Apocalyptic Genre* (Old Testament Message 16; Wilmington, DE: M. Glazier, 1931), 310; similarly, G. W. E. Nickelsburg calls it the "linchpin" of the book, in "1 and 2 Maccabees: Same Story, Different Meaning," *CTM* 42 (1971): 522.

21. The bulk of this chapter is probably an insertion, as Habicht and Doran suggest. Yet the precise origin remains debated. The insertion was probably the work of the same epitomist who abridged the work of Jason of Cyrene. C. Habicht, *2 Makkabäerbuch* (JSHRZ 1.3; Gütersloh: Gütersloher Verlagshaus G. Mohn, 1976), 175ff.; Doran, *Temple Propaganda*, 22; idem, "The Martyr: A Synoptic View of the Mother and Her Seven Sons," in *Ideal Figures in Ancient Judaism: Profiles and Paradigms* (ed. J. Collins and G. Nickelsburg; Chico, CA: Scholars Press, 1980), 189–221; U. Kellermann, *Auferstanden in den Himmel: 2 Makkabäer 7 und die Auferstehung der Märtyer* (Stuttgarter Bibel-Studien 95; Stuttgart: Verlag Katholisches Bibelwerk, 1979), 13–17. On the history of approaches to this textual problem, see Puech, *La croyance*, 1:85n144.

22. See J. Goldstein, "The Origins of the Doctrine of Creatio Ex Nihilo," *JJS* 35 (1984): 127–35.

23. For additional approaches to theodicy in early Jewish writings, see J. H. Charlesworth, "Theodicy in Early Jewish Writings: A Selected Overview," in *Theodicy in the World of the Bible* (ed. A. Laato and J. de Moor; Leiden: Brill, 2003), 470–508.

24. On this writing, see D. Dimant, "Resurrection, Restoration and Time-Curtailing in Qumran, Early Judaism and Christianity," *RevQ* 19 (1999–2000): 527–48; Puech, *La croyance*, 2:605–16. In what follows, I am influenced by their incisive treatments of *Pseudo-Ezekiel*.

25. R. Reitzenstein, *Das iranische Erlösungsmysterium* (Bonn: Marus & Weber, 1921).

26. See A. Hultgård, "Persian Apocalypticism," in *The Encyclopedia of Apocalypticism*, vol. 1, *The Origins of Apocalypticism in Judaism and Christianity* (ed. J. Collins, B. McGinn, S. Stein; 3 vols.; New York: Continuum, 1998); J. Collins, *The Apocalyptic Imagination: An Introduction to Jewish Apocalyptic Literature* (2d ed.; Biblical Resource Series; Grand Rapids: Eerdmans, 1998), 29–33.

27. P. D. Hanson, *The Dawn of Apocalyptic* (Philadelphia: Fortress, 1975). Hanson reports others who developed similar proposals, "Apocalyptic Literature," in *The Hebrew Bible and Its Modern Interpreters* (ed. D. Knight and G. Tucker; The Bible and Its Modern Interpreters; Minneapolis: Fortress, 1985), 465–88.

28. Nickelsburg, *Resurrection, Immortality, and Eternal Life*, 18–23.

29. For this and other examples, see van der Horst, *Ancient Jewish Epitaphs*, 114–26; Park, *Conceptions of Afterlife in Jewish Inscriptions*; Puech, *La croyance*, 1:182–99; Cavallin, *Life after Death*, 99–101, 166–70.

30. For other denials of life after death in the Hebrew Bible, see Prof. Crenshaw's contribution to the present volume (ch. 3).

31. Puech, *La croyance*, esp. vol. 2; idem, "Messianism, Resurrection, and Eschatology," in *The Community of the Renewed Covenant: The Notre Dame Symposium on the Dead Sea Scrolls* (ed. E. Ulrich and J. Vanderkam; Christianity and Judaism in Antiquity 10; Notre Dame, IN: University of Notre Dame Press, 1994), 234–56. See also K. Schubert, "Das Problem der Auferstehungshoffnung in den Qumrantexten und in der frührabbinischen Literatur," *WZKM* 56 (1960): 154–67; Sanders, *Judaism: Practice and Belief*, 302; M. Delcor, *Les Hymnes de Qumran (Hodayot): Texte hébreu, introduction, traduction, commentaire* (Paris: Letouzey et Ané, 1962), 180–84.

32. J. Collins, *Apocalypticism and the Dead Sea Scrolls* (Literature of the Dead Sea Scrolls; New York: Routledge, 1997), 110–29; G. W. E. Nickelsburg, "Resurrection," in *Encyclopedia of the Dead Sea Scrolls* (ed. L. Schiffman and J. Vanderkam; 2 vols.; Oxford: Oxford University Press, 2000), 2:764–67; Cf. also R. Laurin, "The Question of Immortality in the Qumran 'Hodayot,'" *JSS* 3 (1958): 344–55; J. Le Moyne, *Les Sadducéens* (Paris: Gabalda, 1972), 167–68; P. Grelot, "L'eschatologie des Esséniens et le livre d'Hénoch," *RevQ* 1 (1958–59): 113–31; Hengel, *Judaism and Hellenism*, 1:198–99; J. van der Ploeg, "The Belief in Immortality in The Writings of Qumran," *BO* 18 (1961): 118–24; Cavallin, *Life after Death*, 60–68; J. Bremmer, "The Resurrection between Zarathustra and Jonathan Z. Smith," *NTT* 50 (1996): 89–107.

33. See also the discussion of numerous biblical and pseudepigraphic writings (possibly) attesting resurrection in the Community, in Puech, *La croyance*, vol. 1; and J. Hobbins, "Resurrection in the Daniel Tradition and Other Writings at Qumran," in *The Book of Daniel: Composition and Reception*, 2:385–420.

34. For this and other examples, see van der Horst, *Ancient Jewish Epitaphs*, 114–26; Park, *Conceptions of Afterlife in Jewish Inscriptions*; Puech, *La croyance*, 1:182–99; Cavallin, *Life after Death*, 99–101, 166–70.

35. W. D. Davies, *Paul and Rabbinic Judaism: Some Rabbinic Elements in Pauline Theology* (2d ed.; London: SPCK, 1958), 285–320.

36. R. Brown, *The Virginal Conception and Bodily Resurrection of Jesus* (New York: Paulist Press, 1973), 87.

37. See J. Polkinghorne, *The God of Hope and the End of the World* (New Haven, CT: Yale University Press, 2003).

Chapter 3

Love Is Stronger Than Death: Intimations of Life beyond the Grave

James L. Crenshaw

It can be argued that in scholarly pursuits ink is spilled on a given topic in inverse proportion to what can actually be known about it. Hence the large number of articles and books dealing with belief in life after death.[1] All such investigations stand under the honest assessment that for now we possess blurred vision, or to quote Paul, we see "in a mirror dimly" (1 Cor 13:12 NRSV). Whether or not he was correct in contrasting "now" with "then," our present enigma with a future clarity of vision in face-to-face encounter must await the unfolding of history and the final tick of our personal clocks.

In all probability, Paul echoes the legendary elevation of the prophet Moses over all lesser prophets. In the narrator's eyes, Moses experienced the Deity through the immediacy of a one-on-one dialogue, but everyone else encountered riddles, visions, and dreams, which required an act of de-mystification (Num 12:6–8).[2] Paul seems to apply the ancient distinction between modes of receiving an inspired word to the supreme hidden mystery and to the ultimate question facing humanity. Like God, that mystery belongs to the frag-ile realm of faith; and the question, "Is death final?" always retains the utmost in urgency.[3]

What did the peoples of the ancient Near East believe about the destiny of those who succumbed to time's rav-ages? Two views vied with one another, and they have been traced back to the Paleolithic and Neolithic periods.[4] Wander-ing seminomads[5] seem to have thought that the dead rested in their graves as "living corpses." The principle articulated in Gen 3:19 that dust returns to dust has as its corollary a conviction that the animating breath was reclaimed at death by its original owner (Eccl 12:7).[6] A competing conception seems to have characterized the city dwellers in ancient Mesopotamia, who believed that their dead descended to a watery underworld, which corresponded to the biblical Sheol.[7] Considerable ambiguity exists as to the exact condi-tions thought to have pertained to both locations, but on one thing all were in agreement: no one returned from that world.

The Hebrew Bible (or Old Testament) does record an instance of momentary respite, the result of King Saul's desperate resort to assistance from the medium of Endor. Samuel's apparition does not take kindly to someone's dis-turbing his sleep (1 Sam 28). This understanding of the netherworld as a place of rest finds utterance in poetry de-scribing a longing for a sense of closure to every discomfiture. The sufferer envisions an end to all inequities endured in the present lifetime, a belief at odds with the notion that a king of terrors ruled the underworld (Job 18:14).

No shuttle connected the present world with the domain of the dead, nor did the shadowy inhabitants of Sheol give any thought to those remaining behind. Worshippers down on their luck used this bit of lore to argue that Yahweh should act promptly to maintain a steady stream of praise on earth for the Deity. Just as mortals on earth had no commerce with the underworld and its residents, the Lord of the living was thought by some to have nothing to do with Sheol.[8] Amos's hypothetical statement, to the contrary, interposes a serpentine creature between its commissioner and imaginary persons hiding in Sheol (9:3). The prophet's point has more to do with power than with establishing a relationship between Yahweh and the inhabitants of Sheol.

Probably the most widespread picture of the underworld involved tempestuous waters. The notion that its boisterous waves even threatened citizens of the present world caused some slippage in the belief that a radical wall separated the living from the dead. This idea led to gradations of life, as if persons under the power of sickness, physical threat, and the like have descended into the depths of Sheol. Deliverance from any of these threats was attributed to Yahweh's compassion and power. Those caught in the dreaded waters lifted up their petitions to the heavens in the belief that Yahweh possessed the ability to rescue them, even if for some unknown reason the one being implored has, until this moment, lacked the will to save.

This, then, is what the Israelites believed about the lot of the dead. These unfortunate creatures either returned to dust or wandered in Sheol as shades of what they once had been. Yahweh, the living one, had nothing to do with the dead. For this reason, funerary rites associated with cults of the dead were officially proscribed, although they may have enjoyed high regard in areas of ancient Israel that were far from governmental control.

A Daring Breakthrough

Over time, this unpromising picture yielded to a stunning reformulation of Yahweh's conduct vis-à-vis the dead. Two seeds lay in fertile soil awaiting the moistening dew that would act as a catalyst to promote germination. These seeds

were (1) a profound sense of community with Yahweh that
could withstand any obstacle, and (2) the conviction that
there was no limit to this object of devotion's power. The catalyst: grievous injustices, and ultimately martyrdom, which
intensified the problem of theodicy. The peculiar nature of
these two seeds yielded unique plants, each with its own
individual characteristics.

The former seed, passionate communion with the Deity,
gave rise to bold reflection about the possibility that we may
have some innate capacity deep within us that unfailingly
responds to divine wooing. The natural outcome of such speculation is belief in an immortal *nepeš* (like the Egyptian *ba*).
Sometimes this idea carries with it a disparaging of the physical.[9] The latter seed, Yahweh's unlimited might, eventuated in
the affirmation that death will finally succumb to that force:

> He has swallowed death forever;
> Lord Yahweh has wiped away every tear from their faces;
> the reproach of his people he has expunged from the earth,
> for Yahweh has spoken. (Isa 25:8)

In retrospect, a victory over death might suggest immortality, but the concept of death's finality also raises the question:
What about all those who have already surrendered to its
sting? That query was intensified by martyrdom. Justice
seemed to require that individuals who had forfeited their
lives through fidelity to the Deity should be given a chance
to live out a normal life span. Therefore, a daring thinker
uttered the unspeakable, the mind-boggling notion of resurrection, prompting a modern intellectual, Ernst Renan, to
write: "The blood of the martyrs was the veritable creator of
belief in a second life."[10]

Here and there, tiny cracks became visible in the hardened
crust of belief about two distinct realms, this world and the
next. Legends about occasional resuscitation of the dead by
revered prophets functioned primarily to enhance the pres-
tige of Elijah and Elisha, but they also express the author's
belief that Yahweh held the keys to life and death:

> See now that I myself am He,
> There is no god beside me;
> I kill and I enliven;
> I wound and I heal;
> No one can snatch from my grasp.
> (Deut 32:39)

From this assertion about the source of both weal and woe in a single Deity flows a recognition that the instruments of human distress are subject to Yahweh's command. That includes sickness in varying degrees, but also other kinds of physical distress.

Graphic imagery for the various threats poetically convey the idea that against their volition individuals are caught up in a battle of mythic proportions. The dominant image, that of raging waters engulfing its victim, has roots in ancient Near Eastern mythology.[11] The prophet Jonah, according to the psalm in Jonah 2, finds himself at the mercy of the deep. In the view of the author, neither these waters nor their awesome creatures could hold the reluctant prophet. Small wonder that this narrative of Jonah's rescue from the sea and his unusual vessel assumed such significance in later reflections about resurrection.

The figures of Enoch and Elijah illustrate slippage in yet another way: a willingness to conjecture that rare individuals managed altogether to elude death's long tentacles. In both instances the Hebrew verb *lāqaḥ* occurs; its usual meaning, "to take or receive," assumes new dimensions through the identity of the one doing the receiving: God, in both stories:

> Enoch walked with God; and he was not, for God took him.
> (Gen 5:24 RSV)

> Now the sons of the prophets at Bethel went out to Elisha and said to him: "Are you aware that today Yahweh is going to take your master from being your leader?" He responded: "I am informed. Keep it down." (2 Kgs 2:3; cf. 2:5, 9–10)

The mystery associated with Enoch's vanishing is conveyed primarily through understatement, while the opposite literary style produces a similar effect in the story about Elijah's

departure in a fiery chariot. In the former account, a Hebrew particle of nonexistence, "He was not," is followed by
an explanatory declaration: "For God took him." The latter
narrative uses repetition to create an air of eager expectation,
and the explosive finale does not disappoint. On seeing the
extraordinary chariot with a whirlwind as its mode of loco-
motion, an awestruck Elisha cannot follow his earlier advice
and keep quiet.

> Elisha kept on watching, crying out,
> "My father! My father! The chariot of Israel and its horses."
> (2 Kgs 2:12)

The strange story concludes with a linguistic equivalent of a
particle of nonexistence: "He saw him no more."

This peculiar use of the verb *lāqaḥ* with God as subject
forges an impressive link with three additional contexts, two
of them in the book of Psalms (49:16 [15 ET]; 73:24) and the
other in Isaiah (53:8). In combination, they make a tentative
step toward challenging the dominant worldview with respect to human destiny. At the same time, one can hardly
miss the authors' reluctance to come right out and openly
affirm such a radical notion.

Psalm 49:16 (15 ET)

The combination of subject matter, language, and style in
Psalm 49 resembles wisdom literature.[12] The main topic,
life's fleeting character, receives fuller treatment in Qoheleth,
but without the exquisite metaphor of death as a personal
shepherd (49:15 [14 ET]). Structurally, the psalm consists of
two units, each ending with a common refrain comparing
human beings' mortality with that of animals (49:13 [12],
21 [20]). The initial four verses comprise a rhetorical introduction utilizing both prophetic and wisdom terminology.
The universalizing summons to attention is balanced by an
individualizing expression of personal introspection.

The extraordinary language of this introduction matches the singularity of the entire psalm's boldly innovative thought: the twofold reference to humankind as children of *'ādām* and *'îš* (man); the contrasting but unified (*yaḥad*) rich and poor; the plural words for "wisdom" and "understanding"; the two terms of escalating complexity, "proverb" and "riddle" (vv. 3–5 [2–4]). These references to the importance of the human body — mouth, ear, and heart — in communicating anomalies stand over against the final assessment of the psalm: "Humans in their splendor cannot understand; they resemble animals that perish" (v. 21 [20]).

The first unit (49:6–13 [5–12]) addresses the perennial problem presented by cruel persons of financial means and thus power. In essence, the psalmist insists that their possessions cannot purchase release from death's sure clutches. Because no amount of money suffices to stave off that dreaded predator, rich landholders will relinquish their estates for the grave, where they cannot lay claim to a single particle of dust. Why, then, should anyone fear such powerless creatures? The psalmist refuses to universalize the experiences of Enoch and Elijah, instead insisting that none can avoid the grave. The same fate awaits both fools and wise: endless residence in the pit. The cost of ransom exceeds their capacity.

The second unit (49:14–21 [13–20]) breaks away from this dismal picture momentarily, although treating the same theme somewhat differently. Suddenly, the psalmist contrasts the fate of the foolish with his own destiny. They will rot in the grave, while he envisions being ransomed by God, indeed being received (like Enoch and Elijah).

> Surely God will ransom me from Sheol's grasp,
> for he will receive me. (49:16 [15])

The psalmist then draws a conclusion with respect to others struggling with the question of the prosperity of the wicked. These oppressors need not be feared, for they are destined to spend their last days in Sheol, having left all their possessions behind. Like their ancestors whom they now join, they will never again look upon the light.

The ambiguity of this psalm makes it impossible to say with certainty that it contemplates life beyond the grave. On the one hand, it seems to include everyone in its gloomy picture of mortals' fate. On the other hand, the psalmist thinks God will make an exception in his case. If *'aḥ* in 49:8 [7] is an aural mistake for *'ak,* the contrast becomes even more explicit.[13]

> Surely a person can never ransom him,
>   cannot give his price to God....
> Surely God will ransom me from Sheol's grasp,
>   for he will receive me. (49:8 [7], 16 [15])

The addition of "he will receive me" introduces the possibility that the psalmist has advanced beyond the usual understanding of divine deliverance from the power of Sheol. At the same time, the contrast between being received by God (*yiqāḥēnî,* v. 16 [15]) and the fools' inability to "take" (*yiqāḥ,* v. 18 [17]) anything with them provides a nice play on the verb *lāqaḥ.*

Psalm 73:24

The other psalm that uses language reminiscent of that associated with the departure of Enoch and Elijah throws into relief the vexing problem addressed in the book of Job. The inclusion of Psalm 73 in wisdom literature is based almost exclusively on thematic considerations. It ponders the issue of theodicy, offering fresh insight into the true nature of love for God. That advance comes, however, after mind-stretching struggle.[14]

The psalm juxtaposes a ruthless throng and a worshipper who comes perilously close to joining them, if not actually, then at least intellectually. The frame narrative (vv. 1–3, 27–28) articulates the creed that seems to be crumbling and reformulates it to accord with experience. "Truly God [*'ēl*]

is good to the upright, God [*'ĕlōhîm*] to those whose hearts
are pure" (v. 1) becomes "But for me, God's drawing near
is good to me" (v. 28). Having taken refuge in Yahweh, the
psalmist imagines the gradual dissipation of those he had
earlier envied.

The word "heart" functions thematically in the psalm. It
occurs six times, all with a cognitive sense (vv. 1, 7, 13, 21,
26 [2x]). The problem is an intellectual one: how to maintain
integrity in the face of apparent disconfirmation of a religious dogma. In the nick of time the psalmist recognizes the
power of the temptation to join those who question the Deity's knowledge of human activity. Therefore, he enters the
sanctuary, where lofty thoughts drive out the previous bestial
ones (v. 17).

A threefold repetition of the adverb "truly" (*'ak*) focuses
a spotlight at decisive moments: (1) the opening creed (v. 1);
(2) its negation (v. 13); and (3) a reaffirmation of the original creed, but now with the emphasis on the removal of the
reason for the earlier doubt (v. 18).

The solution to the psalmist's anxiety is only partially due
to the discovery that sinners are no more substantial than
figments of a divine dream. The real resolution comes from
a sense of divine nearness, one so real that it seems as if God
takes him by the hand, offers guidance in counsel, and more.
What is that "more," the third source of consolation? "And
afterward you receive me (in) honor" (v. 24b). After what?
The act of taking the psalmist by the hand and giving vital
advice like that found in Isa 30:20–21?

> The Lord will give you bread of adversity
>   and water of affliction,
> but your Teacher will no longer be hidden,
>   for your eyes will behold your Teacher,
> and your ears will hear a word from behind:
>   "This is the path; walk in it,"
> when you veer either to the right or to the left.

The notion of unmediated divine instruction that keeps one
safe from all harm has enormous appeal. Even if that is all the

psalmist hopes for, we need not view it as lacking in religious profundity.

The word "after" invites comparison of this text with Job 19:26; but there, too, the meaning escapes us. The textual problems in Job 19:23–27 did not prevent the early church from using this unit to argue for a physical resurrection, although modern scholars have been more cautious. Early in his argument with his friends, Job recognizes the importance of a permanent witness to injustice, one that endures long after his death (16:18–22). In 19:23–27 he takes up this issue again and imagines the improbable: a future day when his words will stand as a lasting testimony to his claim of innocence. The precise nature of this witness is unclear. It takes the form of a record preserved on three kinds of writing material — scroll, engraved tablet, rock — or more likely a stela on which a message has been carved with iron stylus and lead inlay.[15]

Job considers this written record unlikely, as the introductory "Would that" implies; but he expresses certainty that a redeemer stands ready to avenge wrongdoing directed at him. The same confidence pervades the earlier discussion of a heavenly witness in 16:18–19. Job's choice of the expression *gō'ēl* carries heavy irony, in light of an epithet for Yahweh, "the champion of widows and orphans" (Prov 23:11; Jer 50:34).[16] A victim of injustice, Job stands in need of help from a kinsman and fantasizes that a heavenly redeemer will champion his cause against God, the wrongdoer (19:25).

When does Job think this forensic event will take place? The phrase "after my skin has been stripped off thus" (19:26a) suggests that one think of Job's death. Does he actually believe that he will be raised from the grave or, like Samuel's ghost, will be brought back from Sheol for a special occasion in which Eloah eats crow?

For at least two reasons, this interpretation is unlikely. First, Job's rejection of life beyond the grave in 14:1–22 leaves no room for any hope; and second, such a resolution would make his cry throughout the book ring hollow. An answer to the difficulty presented by the text has been found by distinguishing between two opposing scenes. In 19:25–26a Job imagines a postmortem vindication, whereas in 19:26b–27 he expresses his preference to see things set right before death.[17] In short, over against Job's assurance that the redeemer will vindicate him after his skin has been peeled off, he says: "But I would [i.e., 'want to'] see God from my flesh, whom I would see for myself; my eyes would see, and not a stranger" (vv. 26b–27).

The adverb "afterward" (*'aḥar*) in Job 19:26 does not require that one read Ps 73:24 (with *'aḥar*) as a reference to life beyond the grave, but neither does it rule out such an interpretation. A combination of features points to this bold interpretation: the words "glory," "forever," "rock," and "portion." If by *kābôd* the psalmist meant "earthly honor," one expects something like "he will give me honor." The adverb *lĕ'ôlām* (73:26b) normally refers to this world but comes to mean the next age. In conjunction with the predicate adjective *ṣûr* (rock/strength), it may have the more exalted sense, for both it and the rock of ages endure. Even the adjective "portion" may have this deeper meaning, for in sacred narrative the land as Israel's portion survived the death of generation after generation.

Anyone for whom God is the sole "possession and desire" in heaven and on earth has reached the stage where asking about the permanence of such a relationship is natural, like breathing. The fervor of this intimate relationship seems to have given rise to the unthinkable. Death cannot blot out this love. It follows that the psalmist dares to hope for survival beyond death.

Isaiah 53:8

If Ps 49:16 (15 ET) leaves some doubt about whether or not the psalmist thinks of being received by God after death, as opposed to being rescued from dire threat, and Ps 73:24 only

obliquely refers to dying prior to Yahweh's receiving the worshipper in glory, Isa 53:8 explicitly mentions the servant's
demise:

> By a miscarriage of justice he was taken away,
>   who could have imagined his future?
> For he was cut off from the land of the living,
>   smitten for my people's offenses.

The point is pressed by specific references to his grave and
death (vv. 9, 12).

The question remains whether or not the verb *lūqāḥ* simply
means "taken away," a euphemism for "he died," or carries
a weightier sense of "being received by Yahweh." Even if one
inclines toward the latter interpretation, the exceptional nature of this servant, whether the ideal Israel or an individual,
rules out any universalizing of his fate.[18] The emancipation of
an exiled Israel paints Yahweh's deliverance of an individual
from Sheol's raging waters on a broader canvas. The slippery
use of metaphorical language in discussions of death further
complicates matters.[19] Exile, however unpleasant, differs from
death; life went on, and death awaited the dispossessed just
as it did those who took over their land. If the servant was
an individual, death had already come, and *lūqāḥ* may echo
its uses in Pss 49:16 (15 ET) and 73:24.

Isaiah 26:19

Such modes of discourse combining covenantal relationship
with the ardor of intimacy find expression in Ezekiel's vision of national revivification (ch. 37). Dry bones receive new
life through the activity of Yahweh's spirit, and an exiled
people lives again. The same idea takes up residence in the
little apocalypse embedded within First Isaiah (chs. 24–27).
The much-quoted proof text for belief in resurrection within
the Old Testament, Isa 26:19, can be explained as a poetic
reference to national resuscitation. Is it more than that?[20]

Several observations about this text keep it in perspective.
First, it appears in an apocalyptic unit that bears witness to

the collapsing of myth into metahistory. Events now tran-
spire on two historical planes; ordinary experiences give way
to extraordinary circumstances, this age to a new age. The
Lord prepares a feast on a holy mountain, swallows death
forever, and wipes away all tears (25:6–10).[21] Second, the victory song in chapter 26 both denies and affirms the rising of
the dead (vv. 14 and 19), indicating either a conflicted author
or a gloss on an earlier text. Third, the people are experiencing Yahweh's wrath, which evokes fervent cries for justice (as
in 26:16),[22] especially on behalf of the slain. Fourth, the momentary threat to civilization, expressed poetically in terms
of futile pregnancies (vv. 17–18), will soon ease and the reviving dew will bring new life (v. 19).[23] Fifth, the song ends
with the assuring word that Yahweh will punish murderers,
because the blood of the slain has finally been exposed, like
that of Abel (vv. 20–21). This promise, and not the proclaimed
resurrection, appears to be the main point of the song.

> Your dead will live, their corpses will rise;
> Inhabitants of the dust, awake and exult!
> For your dew is radiant,
> and the earth will give birth to the shades.
> (Isa 26:19)

That may be, but for now the author advises the people to
hide until the divine wrath is past. Clearly, Isa. 26:19 does
not suit the context very well. If it glosses v. 14, it does so in
the spirit of 25:8, the anticipated swallowing of death by a
victorious Yahweh.[24]

Daniel 12:2

The ambiguity vanishes when we turn to Dan 12:2, another
apocalyptic text, this one produced by, and responding to, the
horrific circumstances accompanying the Maccabean revolt
against a Seleucid threat to religious freedom.

> And at that time your people will be delivered,
> all those found written in the book.
> *Many who sleep in the land of dust will awake,*

> *some to everlasting life and others to continual*
> *reproach and contempt.*
> The wise will shine like the radiance
>   of the firmament;
> and those who lead many to righteousness,
>   like stars forever and ever.
>
> (Dan 12:1b–3; italics mine)

Several things make this memorable text a singular moment in the Hebrew Bible. It introduces a new figure, Michael, the angelic protector of God's people. It projects the time of deliverance into the remote future, just as Isa 26:19 does, but views the conflagration of that future date as entirely unprecedented. It suggests that a heavenly book contains a written record of the faithful.[25] It limits the bodily resurrection of the dead to a select group, presumably the exceptionally good and evil (shown by the prefixed *min*, partitive). It echoes the language of Isa 53:12 and 66:24. It expands the concept of a radiant dew in Isa 26:19 to that of the risen dead.[26] And finally, Dan 12:1–3 stresses the witnessing power of such an event "to lead many to righteousness."[27]

2 Maccabees 7:1–42

Daniel's daring solution to the problem of theodicy is matched by the martyrology in 2 Macc 7:1–42. Readers of this fictional account of the death of seven brothers and their mother at the instigation of the Seleucid ruler Antiochus may concur in the closing sentiment that enough has been said about such hideous persecution. Despite the vivid details of a fertile imagination, the rhetoric functions to encourage Jews to remain faithful to the law even if doing so leads to violent death.

The several speeches attributed to the martyrs reinforce their hope in the resurrection, together with their conviction that God will punish their persecutors. That twofold belief is grounded in a theology of Yahweh's power and character. The mother speaks about the wonderful mystery of birth, concluding that life comes originally from an act of divine benevolence, and that the giver of life can bestow it again on those from whom it has been taken. An affirmation of Yahweh's mercy accompanies this first explicit biblical reference to *creatio ex nihilo* (creation from nothing). The narrator cannot resist observing that the devout mother reinforced her woman's reasoning with a man's courage. This surprising acknowledgment that women are appreciated for their intellectual astuteness (and men for courage) contrasts pleasantly with proverbial wisdom in the ancient Near East that disparages women's minds.[28]

The third son thrusts his hands forward, sticks out his tongue, and insists that they are divine gifts, which he hopes to get back. The recurring theme of the final four brothers concerns the question of divine justice. In short, the sons admit that their death is the result of sin; at the same time, they insist that God will eventually punish the murderers, excluding them from the hope of the resurrection. The seventh brother affirms present victory over death's sting; in his view the brothers and mother have already drunk ever-flowing life under the covenant.[29]

Wisdom of Solomon

The Hellenistic author of Wisdom of Solomon drew upon a different intellectual tradition to answer the challenge to divine justice.[30] Death, in his unprecedented view, did not derive from God (1:13) but resulted from the devil's envy, and humankind was created in the divine image, hence immortal (2:22–24). A perishable body (9:15) weights down the pure soul, resulting in ignorance of divine mystery; but Wisdom bestows immortality (8:13, 17). Faithfulness to the law also brings immortality (6:18–19). Alongside the Platonic disparaging of the body exists a tinge of Docetism. The author insists that the righteous dead only seem to have died, for they have the hope of immortality, and their souls will shine forth, running like sparks in stubble (3:7).

The wicked persons evoking this portrait of the righteous vocalize the old-fashioned view that no one returns from Sheol (2:1), and that the dead are extinguished, their separable parts becoming ashes and dissolving into thin air (2:3). Images from nature conjure up the gloomy fate of the dead — clouds dissipating and shadows vanishing. In short, the opponents of the wise believe that nobody returns from the grave, for the dead are sealed in a tomb, preventing their return (2:4–5). Consequently, they advocate and practice the concept usually referred to as carpe diem ("seize the day," enjoy the present and do not fret about tomorrow).

According to Wisdom of Solomon, the test presented by these greedy opportunists became an occasion for the virtuous to demonstrate the reality that they have found shelter in the divine hand. Safe from torment (3:1–4), they claim the promise of eternal life (5:15). Clearly, belief in an immortal soul did not imply future bliss for everyone. On the contrary, only the righteous reaped its benefits.

The views expressed here are thoroughly Greek, but they lack consistency. On the one hand, the soul is immortal; but on the other hand, immortality is bestowed only on the deserving. Similar ambiguity surrounds the author's concept of death.[31] For the righteous, death is only apparent, as if spiritual, but the wicked experience it as real. The author does not describe the fate of the wicked, whether as complete obliteration or eternal punishment. In 8:20 Solomon makes an astonishing admission, correcting himself to include a notion of preexistence alongside the concept of an immortal soul.

Resistance to Belief in a Resurrection

Ancient tradition was not easily overturned, even by an apparent answer to the perplexing problem of theodicy. Those who valued the insights of ancestral heroes more than modern innovations registered an emphatic "no" to belief in life after death. The issue came to divide Jews along party lines,

the Pharisees opting for the new ideas and the Sadducees re-
fusing to accept them. An explanation for these differences
along sociological lines oversimplifies the issue. For some, the
evidence of nature itself implies that death is final.

Possibly the most extensive expression of this view occurs
in Job 14:1–22. Here the question is posed in its simplest
form: "If mortals die, will they live again?" (v 14). In ancient myth the gods died and rose again, and their fecundity
was celebrated annually in the royal cult. Mortals, however,
fell into a different category; access to the tree of life was
withheld from them, except for Utnapishtim, the hero of the
flood in Mesopotamian lore. In the Ugaritic Tale of Aqhat,
the hero makes the point emphatically when promised eternal life in exchange for his bow. He rejects Anath's offer with
these words:

> Further life — how can mortal attain it?
>   How can mortal attain life enduring?
> Glaze will be poured [on] my head,
>   Plaster upon my pate;
> And I'll die as everyone dies,
>   I too shall assuredly die. (*ANET* 151)

To reaffirm the limitation of resurrection to the gods, Job
reflects on life's brevity and undesirable limitations (14:1–
6), death's finality (14:7–12), and the Deity's destruction of
human hope (14:18–22). For a brief moment, Job is drawn
into the language of prayer (14:13–17), but he does not
linger there.

Job establishes the fact of human brevity by recognizing
the kinship with nature. The similes of a flower and a shadow
point to ephemerality and insubstantiality (v. 2). Mortals'
limited life spans, known only to God, remind one and all
that they do not exercise exclusive control over their destiny.
Complicating matters further, divine surveillance shortens
the lives of hapless offenders and innocents alike.

It occurs to Job that the link with nature could suggest permanence. He thinks of a stately tree that has been cut down

and recalls the way a stump, when given sufficient moisture, produces new growth (vv. 7–9). Can mortals anticipate a similar resuscitation? Job replies with a categorical negative, then proceeds to point out that the revivifying agent, water, dries up even in large quantities. This suggests to him that mortals vanish for all eternity.

He finds additional analogies from nature in 14:18–22; this time Job contemplates durable entities such as mountains and rocks, which over time succumb to the eroding power of cascading streams. God's excessive force works like water on rocks, effacing human affection and reducing mortals to perceived pain.

Facing this grim prospect, Job wishes that God would hide him in Sheol until his wrath passed and then remember him (v. 13). In this imaginary world God would not spy on him but would have compassion on his miserable subject. That perfect world would result in mutual calling and answering (v. 15). In his mental turmoil and physical distress, Job refuses to take comfort in unrealistic fantasy.[32]

Job's soul mate, Qoheleth, takes up the issue of life beyond the grave and responds with cool detachment: "Who knows?" His linking of humans and animals suggests, however, that he thinks of death as final. Indeed, Qoheleth's question, "Who knows whether the human breath goes upward and the breath of animals goes down to the earth?" (Eccl 3:21), may constitute his rejection of belief in immortality.[33] If mortals awaited blissful existence beyond this veil of tears, Qoheleth's skepticism would have lacked credibility. Nothing in the book indicates that Qoheleth's teachings were hollow; instead, his words are said to have carried sharp barbs that pricked those who, like him, dared to think radically (12:11).

Ben Sira continued his predecessors' resistance to the notion that the dead return from the grave. One could hardly express the view more strongly than Ben Sira does in observing that at death a person inherits creeping things, wild beasts, and worms (Sir 10:11). As he understood things, death ushered one into eternal rest (30:17; 38:23), a state preferable to chronic illness, the disabilities associated with aging, and poverty. "Do not forget, there is no coming back" stands alongside an epitaph: "Mine yesterday, yours today" (38:21–23). Behind this grim humor stood a divine decree, "You must die," and curse, "Unto dust you must return" (8:6–7; 41:9–10). Ben Sira subscribed to the earlier theory that in Sheol no one inquired about things that occupy the daily thoughts of earth's occupants. Nevertheless, Ben Sira thinks God's attitude toward humankind is compassionate precisely because of life's brevity and the unwelcome end awaiting all (18:8–14).

Like Job, Ben Sira uses an analogy from nature to get his point across. Life, he writes, resembles a tree in that it constantly throws off leaves and grows new ones in their place. Like a used garment, the old ones decay and pass away (14:14–19). Modern naturalists say that nature recycles the old, and new organisms emerge from the decaying matter. Ben Sira would probably agree, although emphasizing the adjective "new."

The conviction that death inaugurates an era of eternal rest does not lead Ben Sira to rule out exceptions. He recalls Elijah's raising of the dead (48:5) and assigns to this prophet a special role, that of calming the divine fury at the decisive eschatological moment. Ben Sira also mentions Enoch as one who escaped death like Elijah, observing that Enoch provides an example of repentance (44:16).[34]

Conclusion

This analysis of Israelite belief in the resurrection of the body and in immortality of the soul has emphasized the biblical sources for both views. It argues that the powerful sense of communion with Yahweh and belief in the Deity's creative might and justice provided the basis for the idea of an immortal soul and resurrection of the body. The catalyst that broke these ideas open and produced full-blown concepts of immortality and resurrection was apocalyptic theology, and its accompanying persecution of the righteous. The driving force and intellectual dynamic was the problem of theodicy. Greek influence, hardly generative here, did bring decisive innovations. Old views exercised surprising tenacity in the face of attractive concepts, as if striving to keep theological discourse honest.[35]

Notes

1. See the selected bibliography at the end of this volume. Among the many books and articles on the subject of life after death in Old Testament thought, a few have been particularly useful: R. Martin-Achard, "Resurrection (OT)," in *ABD* 4 (1992): 680–84 and his earlier *From Death to Life* (Edinburgh: Oliver & Boyd, 1960); G. Johannes Botterweck, "Marginalien zum alt. Auferstehungsglauben," in *Wiener Zeitschrift für die Kunde des Morgenlandes* (ed. Herbert W. Duda; vol. 53; Vienna: Im Selbstverlag des Orientalischen Institutes, 1957), 1–8; V. Maag, "Tod und Jenseits nach dem Alten Testament," in *Kultur, Kulturkontakt und Religion* (Göttingen: Vandenhoeck & Ruprecht, 1980), 181–202; L. Rost, "Alttestamentliche Wurzeln der ersten Auferstehung," in *In Memoriam Ernst Lohmeyer* (ed. Werner Schmauch; Stuttgart: Evangelisches Verlagswerk GmbH., 1961), 67–72; O. Kaiser, "Die Zukunft der Toten nach den Zeugnissen der alttestamentlich-frühjüdischen Religion," in *Der Mensch unter dem Schicksal* (Berlin: de Gruyter, 1985), 182–95; H. Dietrich Preuss, " 'Auferstehung' in Texten alttestamentlicher Apokalyptik (Jes. 26, 7–19; Dan. 12, 1–4)," in *"Linguistische" Theologie* (ed. U. Gerber und E. Güttgemanns; Bonn: Linguistica Biblica, 1972), 103–333; E. Haenchen, *Die Bibel und Wir* (vol. 2; Tübingen: Mohr [Siebeck, 1968], 73–90; G. Hasel, "Resurrection in the Theology of Old Testament Apocalyptic," *ZAW* 92 (1980): 267–83; J. Collins, "The Root of Immortality: Death in the Context of Jewish Wisdom," *HTR* 71 (1978): 177–92; and idem, "Apocalyptic Eschatology as the Transcendence of Death," *CBQ* 36 (1974): 21–43.

2. J. Barton, *Oracles of God: Perceptions of Ancient Prophecy in Israel after the Exile* (New York: Oxford University Press, 1986), discusses the shift in understanding prophecy as twice-removed from its divine source, a late phenomenon that elevated earlier prophets above postexilic exemplars. In his view, this difference in immediacy, with a sacred text replacing a sense of having received the divine word directly, was accompanied by increased emphasis on miraculous acts by

the prophets. One can already see this principle at work in Num 12. Perhaps it represents a heightened sense of awe that certain groups always nurtured with respect to prophetic figures, some of whom invariably towered over their peers.

3. N. Gillman, *The Death of Death* (Woodstock: Jewish Lights Publishing, 1997), examines Jewish views about the afterlife from biblical times to the present and identifies two competing concepts: resurrection and immortality. He beautifully illustrates this ambiguity within modern liturgical prayers.

4. Kaiser, "Die Zukunft der Toten," 186. The persistence of these concepts, a "living corpse" resting in the grave and a "shade" wandering in Sheol like the restless movement of humans on earth, can be observed in later understandings of life after death. The funerary cult of the dead aimed at providing the necessities of the living dead, particularly fluids (C. Kennedy, "Dead, Cult of the," *ABD* 2 [1992]: 105–8).

5. The ease with which interpreters during the first half of the twentieth century envisioned seminomadic existence in Israel's remote ancestry has tightened considerably as a result of competing theories about its origins. Critics nowadays question the older assumption that seminomadism preceded cultivation of the land.

6. On Qoheleth's views about the finality of death as a powerful force in shaping conduct, see my article, "The Shadow of Death in Qoheleth," in J. Crenshaw, *Urgent Advice and Probing Questions* (Macon: Mercer University, 1995), 573–85; originally appearing in *Israelite Wisdom* (ed. John Gammie et al.; Philadelphia: Fortress, 1978), 205–16. This oppressive shadow prefigured (foreshadowed!) the kind of existence everyone was destined to endure in the next life.

7. While biblical authors were reluctant to depict the underworld, graphic accounts appear in Egypt and Mesopotamia. Besides these descriptions, Egyptian literature includes books that lead the dead through various gates and caverns, while Mesopotamian texts describe Ishtar's descent into the netherworld. The name "Sheol" seems to derive from *šā'al* (to ask, inquire) and to reflect the practice of necromancy. On this hypothesis, see T. Lewis, "Dead, Abode of the," *ABD* 2 (1992): 101–5. N. Tromp, *Primitive Conceptions of Death and the Nether World in the Old Testament* (BibOr 21; Rome: Pontifical Biblical Institute, 1969), draws on Ugaritic literature to provide a comprehensive examination of biblical views about Sheol and the denizens of that world, the Rephaim (*rĕpā'îm*).

8. Although frequently expressed in the Psalms (6:6 [5 ET]; 30:10 [9]; 88:6 [5]; 11 [10]), this belief (that the dead are cut off from Yahweh) pervades the prayer attributed to King Hezekiah in the book

of Isaiah (38:11, 18–19) and even surfaces in a wisdom setting (Sir 17:27–28). H. Gunkel explains the rationale for this view: "Das Licht ist der erste Schöpfung; ohne Licht kein Leben und keine Ordnung. Vor dem Licht war die Welt dunkel, leblos, wirr; Finsternis und Chaos sind grauenwoll; grauenvoll ist auch die Sheol, die kein Licht hat; das Licht ist gut und heilsam" (*Genesis* [HAT 1; Göttingen: Vandenhoeck & Ruprecht, 1965]).

9. The Platonic concept of heavenly ideas, together with their pale reflection on earth, and Pythagorean teachings have influenced the author of the Wisdom of Solomon, the fullest representative in biblical literature of such disparaging of the material world. Similarly, 1 Esd 4:36–38 contrasts everything earthly with eternal truth. All things and people of this world are *adika/oi*, "unrighteous."

10. The citation derives from Martin-Achard, "Resurrection (OT)," 683. The question of theodicy lies at the heart of this revolutionary development. On Isa 26:19 Preuss writes, " 'Auferstehung' ist aber in diesem Text nicht Ziel oder Zweck als solche, sondern sie steht im Dienst der Theodizeefrage." Similarly, on Dan 12:1–4 he states, " 'Auferstehung' begegnet auch hier als gewagter Glaube, als Glaubenspostulat,... als Heilszusage, also Sprache des Glaubens, als Trost....Das Theodizeeproblem ist folglich auch hier (vgl. Dan 9,24) für das Entstehen der Zusage 'Auferstehung' konstitutiv" (in " 'Auferstehung' in Texten alttestamentlicher Apokalyptik," 122 and 130).

11. G. Fuchs, *Mythos und Hiobdichtung* (Stuttgart: W. Kohlhammer, 1993); and Jon D. Levenson, *Creation and the Persistence of Evil* (San Francisco: Harper & Row, 1988).

12. L. Perdue, "The Riddles of Psalm 49," *JBL* 93 (1974): 533–42, detects hidden meaning beneath the surface of the language, a weighty endeavor to intensify the gloomy aspects of the human situation. In v. 5 [4 ET] the psalmist uses *ḥîdātî* (my riddle) in parallelism with *māšāl* (proverbial saying). In this psalm rival understandings of the realm of the dead may be detected. That place is the pit; corpses remain in graves forever; the dead waste away in Sheol, with Death as shepherd; they go to the ancestors, dwelling in darkness. On the characteristics of wisdom literature and wisdom psalms in particular, see J. Crenshaw, *Old Testament Wisdom: An Introduction* (rev. ed.; Louisville: Westminster John Knox, 1998).

13. The commentaries generally favor this change, supported by a few manuscripts (e.g., Briggs, Kraus, Craigie, Weiser), although Dahood defends the Masoretic Text's *'āḥ*, translating "alas." He thinks terms of intimacy occasionally express dismay.

14. For analysis of the theological struggle that Psalm 73 plots, see M. Buber, "The Heart Determines [Psalm 73]," in *On the Bible* (New York: Schocken Books, 1968), 199–210; and J. Crenshaw, "Standing Near the Flame: Psalm 73," in *A Whirlpool of Torment: Israelite Traditions of God as an Oppressive Presence* (Philadelphia: Fortress, 1984), 93–109.

15. The alternative view, that Job refers to the preservation of a permanent witness on progressively more enduring surfaces, highlights his growing frustration over unfair treatment on both fronts, heavenly and earthly. On the larger problem of literacy, see J. Crenshaw, *Education in Ancient Israel: Across the Deadening Silence* (ABRL; New York: Doubleday, 1998).

16. Perhaps the example from Proverbs (23:11) should be deleted, for it belongs to the section strongly influenced by the Egyptian Instruction of Amenemope and does not identify the divine (?) redeemer who takes up (adjudicates) the cause of the widow (reading *'almānâ*) and orphans. The text from the book of Jeremiah (50:34) uses a stereotypical formula, *YHWH ṣĕbā'ôt šĕmô*, in identifying this powerful litigator. On this refrain, see J. Crenshaw, "*YHWH sĕba'ôt šĕmô:* A Form Critical Analysis," *ZAW* 83 (1969): 156–75; and idem, *Hymnic Affirmation of Divine Justice* (SBLDS 24; Missoula: Scholars Press, 1975).

17. D. Clines, *Job 1–20* (Dallas: Word Books, 1989), 457–58, 461–62, and C. Newsom, "Job," *NIB* 4 (1996), 479.

18. The monumental step from believing in the resurrection of exceptional victims of malevolence to a general raising of all the dead suggests an easing of theodicy as the driving force. Nevertheless, divine character continues to be central, inasmuch as the destiny of mortals reflects on the Deity's power and benevolence.

19. For modern readers, personal time marches inevitably onward to the beat of muffled drums until it comes to the last milestone, a decisive end. Prior to that final heartbeat, one is alive; after that second, a person is dead. The Israelites did not think that way. Individuals frequently dropped into the realm of the dead, being transported there by adversity of some sort, later experiencing rescue and restoration to full life, like the ebb and flow of the sea. Poets employed vivid images to portray this hazardous existence on the threshold, often choosing extreme language of distress to improve the chance of being heard by the Deity.

20. D. Polaski, "Authorizing an End: The Isaiah Apocalypse and Intertextuality" (Leiden: Brill, 2001), views this text as similar to Ezek 37, the restoration of a nation. He thinks Isa 26:19 functions to contain

social tensions by creating a present moment that blends both effectiveness and ineffectiveness (vv. 14 and 19). In short, the righteous are far more powerful than they think, and the wicked have less might than meets the eye.

21. Jewish weavers of fantasy played with this idea of an eschatological banquet and came up with intriguing scenarios (cf. Isa 25:6, 8; 55:1–5; Prov 9:1–6; *2 En.* 42:5; *2 Bar.* 29; and *Pss. Sol.* 17:40). At this feast the final consumption of Leviathan (Chaos personified) is the supreme irony, because Death was notorious for swallowing its victims (cf. 1 Cor 15:54). In a Hellenistic context, banquets assumed enormous social significance, even receiving favorable comments from Ben Sira (Sir 31:12–32:13).

22. On the prominence of this theological problem in wisdom literature, see my *Urgent Advice and Probing Questions,* 141–221. I address this issue more broadly in "The Sojourner Has Come to Play the Judge: Theodicy on Trial," in *God in the Fray: A Tribute to Walter Brueggemann* (ed. T. Linafelt and T. Beal; Minneapolis: Fortress, 1998), 83–92. See also my *Defending God: Biblical Responses to the Problem of Evil* (New York: Oxford University Press, 2005).

23. F. J. Helfmeyer, " 'Deine Toten — Meine Leichen': Heilszusage und Annahme in Jes. 26.19," in *Bausteine biblischer Theologie: Festgabe für G. Johannes Botterweck zum 60. Geburtstag dargebr. von seinen Schülern* (ed. B. G. Weiss and J. Welch; BBB 50; Bonn: Hanstein, 1977), 254–57. The dew of heaven plays prominently in rabbinic legend about the resuscitation of Isaac in the Garden of Eden, to which he has been transported following Abraham's actual sacrifice of his son. On this speculation, see S. Spiegel, *The Last Trial* (New York: Schocken Books, 1969); and J. Ebach, *Gott im Wort: Drei Studien zur biblischen Exegese und Hermeneutik* (Neukirchen Vluyn: Neukirchener Verlag, 1997), 1–25.

24. See the depiction of a pugilistic Yahweh in Isa 27:1–5, a text in counterpoint with the earlier song of the vineyard in 5:1–7. The eschatological reference in 27:2 (in that day) is unmistakable; here Yahweh finally slays Leviathan (v. 1), the coiling serpent lurking in the sea. Ugaritic texts also lurk in the background, for they feature the twisting serpent and hostile Yam (god of the sea).

25. S. Paul, "Heavenly Tablets and the Book of Life," *JANESCU* 5 (1973): 345–53, demonstrates the scope of this belief in the existence of celestial scribal activity with grave consequences for mortals.

26. The religiohistorical significance of radiant souls is attested by its presence in Zoroastrianism, where the dead pass through a fiery stream and are purified; Qumran eschatology; various Hellenistic

depictions of heavenly sparks that become trapped in human bodies until their liberation through *gnōsis;* and Jewish mysticism generally. Does the biblical author know the concept of stars as personal beings (cf. Isa 14 [Lucifer, son of the Day Star] and a similar tradition in Ugaritic literature)?

27. J. Collins, "Apocalyptic Eschatology as the Transcendence of Death," *CBQ* 36 (1974): 33–35, thinks that the resurrected ones are elevated to the ranks of angels. G. W. E. Nickelsburg Jr., *Resurrection, Immortality, and Eternal Life in Intertestamental Judaism* (HTS 26; Cambridge: Harvard University Press, 1972), 19, observes a difference between Isa 26:19, where resurrection is itself the vindication of righteousness, and Dan 12:1–3, where "resurrection is a *means* by which both the righteous and the wicked dead are enabled to receive their respective vindication or condemnation."

28. "Instructing a woman is like having a sack of sand whose side is split open" (Instruction of Ankhsheshonq 13.20, from Egypt). A single example of such nonsense is one too many.

29. Nickelsburg, *Resurrection, Immortality, and Eternal Life,* 93–109, thinks that the original of this genre referred to a father and his seven sons, to which were added traditions of apocalyptic catastrophe and Isaianic exaltation. The figure of the mother, in Nickelsburg's view, derived from another contemporary tradition, which has been enriched from the language of the Isaianic servant. For an exhaustive discussion of this story about a mother and her seven sons, see Jonathan A. Goldstein, *II Maccabees* (AB 41A; Garden City, NY: Doubleday, 1983), 289–317.

30. On the Diaspora setting of Wisdom of Solomon, see J. Collins, *Jewish Wisdom in the Hellenistic Age* (Louisville: Westminster John Knox, 1997), 135–57.

31. M. Kolarcik, *The Ambiguity of Death in the Book of Wisdom 1–6* (AnBib 127; Rome: Pontifical Biblical Institute, 1991), thinks the author works with quite different concepts of death: actual death and spiritual death. Kolarcik tries to show that the Christian notion of transcending physical death is philosophically valid.

32. For further discussion of Job 14:13–17 in its larger context, see J. Crenshaw, "Flirting with the Language of Prayer (Job 14:13–17)," in *Worship and the Hebrew Bible: Essays in Honor of John T. Willis* (ed. P. Graham, R. Marrs, and S. McKenzie; Sheffield: Sheffield Academic Press, 1999), 110–23.

33. See my article, "The Expression *mî yôdēa'* in the Hebrew Bible," *VT* 36 (1986): 274–88 (also in *Urgent Advice and Probing Questions,* 279–91).

34. For my understanding of Ben Sira, see "Sirach," *NIB* 5 (1997), 601–867.

35. The facile liturgy in Hos 6:1–3, with its explicit imagery from nature, looks to national restoration after three days, a symbolic number in mythic texts of the ancient Near East signaling a decisive event. The text has nothing to do with life after death.

Chapter 4

The Resurrection Passages in the *Testaments of the Twelve Patriarchs:* Hope for Israel in Early Judaism and Christianity

C. D. Elledge

From an existential perspective, the reality of death has posed one of the most enduring problems and prospects of human religion. The literature of Early Judaism and Christianity attests to the development of responses to death that for centuries have proved to be of especial importance in the history of religions in the West. Over the last century historical surveys of the resurrection, immortality, and eternal life have repeatedly demonstrated that early Jewish and Christian reflection upon the problem of death and the future life did not take the form of a static concept or doctrine.[1] Instead, hope in the future life was a flexible, living tradition and took a fascinating variety of expressions. If we would gain a more profound appreciation of this monumental development, it therefore is necessary

79

to describe the distinctive contours of the resurrection hope
in the literature of Early Judaism and Christianity on a
document-by-document basis.

The collection we now call the *Testaments of the Twelve
Patriarchs* provides an instructive example of how an individual document develops appeals of hope in the resurrection
in order to suit its own apologetical aims. The contemporary English reader may study the *Testaments* in volume 1
of James H. Charlesworth's *Old Testament Pseudepigrapha*, in
a fine edition by Howard Clark Kee.[2] Among the numerous documents that attest hope in the resurrection during
the formative period of Judaism and Christianity, this collection has shaped its own presentation of the resurrection in a
way that is distinctively nationalistic and attempts to come
to terms with the problem of Israel's ultimate destiny at the
end of days.

The *Testaments* contain four resurrection prophecies, in
which the biblical patriarchs Simeon, Judah, Zebulon, and
Benjamin declare their faith in a future resurrection of the
dead. These four passages present formidable challenges for
analysis, since the origin of the *Testaments* has remained a disputed issue in critical scholarship. On the one hand, aspects
of the *Testaments* must have existed at a pre-Christian and
Jewish stage of development; on the other, the collection was
edited over time as it was handed down in a variety of ancient
and medieval Christian communities.[3] Unfortunately, the evidence for the *Testaments* among the Dead Sea Scrolls proves
ambiguous and has not solved this problem.[4] Questions thus
remain about the extent to which a pre-Christian Semitic
original remains accessible despite Christian rewriting.[5] This
often makes it difficult to discern whether one is reading Jewish or Christian theology in the *Testaments,* or a combination
of both.

Despite these challenges for interpretation, the speeches
of the *Testaments* are worthy of careful study. They provide
an intricately woven and colorful strand within the much
larger historical and theological fabric of ancient resurrection

faith. This chapter begins with a survey of the resurrection prophecies in the *Testaments,* followed by a description of the concept of the resurrection assumed in these texts, and finally a constructive proposal for assessing the rhetorical function of these resurrection passages within the *Testaments.* This approach is specifically designed to familiarize the general reader with how one document can broaden our current understanding of the language, theology, and purpose of ancient resurrection faith.

Survey of Passages

At least four passages of the *Testaments* directly refer to a future resurrection of the dead:

> *Testament of Simeon* 6:7
>
> *Testament of Judah* 25
>
> *Testament of Zebulon* 10:1–4
>
> *Testament of Benjamin* 10:6–10[6]

Each of these references surfaces among the discourses in which the patriarchs make eschatological predictions on the verge of their imminent deaths. The first passage in the *Testament of Simeon* is brief, as is *Testament of Zebulon;* but the *Testament of Judah* and the *Testament of Benjamin* expand and magnify the resurrection motif into a visionary prophecy for the reconstitution of Israel. Though the first three examples may well preserve originally Jewish traditions of the resurrection prophecies, the *Testament of Benjamin* demonstrates how later Christian scribes adopted and revised Jewish resurrection hopes for their own theological purposes.

Simeon's Prophecy (*T. Sim.* 6:7)

The *Testament of Simeon* opens with an introduction describing the occasion of his words "to his sons before he died."[7] A biographical sketch of Simeon's life comprises the first main element of his speech (ch. 2). Within this sketch, Simeon's reflections upon his role in his brothers' crime against Joseph (2:6–14) lead to a moral exhortation against "envy" (ch. 3), which H. Hollander and M. de Jonge rightly describe as the "central theme" of Simeon's story.[8]

Simeon then turns his attention from the past to Israel's future, as he warns his children with prophetic tone concerning coming apostasy and God's ultimate renewal of Israel in the latter days (5:4–7:3). It is within this extended section that his resurrection prophecy takes place (6:7). Finally, chapters 8–9 describe the details of Simeon's death and burial, as his last words come to a close.

Within the extended eschatological section of 5:4–7:3, the resurrection prophecy of Simeon occurs after the suggestion of his own descendants' apostasy (5:4–6) and the prediction that Israel's political enemies will all be destroyed (6:3–4),[9] giving way to a period of universal peace in which Shem (presumably his descendants) will be glorified and humans will rule over evil spirits (6:5–6). Israel's enemies, both political and supernatural, will all thus be destroyed. At this point, Simeon prophesies:

> Then *I shall arise in joy,* and I shall bless the Most High, because of his marvelous (works). (6:7)[10]

This is the only clear resurrection passage within the *Testament of Simeon* and the first resurrection prophecy of the collection. Though very brief, it uses a recognizable terminology for the resurrection (I shall arise) that is maintained in the prophecies of Judah, Zebulon, and Benjamin. Furthermore, it links the resurrection to eschatological joy and worship (a recurrent motif in what follows), as the patriarch rises to "bless the Most High." The patriarch will thus one day join his future descendants in an Israel that has been delivered from both its external political threats and its own internal apostasy from God.

Judah's Prophecy (*T. Jud.* 25)

In the testament that Judah bequeaths to his descendants, one finds a clear example of this collection's special concern with Judah and his offspring. His testament is especially long. The first twelve chapters contain a biographical reminiscence of the patriarch's life and courage, followed in chapters 13–20 by a section that intermingles biographical details about the Tamar affair of Gen 38 and exhortations against drunkenness, greed, and impurity. These moral teachings are illustrated through Judah's personal, and occasionally humorous, reflections upon the biblical Tamar episode. After a description of "the spirits of truth and evil" in chapter 20, the next section (chs. 21–25) turns to prophesy future events, including the coming sins of Judah's descendants (21:6–22:2) and the emergence of a king from his seed who will rule the whole world in peace and righteousness (22:2–24:6). Immediately after this passage the patriarch describes his own future resurrection in the extended discourse of chapter 25. Finally, chapter 26 concludes the testament with an exhortation to keep the law, since there is much "hope"[11] in the future for those who are steadfast. Judah also gives precise instructions for his burial, which his children execute by returning him to Hebron.

Judah's prophecy of resurrection introduces a new hope that could not have been predicted from Simeon's earlier prophecy. Judah is not the only one whom God will raise from the dead:

> And after these things, Abraham and Isaac and Jacob *shall arise*
> *unto life*,
> And I and my brothers will be rulers over our tribes in Israel:
> Levi first, second I, third Joseph, fourth Benjamin, fifth Simeon,
> sixth Issachar, and so all in order.[12] (25:1)

This resurrection (after these things)[13] takes place after a new ruler has brought a universal reign of peace to Israel. The patriarchs arise from the dead for participation in this restored Israel. They will preside over their original tribes and territories in the land, with Levi and Judah taking positions of authority above the others. The author carefully describes a hierarchy of resurrections that Hollander and de Jonge attribute to reflection upon Deut 27:12: first Levi, then Judah, and the others.[14] In what follows, the entire cosmos in heaven and earth will bless the risen patriarchs (25:2).[15] "There will be one people of the Lord and one tongue," and Beliar (Satan) shall be punished forever (25:3). Thus, the restored Israel that the risen patriarchs govern will be a people united and free of evil.

The resurrection also extends beyond the patriarchs to encompass many others, for whom the resurrection will mark a complete reversal of fortunes in the world to come:[16]

> And those who died in sorrow *shall arise in joy;*
> And those who were in poverty because of the Lord *shall be made rich;*
> And those who were in want *shall be fed;*
> And those who were in weakness *shall be strong;*
> And those who died because of the Lord *shall be awakened unto life.* (25:4)

This passage, which so carefully juxtaposes five parallel reversals of fortunes, proclaims the resurrection day as a time for joy, prosperity, nourishment, strength, and life. This prophecy is aimed especially at those who suffer sorrow, poverty, lack, weakness, and death amid current afflictions. The prophecies of Simeon and Judah thus envision the resurrection of the patriarchs to a restored Israel. Both the patriarchs and their suffering descendants shall be raised to a new life in the land of Israel, in which God will reverse their previous status of sorrow, poverty, hunger, sickness, and death. This life will include a just political rule in the land of Israel. Judah encourages the righteous to remain steadfast in light of these hopes.

Zebulon's Prophecy (*T. Zeb.* 10:1–4)

Yet another resurrection passage is to be found in the *Testament of Zebulon,* which employs this patriarch's biographical reminiscences (1:4–4:13; 5:5–7:4) in order to exhort its readers toward greater compassion and mercy (5:1–4; 7:2–3; 8:1–3). Like the other testaments, the *Testament of Zebulon* also concludes with eschatological prophecies (9:5–10:4), including the foretelling of his own future resurrection. This expectation is directly connected with the patriarch's imminent death (10:1, 4). As in the previous examples, the patriarch's death and burial conclude the entire testament (10:6–7).

Zebulon's resurrection prophecy also proclaims that the patriarch will rule politically over a restored Israel in the land of promise:

> And now, my children, do not sorrow that I am dying,
>   nor grieve that I am perishing.
> For *I shall arise again in your midst,*
>   as a ruler in the midst of his sons,
> And I shall rejoice in the midst of my tribe,
>   as many as keep the law of the Lord
>   and the commandments of Zebulon their father.
> But upon the ungodly, the Lord will bring everlasting fire,
>   and he will destroy them throughout generations.
> But as for *now, I am going away into my rest,* as my fathers.
>
>   (10:1–4)

Zebulon's restored rule over his tribe is linked with his rejoicing, a theme already established in the prophecies of Simeon and Judah (see also "gladness" in *T. Ben.* 10:6, below). The passage also seems to assume that all those who keep the law will participate in this restored rule. But as for the wicked, they will suffer retributive judgment (cf. *T. Jud.* 25:3). These prophecies lead to Zebulon's final exhortation to his children: "But as for you, fear the Lord your God with all your might all the days of your life" (10:5). This fear of God and adherence to the commandments provide the definitive criterion for participation in the eschatological blessings that the patriarch promises his descendants.

Benjamin's Prophecy (*T. Ben.* 10:6–10)

The final passage of the *Testaments* that contains a clear reference to the future resurrection of the dead occurs near the

end of the *Testament of Benjamin,* which is the last discourse
of the entire collection. Since the *Testament of Benjamin* is, in
part, a kind of résumé of previous claims expressed throughout the collection, its structure is rather cursory and lacks
an ultimately consistent topical focus.[17] Chapters 1–2 lead to
the reminiscence of a dialogue between Benjamin and Joseph,
followed in chapters 3–8 by an exhortation that also includes
scattered biographical references illustrating the virtues of a
pure mind. Eschatological topics, including the last temple,
the Messiah, and the giving of the spirit to the Gentiles,
conclude the *Testament of Benjamin* in chapters 9–11. In this
context, the patriarch also gives his prophecy of a future resurrection of the dead. After a final exhortation to carry his
bones back to Hebron, Benjamin, the youngest son of Israel,
dies; and the entire collection comes to an end (ch. 12).[18]

After several exhortations to keep the commandments
(10:2–5), Benjamin describes the reward the righteous will
have when God reveals his savior to all the nations. This
resurrection prophecy, more than any previous example, illustrates how Christian scribes expanded and reinterpreted
the resurrection traditions in the *Testaments:*

> Then you will see Enoch, Noah, and Shem,
>   and Abraham and Isaac and Jacob
>   standing on the right hand in gladness.
> Then *we also shall arise,* each (of us) over our tribe,
>   worshipping the king of the heavens,
>   who appeared on earth in the form of a man of lowliness.[19]
> And as many as believed in him on earth shall rejoice
>   together with him.
> Then also *all shall rise,* some unto glory and some unto shame.
> And the Lord will judge Israel first concerning (her) iniquity
>   against him,
>   for they did not believe that God appeared in the flesh
>   as a deliverer.
> And then he shall judge all the nations,
>   as many as did not believe in him who appeared on earth.
> And he will convict Israel by the elect ones of the nations,
>   even as he convicted Esau by the Midianites,

who refused to be their brothers through impurity and
  idolatry,
and they were alienated from God,
not becoming children in the portion of those who fear the
  Lord. But you, if you walk in holiness before the Lord,
you shall also dwell again in hope with me.
And all Israel shall be gathered unto the Lord.[20] (10:6–11)

This passage, containing obvious christological elements
(underlined above), reiterates previous expectations of a resurrection in "joy" or "gladness" found in the *Testaments of
Simeon* and *Judah*. The resurrection also leads the righteous
into a state of eschatological worship "on the right hand."

A careful progression of resurrections is prophesied,[21] beginning with Enoch and continuing until all are raised. First,
Enoch, Noah, and Shem arise, the faithful servants of God
who lived before Abraham. Then, the trio of Abraham, Isaac,
and Jacob arise. Third, the twelve patriarchs themselves (we)
arise to preside over their original tribes, as in earlier examples. Fourth, "all shall rise" — both the wicked and the
good — and God will judge Israel and the nations according
to whether or not they believed in the Messiah. More than
any other previous example, the *Testament of Benjamin* asserts
the universalist dimensions of the resurrection, not simply for
the patriarchs or even just for Israel, but for all.[22] The passage
closes with a final exhortation that if Benjamin's descendants
will continue in holiness, they will "dwell again in hope"
with the patriarch, as all Israel is gathered together before
the Lord.

The Concept of the Resurrection

As the introduction to this chapter suggests, the study of the
Testaments continues to deal with the relationship between
Jewish and Christian theology in the collection. It is a vast
and complex problem that specialists continue to study. This
aspect of the *Testaments* as a whole is reflected in the four

resurrection passages we have treated above. Whereas two of these (*T. Sim.* 6:7; *T. Ben.* 10:6–10) contain clearly Christian references in the immediate context of the resurrection prophecies, the other two do not (*T. Zeb.* 10:1–4; *T. Jud.* 25). Taken together, these four passages illustrate the common interests of both early Jewish and later Christian authors in the development of the resurrection passages in the collection. In a sense, these four passages illustrate in literary form how Jewish hopes in the resurrection of the dead were taken up and given further expansion in Christian hands.

The Christian associations of the resurrection prophecy of *T. Sim.* 6:7 come just at the end of the resurrection prophecy, in the form of an explanatory clause that describes the praise that the risen patriarch will give to God in eschatological rejoicing: "for God, taking a body and eating with men, saved men." Though the presence of this christological statement of praise at the conclusion of the resurrection prophecy would suggest its Christian origin, the Christology of the explanatory clause does not directly occur within the resurrection prophecy itself and may, in fact, have originated separately from it.[23] Thus, the resurrection passage itself need not have originated from a Christian author.

A more decisively Christian resurrection passage is in *T. Ben.* 10:1–4, where christological statements are more naturally integrated throughout the entire resurrection prophecy. In this passage, belief in the one "who appeared on earth in the form of a man of lowliness" has become the supreme criterion of future judgment both for Israel and for the Gentiles. This Christianizing tendency is so strong throughout the passage that one cannot easily separate the christological statements from an originally Jewish resurrection prophecy.[24]

Two other passages, however, do not contain clearly recognizable christological statements. Despite its length, the resurrection prophecy of *T. Jud.* 25 lacks a definitive christological reference.[25] Instead, it is primarily concerned with the restoration of patriarchal rule over the tribes in the land of Israel and with the reversal of fortunes for the faithful in the future life.[26] Furthermore, *T. Zeb.* 10:1–4 lacks any christological references in its resurrection prophecy. Instead, it is more directly concerned with the physical death of Zebulon and the destruction of the wicked. Keeping the law of God and the words of the dying patriarch will be the criterion for future judgment — not faith in any Messiah. It is probable, then, that hope in the future resurrection existed in the collection at a pre-Christian stage of development and underwent gradual christological expansion over the course of its tradition history.[27]

Having established that the resurrection prophecies attest originally Jewish hopes that were adopted and expanded among Christians, what can we say of the theology of the resurrection in these passages? One must observe, first of all, that the theology of the resurrection in all four examples emerges within a biographical context that poses the imminent death of the ancestor as the occasion for these discourses. This narrative context is by far the most consistent characteristic among the four resurrection passages.[28] Hope in the resurrection shines forth the more brightly against these sober testamentary death scenes, as piety meets its final trial in death.

The content of all four prophecies envisions the resurrection as a time of "joy" or "rejoicing." Three factors may account for this use of language for the resurrection. First, as Hollander and de Jonge suggest, the prophecy of Isa 26:19 may have served as a scriptural influence upon the terminology of the *Testaments.*[29] Crenshaw's contribution to the present volume (ch. 3) illustrates the importance of this passage for understanding ancient Israel's theology of life and death. Rejoicing at the time of the resurrection is also reflected in a broader array of parabiblical literature contemporaneous to the development of the *Testaments.*[30] Second, the very pathos of the patriarch's death may raise the expectation for its opposite, joy, at the resurrection. Zebulon, for example, must counsel his children not to be "sorrowful" and "downcast" at his death. Third, the language of joy may also reflect the expectation that the resurrection will involve worship, since both the *Testament of Simeon* and the *Testament of Benjamin* prophesy that they will "bless" and "worship" God in the resurrection (cf. *Pseudo-Ezekiel*). The place of this worship in the *Testament of Benjamin* is "at the right hand" of God, where the worshipping patriarchs enjoy the ultimate position of human honor.[31]

If this vision of the resurrection is at least somewhat "liturgical," it also possesses "political" dimensions. Three of the four passages (*Testaments of Judah, Zebulon,* and *Benjamin*) prophesy that the patriarchs will arise to reign over their original territorial portions in the land of Israel. This understanding of the resurrection is thus both nationalistic and restorationist. It envisions a restoration of Israel's original tribal constitution at the end of days. This must come as a surprise to modern readers, whose popular assumptions about the future life have become so etherealized that they often lack any practical implementation upon the earth. For the authors of the *Testaments,* both Jewish and Christian, this was not so. Instead, the *Testaments* portray a vision of the resurrection that combines aspects of Charlesworth's types 1 and 15: A national, political restoration accompanies personal hope in the resurrection.

The timing of the resurrection complements these nationalist and restorationist concerns. Simeon, for example, prophesies that the patriarch's resurrection will occur after Israel's political enemies have been destroyed (6:3–4). Even evil spirits will be subdued (6:5–6) in a period of universal peace. The patriarch will arise to enjoy this time of victory over Israel's national and supernatural enemies. In similar fashion Judah's prophecy places the resurrection after one of his own descendants has emerged to rule the whole world in peace and righteousness (22:2–24). Once again, the patriarchs are raised to enjoy and govern their hereditary portions in Israel as part of a new and universal kingdom. The prophecies thus reflect a sophisticated conception of the eschatological timing of the resurrection, which will restore the patriarchs to govern their tribes in the land of Israel after a period of universal peace has ensued. Rather than an escape from the world, the resurrection will mark a return to the earth to enjoy the blessings of a world now liberated from evil.

Two of the prophecies (*Testaments of Judah* and *Benjamin*) extend the resurrection to others besides the patriarchs. Judah's resurrection hope envisions an eschatological reversal for those who have suffered in life. The resurrection will be joy for the sorrowful, riches for the poor, food for the destitute, strength for the weak, and life for the dead (25:4). The highly christological *Testament of Benjamin* is the only prophecy among the four that prophesies a general resurrection of "all" people — "some unto glory and some unto shame," an almost formulaic statement that may reflect the influence of Dan 12:1–3. By prophesying the resurrection of all, the *Testament of Benjamin* adds to the *Testaments* a universalizing dimension that one cannot find in the other resurrection passages.[32] The resurrection the righteous (as opposed to the resurrection of *all* the dead), then, remains the most frequently cited hope in the collection, with only the *Testament of Benjamin* expecting a more universal and general resurrection.

The terminology of "hope" surfaces in the context of at least two resurrection prophecies. Judah's resurrection prophecy leads to the following exhortation: "Keep, therefore, my children, the whole law of the Lord, for there is hope for those who make straight their ways" (26:1). The term "hope" encompasses the resurrection and the reversal of fortunes after death. A more subtle reference to "hope" occurs at the end of Benjamin's resurrection prophecy (10:11), where the patriarch promises, "If you walk in holiness before the Lord, *you shall also dwell again in hope with me.*" Hollander and de Jonge have traced this expression to scriptural prophecies for the political restoration of Israel, such as Ezek 28:25–26.[33]

Finally, one must account for what the patriarchs have not described about the resurrection. They lack any of the cosmic or anthropological aspects of the resurrection hope encountered on repeated occasions in the study of the New Testament and related literature (e.g., *1 En.* 51, 92, 104; Dan 12:1–3; 1 Cor 15).[34] They are far more content to locate the resurrection life on earth and in Israel. The only concern for the body of the resurrection is implied in the transference of the patriarchs' physical remains to Hebron, whence, presumably, they shall arise. Otherwise, the resurrection is only described as an entrance "into life." Though the timing of the resurrection is carefully described with surprising consistency, the prophecies lack any kind of impending eschatological imminence. Yet there is a fervent certainty about the event, when one recognizes that the patriarchs have already described accurately the course of Israel's history that had presumably occurred before the composition of the *Testaments.* The accuracy of the patriarchs in prophesying the ongoing of history of Israel beyond their own ancient deaths lends credence, even an air of inevitability, to unfulfilled events in the future, including the resurrection of the righteous in the promised land, with national Israel triumphant.

From the perspective of Christian history and theology, the resurrection hope in the *Testaments* contains a remarkable surprise. *Supersessionism* — the belief that the Christian Church has replaced Israel in the plan of God — is generally avoided in the Christian editing and transmission of the collection. This is surprising, since Christianity in late antiquity often exhibits strongly supersessionist tendencies, including the idea that God has forsaken Israel and chosen the Gentile Church as his elect people (e.g., Justin Martyr, *Dial.* 11, 119, 123, 135; Origen, *Cels.* 2.8; 4.22; idem, *Comm. Matt.* 19). To the contrary, the resurrection passages of the *Testaments* proclaim hope for a future political restoration of Israel — and the Christian scribes who edited and transmitted this work have not undermined this hope.

The *Testaments*, thus, insist that through the resurrection God will somehow keep the promises originally made to Israel's ancestors. Other early Christian writings indicate a similar struggle to affirm God's promises to Israel's ancestors, despite the widespread rejection of the Christian Messiah in Judaism. One may read Paul's struggle with the fate of Israel in this way (Rom 9–11). Justin Martyr, despite his own supersessionist tendencies (*Dial.* 11, 119, 123, 135), also explores the possibility that God will yet remain faithful to Israel's ancestors, even amid the heated conflicts between Judaism and Christianity in the present (*Dial.* 45.2–4, 80–81; 130.1–2).[35] In the book of Acts, one may similarly view Luke's portrayal of Paul, including his own resurrection faith (17:16–34; 23:6–10; 24:15–16; 26:6–8, 22–23; cf. 28:20), as an affirmation of God's faithfulness to Israel's ancestral hopes. Alongside Paul, Justin, and Luke, the early Christian editors of the *Testaments* affirm the divine faithfulness to Israel, from the beginning of the people and even to the end of time, despite the advent of Christianity.[36]

Function of the Future Life

Why did the authors and revisers of the *Testaments* include these repeated references to the resurrection within the eschatological discourses of the dying patriarchs? One can only follow the clues that these texts leave behind in attempting to formulate an answer to this question. Three options for the rhetorical function of these passages are worth pursuing. The first deals with the question of what these prophecies tell us about the patriarchs who offer them. The second treats the question of how these passages relate to the theological presentation of Israel's history in the *Testaments*. The third attempts to identify the rhetorical force of these passages with regard to those who read these texts.

Hope and Imminent Death

As Hollander has recently brought into renewed focus and clarity, the twelve patriarchs serve as ethical models who bequeath examples of righteousness and unrighteousness to contemporary readers through reminiscences upon their own lives.[37] Although they are presented as ideal figures, the patriarchs are also flawed examples, recounting their own mistakes in their biographical narrations, particularly in their crimes against Joseph. They are thus well acquainted with vice as well as virtue. Their experiences qualify them to give ethical instruction to their descendants and to warn with prophetic tone that their descendants will fall into similar vices.

This is especially the case when one considers the close relationship between the resurrection prophecies and the biographical context of imminent death in the four passages treated above. As the previous section suggested, the most consistent textual aspect of the four resurrection prophecies is that each patriarch foretells his future resurrection from his deathbed. In this sense, their prophecies bring to light the patriarchs' steadfast hope in God, even at their very moment of decease. Through the resurrection prophecies, the patriarchs heroically face death through their hope and point beyond it to the future restoration of Israel. Their words are radiant professions of hope in God that the shadows of death do not dim. The sorrows of death, though real, are not the last word on human existence.

Theology of Israel's History

As the ancestral representatives of the Jewish people, the future resurrection of the patriarchs is also the exaltation of Israel over her political and supernatural enemies. This event will mark the definitive reunification of Israel and the end of its recurrent loss of nationhood, which the patriarchs' descendants would suffer throughout subsequent history.[38] Israel as a political kingdom has not, then, passed out of the divine plan for history. God's promises to the patriarchs are steadfast; they, in fact, will be raised from the dead to enjoy their fulfillment in the future.

The *Testaments* communicate this assurance of Israel's future restoration by juxtaposing fulfilled events in Israel's history with unfulfilled events in the eschatological future. Fulfilled events include a broad array of references to key events in Israel's history: the oppression in Egypt (*T. Jos.* 20:1), Israel's original occupation of the land (*T. Lev.* 7:1), the construction of the Temple in Benjamin (*T. Ben.* 9:2), the continuing priestly status of Levi's descendants (*T. Lev.* 8– 9), the divided monarchy (*T. Zeb.* 9:5), the establishment of the kingdom through the tribe of Judah and its later termination (*T. Jud.* 17:6; 22:2), as well as the destruction of the first Temple and exile (*T. Levi* 16; *T. Jud.* 23:3). In addition to these events that had certainly been fulfilled by the time of the collection's origins, Christian editions continue to elaborate upon the fulfilled events of the patriarchs' prophecies by making cryptic allusions to the Messiah's coming. The words of the patriarchs, then, have presumably shown themselves to be faithful prophecies of future events in Israel's ongoing history, up until the time of its ancient readers.

Through the resurrection prophecies, the patriarchs project this vision of Israel's history far into the future, even to the very consummation of the age. From the beginning of Israel's history, they are able to see the ultimate destiny of Israel as a restored political kingdom in the land. The assurance of this prophecy indicates that the recurrent patterns of sin and judgment that have plagued Israel's history cannot have the final word. God will restore the chosen people, not simply by the sword or war, but by supernatural resurrection and judgment. By framing Israel's history from the time of the patriarchs' hopes to the time of their fulfillment in the future, the resurrection prophecies affirm that Israel's sin and dispersion have not wrested history from the control of God. These repeated professions of hope in the resurrection, thus, seem to have been the *Testaments'* attempt to resolve the problem of Israel's ultimate destiny at the end of days.

The resurrection also addresses the plight of the suffering righteous. As the previous section has shown, *T. Jud.* 25:4

extends the resurrection hope to those who suffer affliction
in this world. This concern for the fate of the suffering righteous is reflected more broadly in the collection in a number
of ways, but it is especially in the paradigmatic life of Joseph
(*T. Ben.* 3:1–6) that the collection typically treats this matter.[39]
His story, in his own words, illustrates that "If, then, you also
walk in the commandments of the Lord, my children, he shall
exalt you as a result, and he shall bless you with good things
forever" (*T. Jos.* 18:1). The resurrection prophecy in *T. Jud.* 25:4
has been made to complement this theme. In the resurrection, God will raise up those who, like Joseph, suffer hunger,
affliction, false accusation, and sorrow. They shall have "everlasting joy." The patriarchs affirm to their descendants that
God will not abandon the righteous, but will reverse their current state of afflictions at the resurrection. This same concern
with final justice is replicated in the *Testament of Benjamin*'s
resurrection of all people for judgment (10:8), and in the *Testament of Zebulon*'s destruction of the wicked immediately after
the resurrection of the righteous (10:2–3). The resurrection is
a significant aspect of the divine response to good and evil
in the world. These four prophecies proclaim that God ultimately controls human affairs. They assure the final reward
of the righteous in a world where evil and human failure are
rampant no more.

Association with the Readers

The literary style of a "testament" assumes that the reader
of this collection should learn what the patriarchs have to
share with later generations. If there is a representative for the
readers in the actual text of the *Testaments*, it is the children
of the patriarch, who attend faithfully to the dying words of
their ancestor. The ancestors of the *Testaments* prepare future
generations for the troubles and glory that will come upon
Israel for centuries after their own deaths.

The *Testaments*, however, do not simply frame the contemporary context of the reader with regard to the patriarchal

past. In their predictions of events yet to come, they also frame the readers' position in history with a view to the eschatological future. Like the patriarchs, those who read these texts could look forward in the future to a final resurrection of the dead. The moral exhortations that the ancestors have bequeathed to their descendants come as instructions for participation in the eschatological blessings that the resurrection will inaugurate. Zebulon will rejoice in the resurrection with his tribe, "as many as keep the law of the Lord and the commandments of Zebulon their father" (*T. Zeb.* 10:2). Benjamin's resurrection prophecy also urges faith in the Messiah and walking in holiness as the conditions for being raised "unto glory" rather than "unto shame" (*T. Ben.* 10:2–5). In this sense, the resurrection prophecies are a call of exhortation to later readers of the *Testaments*. They must repent of errors and follow the ethical teachings of the patriarchs in order to be admitted to eschatological life.

The call for obedience to the law and the patriarchs' words, however, is of little benefit for those who keep the law and suffer while doing so. The *Testaments* recognize this situation and proclaim to the suffering righteous that God has not abandoned them to their sorrows. As *T. Jud.* 25:4 promises, "Those who died in sorrow shall rise in joy." The resurrection is one of a variety of ideas that the *Testaments* employ to affirm God's faithful care for the suffering righteous. This affirmation must have embraced the ancient reader as a consolation amid the troubles of life. Through the consolation of the resurrection, the patriarchs promise to their suffering descendants a dramatic reversal of fortunes into eschatological life. Like Joseph during his own life, they will be exalted beyond their afflictions into life, joy, and strength.

Conclusion

In reflection upon the language, theology, and purpose of the resurrection prophecies in the *Testaments,* it is important to recognize how they have been shaped to address a number of larger moral problems in the history of Israel: the problems of human sin and apostasy, the loss of political kingdom, the prosperity of the wicked and the suffering of the righteous, and the finality of individual death itself.[40] The resurrection prophecies of the patriarchs directly address these problems. They affirm for those who would live long after the ancestors that God will not forsake the chosen people to their own apostasy and suffering, but at the end time will restore to them all that they have lost, as they sojourn with hope, in a dangerous world. As a document shared by Christians and Jews in antiquity, the *Testaments* illustrate that this was a message of needed comfort for the two emerging faiths, as they struggled in their own distinctive ways to face both the past and the future with hope.

Notes

1. In this essay, translations of the *Testaments* follow the edition by H. Kee (see note 2, below), with frequent revision from the Greek editions by M. de Jonge and R. Charles (see below).

Surveys of early beliefs about the future life include R. H. Charles, *A Critical History of the Doctrine of a Future Life in Israel, in Judaism, and in Christianity; or, Hebrew, Jewish, and Christian Eschatology from Pre-Prophetic Times Till the Close of the New Testament Canon* (London: Black, 1899); G. W. E. Nickelsburg, *Resurrection, Immortality, and Eternal Life in Intertestamental Judaism* (Cambridge: Harvard University Press, 1972); G. Stemberger, *Der Leib der Auferstehung: Studien zur Anthropologie und Eschatologie des palästinischen Judentums im neutestamentlichen Zeitalter (ca. 170 v. Chr.–100 n. Chr.)* (Rome: Biblical Institute Press, 1972); H. C. C. Cavallin, *Life after Death: Paul's Argument for the Resurrection of the Dead in 1 Cor 15* (Lund: Gleerup, 1974); É. Puech, *La croyance des esséniens en la vie future: Immortalité, résurrection, vie éternelle? Histoire d'une croyance dans le judaïsme ancien* (2 vols.; ÉBib, NS, 21; Paris: Lecoffre, 1993).

2. For an accessible introduction and English translation, see H. Kee, "Testaments of the Twelve Patriarchs," in *OTP* 1:775–828.

3. R. H. Charles argued that the *Testaments* was an originally Jewish document containing Christian interpolations. His conclusions

are articulated in a series of works in 1908–13: R. H. Charles, ed., *The Apocrypha and Pseudepigrapha of the Old Testament in English, with Introductions and Critical and Explanatory Notes to the Several Books* (2 vols.; Oxford: Clarendon, 1913); idem, ed., *The Greek Versions of the Testaments of the Twelve Patriarchs, Edited from Nine MSS, together with the Variants of the Armenian and Slavonic Versions and Some Hebrew Fragments* (Oxford: Clarendon, 1908); "The Testaments of the XII Patriarchs," *Encyclopaedia Biblica* (4 vols.; New York: Macmillan 1899–1903): 1:287–91; idem, "Testaments of the XII Patriarchs," *Dictionary of the Bible Dealing with Its Language, Literature and Contents* (ed. J. Hastings; 5 vols.; Edinburgh: T & T Clark, 1898–1904; reprint, 1909), 4:721–25; idem, "The Testaments of the XII Patriarchs," *HibJ* 3 (1904–5): 558–73; idem, ed., *Testaments of the Twelve Patriarchs, Translated from the Editor's Greek Text and Edited with Introductory Notes, and Indices* (London: Black, 1908); R. H. Charles and A. Cowley, "An Early Source of the Testaments of the Twelve Patriarchs," *JQR* 19 (1907): 566–83. For the term "Charles consensus," see the well-known critical history by H. Slingerland, *The Testaments of the Twelve Patriarchs: A Critical History of Research* (SBLMS 21; Missoula, MT: Scholars Press, 1977).

4. This problem has certainly not been solved by the inconclusive evidence provided in Qumran manuscripts 3Q7, 3Q8, 4Q215, 4Q484, 4Q538, and 4Q539. Fragments of the Aramaic Levi document from Qumran also yield inconclusive results. Though 4Q213 and 4Q213a attest traditions retained in the Greek *Testament of Levi*, the remaining Aramaic Levi materials (1Q21, 4Q213b, 4Q214, 4Q214a, 4Q214b, 4Q540, 4Q541) cannot be consistently identified with portions of the Greek *Testaments*.

5. The urgency of this question is posed by M. de Jonge's work. He has argued that although the *Testaments* bear evidence that the collection existed at a pre-Christian stage of transmission, the precise content of that pre-Christian stage remains unrecoverable due to the freedom of the Christian redactors with their sources; see "Christian Influence in the Testaments of the Twelve Patriarchs," *NovT* 4 (1960): 182–235, esp. 184–89; idem, "The Main Issues in the Study of the Testaments of the Twelve Patriarchs [orig. 1979]," in *Jewish Eschatology, Early Christian Christology, and the Testaments of the Twelve Patriarchs: Collected Essays of Marinus de Jonge* (Leiden: Brill, 1991), 147–63, esp. pp. 159–60, 162–63; idem, "Israel's Future in the Testaments of the Twelve Patriarchs [orig. 1986]," in *Jewish Eschatology,* 164–79, esp. 177–79; idem, "Hippolytus' 'Benedictions of Isaac, Jacob and Moses' and the Testaments of the Twelve Patriarchs [orig. 1985]," in *Jewish Eschatology,* 204–19, esp. 204; idem, "The Testaments of the

Twelve Patriarchs: Jewish and Christian [orig. 1985]," in *Jewish Eschatology*, 233–43; idem, ed., "The Interpretation of the Testaments of the Twelve Patriarchs in Recent Years," in *Studies on the Testaments of the Twelve Patriarchs: Text and Interpretation* (SVTP 3; Leiden: Brill, 1975), 183–92. See also Slingerland, *Testaments of the Twelve Patriarchs*, 60–63. An instructive test case for illustrating the most important critical issues in the debate is provided in J. H. Charlesworth, "Reflections on the SNTS Pseudepigrapha at Duke on the Testaments of the Twelve Patriarchs," *NTS* 23 (1977): 296–304.

6. *T. Lev.* 18.13–14 may also contain a resurrection prophecy since it shares the language of the patriarch's future "rejoicing," which recurs in these four passages; see H. Hollander and M. de Jonge, *The Testaments of the Twelve Patriarchs: A Commentary* (SVTP 8; Leiden: Brill, 1985), 125. Yet it should be noted that this brief passage lacks the specific Greek terminology for "rising" that appears in the other four. Because of this, it is not included among the four definitive references to the resurrection in the current study.

7. The critical edition used in this study is that of M. de Jonge, *The Testaments of the Twelve Patriarchs: A Critical Edition of the Greek Text* (PVTG 1.2; Leiden: Brill, 1978). M. de Jonge's edition is occasionally supplemented by that of Charles, *Greek Versions of the Testaments.* Further reference is also made to the critical edition of all eschatological passages by A. Hultgård, *L'eschatologie des Testaments des Douze Patriarchs*, vol. 1, *Interprétation des texts;* vol. 2, *Composition de l'ouvrage texts et traductions* (Acta Universitatis Upsaliensis, Historia Religionum 7; Uppsala: Uppsala University, 1977), 2:239–87.

8. Hollander and de Jonge, *Testaments of the Twelve Patriarchs: A Commentary*, 109–10.

9. On these peoples, see Hultgård, *L'eschatologie des Testaments*, 1:248–51. Hultgård argues that this expectation is based upon an eschatological source that predicted the extermination of nations hostile to Israel (1:251–52).

10. Unless otherwise noted, all translations are my own.

11. MS l reads "a certain hope." See de Jonge, *Testaments of the Twelve Patriarchs: A Critical Edition*, 79.

12. MS k adds in the margin, "when the Messiah arises to raise them up together." See de Jonge, *Testaments of the Twelve Patriarchs: A Critical Edition*, 77–78.

13. Such phrases often introduce eschatological prophecies in the *Testaments* (cf. *T. Sim.* 6:7; *T. Ben.* 10:4–5); Hultgård, *L'eschatologie des Testaments*, 1:231.

14. Hollander and de Jonge, *Testaments of the Twelve Patriarchs: A Commentary*, 230.

15. As in *T. Jud.* 25:1, there is a clear hierarchy: higher powers in heaven bless the *Testaments'* "favorite" patriarchs, Levi and Judah; see Hollander and de Jonge, *Testaments of the Twelve Patriarchs: A Commentary,* 230.

16. For other traditions that emphasize the resurrection as a reversal of earthly fortunes, see *1 En.* 96:3; 103:1–104:4; *2 Bar.* 51–52; *Apoc. Mos.* 39; Matt 5:3–12; Luke 6:20–23; see Hollander and de Jonge, *Testaments of the Twelve Patriarchs: A Commentary,* 230. See also *On Resurrection* (4Q521) in chs. 1, 2, and 6 of the present book.

17. Hollander and de Jonge, *Testaments of the Twelve Patriarchs: A Commentary,* 411; Hultgård, *L'eschatologie des Testaments,* 1:231.

18. On the special function of *Testament of Benjamin* as the conclusion of the *Testaments,* see also Hultgård, *L'eschatologie des Testaments,* 1:230–31; J. Becker, *Untersuchungen zur Entstehungsgeschichte der Testamente der Zwölf Patriarchen* (Leiden: Brill, 1970), 380–82; de Jonge, "Israel's Future in the Testaments of the Twelve Patriarchs," 178.

19. MSS k and d add in the margin "concerning the Messiah." See de Jonge, *Testaments of the Twelve Patriarchs: A Critical Edition,* 176.

20. Hultgård reads "unto me"; see *L'eschatologie des Testaments,* 2:271.

21. J. Ulrichsen, *Die Grundschrift der Testamente der Zwölf Patriarchen: Eine Untersuchung zu Umfang, Inhalt und Eigenart der ursprünglichen Schrift* (Acta Universitatis Upsaliensis, Historia Religionum 10; Uppsala: Uppsala University, 1991), 248.

22. Hultgård, *L'eschatologie des Testaments,* 1:231.

23. In 1953, M. de Jonge was even more emphatic: "These [references to the incarnation] are definitely out of place in *T. Sim.* 6.5, 7"; see *The Testaments of the Twelve Patriarchs: A Study of Their Text, Composition and Origin* (Van Gorcum's theologische bibliotheek 25; Assen: Van Gorcum, 1953), 96. Hultgård explains the clause as a secondary Christian gloss, which attempted to explain the "marvels" as the incarnation and Eucharist, whereas previously they had referred only to the other events described in 6:5–7; see *L'eschatologie des Testaments,* 1:252.

24. One must recognize, however, that the Armenian textual tradition altogether lacks these christological statements. If the Armenian tradition preserves a pre-Christian textual tradition at *T. Ben.* 10:6–10, then it is all the more probable that this resurrection passage also existed at a pre-Christian stage of development. See Hultgård, who attempts to mark only 10:7–9 as secondary expansion; *L'eschatologie des Testaments,* 1:232–33. Charlesworth would also make this same proposal in 1981; see J. H. Charlesworth, "Christian and Jewish Self-Definition in Light of the Christian Additions to the Apocryphal

Writings," in *Jewish and Christian Self-Definition*, vol. 2, *Aspects of Judaism in the Greco-Roman Period* (ed. E. P. Sanders, A. Baumgarten, and A. Mendelson; Philadelphia: Fortress, 1981), 27–54, esp. 37. See also more recently, Ulrichsen, *Grundschrift der Testaments*, 142–43.

25. However, de Jonge has suggested that the eschatological reversals in *T. Jud*. 25:4 depend upon the Beatitudes; see *Testaments of the Twelve Patriarchs: A Study of Their Text, Composition and Origin*, 32 and 95. Hultgård responds that one can find similar ideas as easily in the Scriptures and in a broader array of non-Christian eschatological literature (*L'eschatologie des Testaments*, 1:324–45). Hultgård himself concludes, "L'authenticité juive de ce chapitre ne peut être contestée" (1:246). I would add that the *Testament of Joseph*'s biographical reminiscences contain similar sets of reversals (*T. Jos.* 1:2–7). Thus, one need not look outside the collection to identify a source, whether Christian or otherwise.

26. T. Kortweg prefers to state that *T. Jud.* 25 contains some primitive material that promises the patriarchs their own share or portion in the future; see "The Meaning of Naphtali's Visions," in *Studies on the Testaments of the Twelve Patriarchs* (ed. de Jonge), 260–90, esp. 275.

27. The thirteenth-century manuscript of the *Testaments* (MS k) at *T. Jud.* 25:1 shows this very process still at work *in margine:* MS k adds in the margin, "when the Messiah arises to raise them up together." See de Jonge, *Testaments of the Twelve Patriarchs: A Critical Edition*, 77–78.

28. Contrast de Jonge, who argues that "the passages dealing with the resurrection...are so heterogeneous that it is not possible to speak of common patterns"; see "The Main Issues in the Study of the Testaments of the Twelve Patriarchs," 159. Almost ten years later, however, he would conclude that, though the resurrection passages have a variety of applications, they are confined within a variety of other traditional motifs in "a coherent approach to the question" of Israel's future; see "Israel's Future in the Testaments of the Twelve Patriarchs," 178.

29. The terminology is especially close: "The dead shall arise, and those in the tombs shall be raised, and those who are in the earth shall rejoice"; cf. also Isa 25:6–9 LXX.

30. Cf. references to eschatological joy in *1 En.* 25:6; 51:5; *2 Bar.* 30:2; *Apoc. Mos.* 13:4. On these passages, see Hollander and de Jonge, *Testaments of the Twelve Patriarchs: A Commentary*, 125.

31. Hultgård, *L'eschatologie des Testaments*, 1:232.

32. Ibid., 1:231.

33. Hollander and de Jonge, *Testaments of the Twelve Patriarchs: A Commentary*, 441. As examples, they cite Judg 18:7–10; Ps 4:8 (9 ET); 16:9; Prov 1:33; Ezek 28:25; 34:27; Hos 2:20 (18 ET); Zeph 2:15.

34. E.g., cosmic/astral dimensions appear in the resurrection hope of Dan 12:1–3; similarly, see the cosmic dimension of Paul's resurrection theology in 1 Cor 15; Rom 8; 1 Thess 4:16–20.

35. M. de Jonge, "The Testaments of the Twelve Patriarchs: Christian and Jewish: A Hundred Years after Friedrich Schnapp," in *Jewish Eschatology*, 233–43, esp. 237–41; idem, "The Pre-Mosaic Servants of God in the Testaments of the Twelve Patriarchs and in the Writings of Irenaeus," *VC* 39 (1985): 157–70; reprint in *Jewish Eschatology*, 266–72.

36. On this point, see also J. Jervell, "Ein Interpolator interpretiert: Zu der christlichen Bearbeitung der Testaments der Zwölf Patriarchen," in *Studien zu den Testamenten der Zwölf Patriarchen: Drei Aufsätze herausgegeben von Walter Eltester* (ed. C. Burchard et al.; BZNW 36; Berlin: Töpelmann, 1969), 30–61, esp. 41–47.

37. H. Hollander, *Joseph as an Ethical Model in the Testaments of the Twelve Patriarchs* (SVTP 7; Leiden: Brill, 1981), 6–12.

38. The traditions carefully treat these themes in what are typically called the "sin-exile-restoration" passages, such as *T. Lev.* 10, 14–16; *T. Jud.* 18:1 and ch. 23; *T. Iss.* 6; *T. Zeb.* 9:5–7, 9; *T. Dan* 5:4–9; *T. Naph.* 4:1–5; *T. Gad* 8:2; *T. Ash.* 7:2–7; *T. Ben.* 9:1–3); see Hollander and de Jonge, *Testaments of the Twelve Patriarchs: A Commentary*, 53–56.

39. In addition to the *Testament of Joseph* itself, see also *T. Reu.* 4:8–10; *T. Sim.* 4:3–7; 5:1; *T. Lev.* 13; *T. Zeb.* 8:4; cf. *T. Dan* 1:4–9. See Hollander, *Joseph as an Ethical Model*, 51–62.

40. As J. H. Charlesworth shows, these problems recur throughout Jewish literature dealing with the issues of theodicy; "Theodicy in Early Jewish Writings," in *Theodicy in the World of the Bible* (ed. A. Laato and J. de Moor; Leiden: Brill, 2003), 471–508.

Chapter 5

The Meaning of Christ's Resurrection in Paul

Hendrikus Boers

Preliminary Remarks

Two preliminary points clarify my understanding of Paul's historical context:

1. *Paul was as little a Christian as Jesus had been.* Both contributed fundamentally to the religion that later became known as Christianity, but neither of them were Christians: both were Jews. I do not say this to disassociate Paul from Christianity, but as a way of finding a vantage point in our approach to him that accords better with the place where he found himself in the development of Christianity. When we make use of Christian language in interpreting him, we unavoidably read back into him ideas that had not yet developed in his thinking.

The point is that we should not read Paul backward from the perspective of what later developed as Christianity, but forward from the Jewish perspective out of which he came. Instead of using the term "Christian" in interpreting him, we should use "believer," the term that he himself consistently uses and not as an alternative to "Christian." Neither Paul nor his readers had yet become Christians. They were at a place on the trajectory in the development of Christianity where the definition of their identities was still fluid.

2. We can gain an understanding of the situation with regard to Paul's Jewish origins when we consider the retrospective view of the author of Acts, *who reports more than once that the new religious movement was considered a sect* — both critically, in Acts 24:5, where Paul is accused of being "a leader of the sect of the Nazarenes," and sympathetically, in 28:22, where the Jewish leaders in Rome tell Paul that they are interested in hearing from him, "for we are aware concerning *this sect* that it is being contradicted everywhere."

The author of Acts refers to the Sadducees and the Pharisees as sects. According to 5:17, the high priest and all of those with him "were of the *sect* of the Sadducees," and, according to 15:5, within the believing community those "who belonged to the *sect* of the Pharisees said that they [all believers] should be circumcised." In 26:5, Paul refers to his "having lived [previously] according to the strictest *sect* of our religious observance as a Pharisee."

In Acts 24, however, being a sect appears to have something of a negative connotation. In 24:5, when the high priest Ananias and some of the elders accuse Paul of being "a leader of the sect of the Nazarenes," Paul reacts to this in verse 14 by confessing that he serves the God of the Fathers "according to the way which *they* [Ananias and the elders] call a *sect*," seemingly dissociating himself from the use of the term "sect" to designate the religious movement to which he belonged. According to 11:26, "the disciples were first called Christians in Antioch." When the author of Acts, projecting the situation of his own time back onto that of Paul, has Agrippa say to the apostle, "You are confident, within a short time, of making me a Christian" (26:28), "Christian" has attained its designation for those who belong to the new religion.

We cannot draw precise exegetical conclusions about the author of Acts' understanding of "sect," but from what he reports in the above statements, some decades after Paul's time, we gather a sense of how the new religious movement was becoming independent of Judaism, shedding its image as a Jewish sect. There is no indication in Paul's letters that this development had already taken place in his time. In order to understand him, thus, we have to interpret him on a trajectory between the origins of this new religious movement as a Jewish sect, and its becoming an independent religion on a level similar to that of the Judaism from which it emerged. It is not possible to establish precisely where Paul found himself on this trajectory, but his thinking was clearly still rooted in Judaism.

By interpreting Paul from the point of view of his origins in Judaism, and not backward from that of an established Christianity, we become sensitive to the fact that the subject matter of his thoughts was still in motion, that in his thinking he was engaged in a process of discovery, seeking to find clarity about the implications of what it meant to believe that God revealed himself decisively in Christ Jesus. In his letters, Paul did not interpret existing doctrines, or develop new ones; instead, he reflected on a variety of concrete issues in the churches to which he addressed himself, guiding his readers into a fuller understanding of what it meant to live the life that had become a new reality in Christ Jesus.

Introduction

Nowhere in his letters does Paul present a teaching *about* Christ. When he brings to expression the meaning of Christ's resurrection, it is always part of his reasoning concerning specific issues for which Christ has meaning. The meanings of Christ in such passages are not expressions of an underlying meaning that Paul recalls, but meanings that arise from his reasoning in those passages. There is, thus, not a single meaning that comes to expression in Paul's letters, but a range of meanings, dependent on the ways Christ functions in each case in his reasoning, similar to the way in which we can use the same word with different meanings in different sentences.

The pervasiveness of Christ in his letters makes it clear that Christ was on Paul's mind almost all the time. His fundamental commitment to Christ made it possible for him to come to new insights about Christ as he engaged with issues in continually changing circumstances. His understanding of Christ was as a real being, as the person whom he encountered at a time when he was still persecuting the church:

> When it pleased [God], who set me aside from the womb of my mother and called me through his graciousness to reveal his son to me, that I should proclaim him to the Gentiles, I promptly did not consult flesh and blood. (Gal 1:15–16)

It is possible to abstract a single, complex meaning of Christ's resurrection for Paul from the variety of his expressions, but that would not be what Christ meant for him in any particular passage. The meanings expressed by Paul are not entirely new, but drawing on the information about Christ which he had in his mind as a resource, he brought out new meanings as they became relevant in each case.

In this chapter, I will not attempt to uncover a single, complex meaning of Christ's resurrection that underlies the variety of Paul's expressions, nor will I attempt to abstract a single meaning from those expressions. Rather than present an understanding of the meaning of Christ in Paul, as abstracted from his expressions of what Christ's resurrection meant for him, I will try to see if we can discover what the meanings are that found expression in what he wrote. The following incident may serve to illustrate what I have in mind.

My father and I were walking in the South African veld, philosophizing about various matters, when he suddenly motioned to me that we should briefly pause our conversation: "There is a little bird who must have a nest somewhere close by," he said. "She is trying to prevent us from finding her nest." It took my father very little time to find the nest, with two little blue eggs. He explained that the closer we came to the nest, the less excitement the bird demonstrated as a way of pretending that we were already leaving the scene. She would have done the same if we had actually moved further away from the nest. The critical area was when we were a certain distance from the nest. By observing her behavior, my father allowed the bird to guide him to her nest. What is most important for us about this story is what happened next. Having seen the nest and shown it to me was all that interested my father. His pleasure was satisfied in seeing the bird's eggs; he had no interest in removing them from the nest.

In our investigation of the meaning of Christ's resurrection in Paul, we will do something similar. We will look at Paul's expressions concerning Christ as a way of discerning the meanings that gave rise to those expressions. Seeing how Christ's resurrection had meaning for Paul completes our task. We will not try to appropriate his meanings by abstracting a general understanding from them. For that reason I will quote extensively from Paul. To put it another way, I do not intend to let you know what I understand about the meaning of Christ's resurrection in Paul, but I hope to show how you can allow Paul's expressions to guide *you* to the meanings of Christ's resurrection for Paul, as the little bird guided my father to her nest. What should concern you is not what I say, but what you can discern from Paul's texts about the meanings that Christ's resurrection had for him.

Paul expresses the meaning of Christ more typically in terms of Christ's death than of his resurrection, including the extreme statement in 1 Cor 2:2: "I decided not to know anything among us except Christ Jesus, and him crucified." In accordance with the theme of this book, however, I will focus on Christ's resurrection, bearing in mind that Christ's death, resurrection, and Parousia did not have distinct meanings in Paul's mind.

We can distinguish two kinds of information on which Paul draws to bring to expression the meaning of Christ's resurrection as it becomes relevant at different points in his reasoning throughout his letters: When he brings to expression the meaning of Christ for himself, he draws on his encounter with the resurrected Christ (cf. esp. Phil 3:2–14 and Gal 1:15–16). He does not have a similar encounter to which he could appeal in his reasoning concerning the meaning of Christ for his readers. In those cases his appeal is always to the actual events of Christ's death, resurrection, and expected Parousia, as for example in 1 Cor 15:3–7 and Rom 6:1–14.

The Meaning of Christ for Paul Himself

We can see how differently Paul could express the meaning of Christ's resurrection when we compare Phil 3:2–11 with Gal 1:15–16, both of which concern the resurrected Christ's appearance to him, marking his transition from an existence under the law to that of a believer. In Philippians, Christ's appearance to Paul functions to bring out what it meant for him to give up his achievements under the law, and in Galatians the same event functions as part of his defense of himself and of the gospel he preached. More significantly, in Phil 3:2–11 Paul refers to the resurrected Christ's appearance to him only indirectly, by expressing what the event meant to him, whereas he refers to it directly in Gal 1:15–16. The meaning of Christ's appearance as expressed in the Gal 1:16b, "in order that I proclaim the gospel among the Gentiles," is sparse compared with the full four verses of Phil 3:7–11.

This discrepancy makes it tempting to discuss Galatians first and then the more developed passage in Philippians. However, Galatians was almost certainly written later, which makes it preferable to discuss the Philippians passage first and then to consider what significance there may be to the fact that Paul is so brief in Galatians, notwithstanding his fuller reflection earlier in Philippians. Discussing the Galatians passage first and then the more developed one in Philippians could also create the false impression that Phil 3:7–11 is an expansion of the briefer Gal 1:16b, which it is not, since what the two passages express are completely different aspects of the meaning of the resurrected Christ's appearance to Paul. In Philippians it means a rejection of his merits as an exemplary Jew in favor of what it means to be found in Christ. In Galatians it means the call to proclaim the gospel.

Philippians 3:2–11

One of the clearest expressions of what Christ's resurrection meant to Paul personally is Phil 3:7–11:

> What was gain for me, I considered a loss for the sake of Christ. What is more, I consider everything a loss for the sake of the superiority of the knowledge of Christ Jesus, my Lord, for whose sake I took everything as a loss, and considered it as waste, in order to gain Christ and to be found in him, not having my own justification, which is from the law, but [justification] through the faith of Christ, justification which is from God on faith; to know him and the power of his *resurrection* and communion with his sufferings, conforming with his death, that I may somehow attain the *resurrection* from the dead.

The gains to which Paul refers are the virtues listed in verses 5–6, which characterize him as an exemplary Jew before he became a believer:

> Circumcised on the eighth day, from the people of Israel, the tribe of Benjamin, a Hebrew from the Hebrews, as to the Law, a Pharisee, as to zeal, a persecutor of the church, as to justice in the law, without blemish.

The statement with which the list culminates in verse 6b, "as to justice in the law, without blemish," does not refer to being justified through "works of the law," but rounds off the entire list. With it Paul claims that his merits under the law covered all requirements for being a perfect Jew. What is at issue in this passage are not the alternatives, justification through works of the law or justification by faith, but Paul's failure, now as a believer, to live in accordance with the law. When he writes about "not having my own justification, which is from the law" in verse 9, he does not mean specifically "works of the law," but the complete list of merits to which he refers in verses 5–6, justification through having achieved everything required to make him an exemplary Jew in the time before he encountered Christ. Justification by faith is not at issue; that comes into the picture only indirectly insofar as Paul's belonging to Christ was characterized by faith. In his defense he does not interpret what faith means, but what it means to be in Christ, "to know him and the power of his resurrection and communion with his sufferings" (v. 10).

Paul's venomous counteroffensive against his accusers (vv. 2–4) reveals that he understood himself as being accused of not measuring up to the law's requirements:

> Watch out for the dogs! Watch out for the evildoers! Watch out for the cutting up! We are the circumcision, who serve God in the Spirit and have pride in Christ Jesus, and who are not reliers on the flesh, even though I have grounds to rely on the flesh. If someone else is confident of relying on the flesh, I even more.

He interprets living by the law as reliance on the flesh, and claims that he had been preeminent in that way of life. We are reminded of Gal 1:13–14:

> For you have heard of my earlier activity in Judaism, that I thoroughly persecuted the church and destroyed it, and advanced in Judaism beyond many of my generation among my people, extremely zealous in the traditions of the Fathers.

Paul's claims to excellence in what he achieved under the law in Gal 1:13–14 and Phil 3:5–6 are closely similar in meaning, but they function differently. In Galatians his claim brings to expression the radical difference between his earlier life as a zealous Jew and his new life as a believer; he uses this difference as proof that his call (vv. 15–16) came from God, contrary to his own intentions. I will give attention to

verses 15–16 in more detail below. In Philippians, Paul's Jewish claim is positive. He asserts that, as far as things Jewish
are concerned, his achievements were second to none: what
he had found in Christ was incomparably more valuable than
his achievements as a perfect Jew. The issue in Philippians
is purely Jewish, and Paul's reasoning never moves outside
that context. He challenges his accusers on their own terrain,
not denying the value of a life under the law, but claiming
it to be inferior, of the flesh, compared with what he found
in Christ.

In Phil 3:7–11 the encounter with the resurrected Christ
meant for him, on the one hand, surrender of everything he
had achieved under the law in exchange for, on the other
hand, the incomparable value he found in Christ Jesus. He
expresses these contrary meanings in a series of informal,
contrasting parallels (italics mine):

[7]What was gain for me, I considered a loss	for the sake of Christ.
[8]What is more, I consider everything a loss	for the sake of the superiority of the knowledge of Christ Jesus, my Lord, for whose sake
I took everything as a loss, and considered it as waste,	in order to gain Christ [9]and to be found in him,
not having my own justification, which is from the law,	but [justification] through the faith of Christ, justification which is from God on faith; [10]to know him and the power of his *resurrection* and communion with his sufferings, conforming with his death, [11]that I may somehow attain the *resurrection* from the dead.

Paul does not simply recall his encounter with the resurrected Christ in Phil 3:7–11. As we saw, he does not even
explicitly refer to it. In the face of the perceived accusation

that he does not live a life worthy of a Jew, he allows that encounter and what resulted from it to attain new meaning. In his defense, he allows Christ to play the central role, a role Christ had come to play in all he did and thought. The verses (12–14) that follow on his defense reveal that he does not quote teaching, but gives expression to the meaning of Christ as he experiences him. The passage expresses the meaning of Christ as the controlling power of his entire life:

> Not that I have already obtained it, or am already perfected, but I endeavor if I can take hold of it, insofar as I have been taken hold of by Christ [Jesus]. Brothers [and sisters], I do not consider myself having taken hold of it, but one thing, I give up what lies behind, reaching out to what lies ahead. In accordance with the objective, I reach for the wreath of the high calling of God in Christ Jesus.

In two additional passages — 2 Cor 11:22 and Gal 2:19–20 — Paul deals with issues that have certain similarities with the issue he addresses in Phil 3:2–14. These texts may put the way he reasons into perspective. In both cases it also concerns Paul's past Jewish identity.

In 2 Cor 11:22 Paul responds to what also appears to be a challenge to his credentials as a Jew, formulated differently: "Are they Hebrews? I too. Are they Israelites? I too. Are they seed of Abraham? I too." In this case, however, the challenge includes his credentials as a "servant" of Christ as well: "Are they servants of Christ? Beyond my wits, I say, I even more" (v. 23a–c). That his accusers consider themselves servants of Christ makes it clear that the issue in this case must have arisen internally within the Jesus movement.

The challenge to Paul's Jewish credentials in both passages makes one wonder if his outburst in Phil 3:2–14 may not have been prompted by persistence of the challenge to which he responded earlier, in 2 Cor 11:22. The differences between the two passages are significant; most noteworthy is the inclusion of being a servant of Christ among Paul's credentials in 2 Corinthians. The list of what he suffered in his service of Christ, which follows immediately in 2 Cor 11:23d–29, focuses on being a servant of Christ as the only issue that he addresses in his defense. As a result, in contrast with Phil 3:2–11, the challenge to his Jewish credentials fades into the background. Paul's defenses in the two passages are entirely different. The extraordinary meaning that he has found in Christ compared with what he achieved under the law, the center of his defense in Philippians, plays no role in 2 Corinthians, with its focus on what he suffered in the service of Christ.

We cannot escape the possibility that the two charges were related. In that case one would have to assume that the charges in Phil 3:2–11 also came from within the believing community. What is significant is that in his defense in 2 Corinthians, he ignored the charge concerning his Jewish credentials. In Phil 3:2–14 he was unable to ignore that charge; it is the only one he mentions and addresses in his defense. Both passages reveal that the behavior of Jewish believers was an issue that Paul could not ignore. In neither of these letters does Paul rely on justification by faith for his defense.

A different kind of parallel to Phil 3:2–11 is found in Gal 2:19–20:

> I, through the law, died to the law, in order to live for God. I was co-crucified with Christ. It is not I who lives; living in me is Christ. What I now live in the flesh, I live in the faith of the Son of God, who loved me and gave himself over for me.

Here too Paul clarifies why he has abandoned an existence under the law. Being in Christ again plays the central role. Two of the elements of the meaning of Christ in this passage have parallels in Phil 3:7–11. "It is not I who lives; living in me is Christ" in Gal 2:20a–b has a parallel in the statement in Phil 3:10a–b, "to know him and the power of his resurrection." Likewise, "I was co-crucified with Christ" in Gal 2:19c has a parallel in Phil 3:10 in the statement of "having become conformed with his death." These parallels reveal that Paul used the same concepts, formulated differently, to express different meanings in different contexts.

In Galatians, Paul does not defend himself against an accusation; instead, he uses his abandonment of the law positively to give expression to the new meaning he has found in Christ. This articulation is clearly a step beyond his earlier defense of himself for having abandoned the law. He does not find it necessary to defend himself here; instead, he makes positive use of his abandonment of the law as an argument in his main reasoning in the letter: justification of the Gentiles without having to submit themselves to the law. It is not as if he has left the earlier reasoning behind, but the new situation requires that his abandonment of the law and his new being in Christ function differently in his reasoning in the two passages.

The three passages we discussed thus far — Phil 3:2–11; 2 Cor 11:22; and Gal 2:19–20 — reveal the multivalence of Paul's abandonment of the law and his new being in Christ. Each situation allows these same events to acquire new meaning for him.

1 Corinthians 15:8–11

Paul's discussion of his encounter with the resurrected Christ in 1 Cor 15:8–11 is a parenthesis in his discourse on the resurrection of the dead. I will discuss the rest of the passage in the following pages in connection with "the meaning of Christ's resurrection for the believer." Paul's list of Christ's appearances to the other apostles in his quotation of the confession of Christ's death and resurrection in verses 3c–7 leads him to add Christ's appearance to himself:

> Last of all he appeared to me too, as to one untimely born. For I am the least of the apostles, who is not worthy of being called an apostle since I persecuted the church of God. But through God's graciousness I am what I am, and his graciousness to me was not in vain, but I labored harder than any of them; not I,

but the graciousness of God with me. Thus, whether I or they,
so we proclaimed and so you believed.

With verse 11, Paul returns to the main topic of his discourse,
his reasoning against those who deny a general resurrection
of the dead.

Nowhere is Paul more vulnerable than in this report of
Christ's appearance to him. He is aware of the precarious-
ness of his previous relationship to the new religion, but he is
even more concerned to assert himself in relationship to the
other apostles. With regard to his Jewish heritage, he was,
with great pride and without hesitation, able to claim, "I advanced in Judaism beyond many of my generation among my
people, extremely zealous in the traditions of the Fathers"
(Gal 1:14).

Probably, Paul would have preferred to claim something
similar for himself as a believer as well, but he is obviously
aware of the doubtfulness of his Jewish past with regard to
the believing community. He also does not appear quite certain about his comparison with the other apostles. And then,
boasting does not appear to be the right thing to do in this
new community. On the one hand, Paul is aware that Christ
appeared to him as to "one untimely born," but on the other
hand, he cannot help priding himself on having achieved
more than any of the others.

The meaning of the appearance of Christ to Paul in 1 Cor
15:8–10 is that it is an embarrassment from which he tries to
extricate himself — first by admitting it, but then by pointing
to his greater achievements, which he is unable to claim quite
as his own. As a believer, thus, he claims for himself the same
superiority in achievement that he claims for himself as a
Jew in Phil 3:5–6 and Gal 1:14. In 2 Cor 11:22–29, as we have
seen, he claims both in a single text. While Paul may have
changed his religious commitment, his personality remained
the same.

Galatians 1:13–16

After discussing Gal 2:19–20 as a parallel to Paul's abandonment of the law in Phil 3:2–11, we now turn to his mention of the appearance of Christ to him in Gal 1:15–16, to which I also referred earlier in a different context. The reference to the resurrected Christ's appearance in this passage is more direct than in Phil. 3:3–11, and it brings to expression a new meaning:

> When it pleased [God], who set me aside from the womb of my mother and called me through his graciousness to reveal his Son to me, that I should proclaim him to the Gentiles, I promptly did not consult flesh and blood.

Here the meaning of Christ's appearance for Paul is in proving that his proclamation of the good news is not a product of his own intentions, but something he does in obedience to God. It is particularly telling since his call came when he had still been persecuting the church, as a sign of his progress in Judaism, as he states in Gal 1:13–14, another text to which I referred previously in a different context:

> For you have heard of my earlier activity in Judaism, that I thoroughly persecuted the church and destroyed it, and advanced in Judaism beyond many of my generation among my people, extremely zealous in the traditions of the Fathers.

Paul's juxtaposition of his advances in Judaism and Christ's appearance to him in these two passages has double significance. Its primary meaning is as proof that his apostleship is from God, and not a product of his own will, a matter of the highest importance for him in this first part of the letter. It is a question of his authority as an apostle, already indicated in the prescript of the letter:

> Paul, an apostle, not of human beings nor through human beings, but through Jesus Christ and God the Father, who raised him from the dead — (1:1)

and reaffirmed in verses 11–12:

> I make known to you, brothers [and sisters], the gospel that was
> proclaimed by me was not according to human beings, nor did
> I receive it from human beings, nor was I taught it, but [I have
> it] through a revelation of Jesus Christ.

He expresses this relationship between Christ's appearance
and his apostleship in a straightforward way in 1 Cor 9:1:
"Am I not free? Am I not an apostle? Have I not seen Jesus,
our Lord?"

The juxtaposition of his advances in Judaism and Christ's
appearance to him has a second meaning for Paul as well,
in some way closer in meaning to what we find in Phil 3:2–
11. The contrast between his previous life as a zealous Jew
who persecuted "the church" (vv. 13–14) and his call to proclaim the gospel among the Gentiles (vv. 15–16) implies that
he gave up his former life under the law for the sake of a life
in Christ. He makes this change explicit in a different formulation in 2:19: "I, through the law, died to the law, in order to
live for God." Here it is not as the result of Christ's appearance to him, but of his having been crucified with Christ: "I
was co-crucified with Christ" (v. 20). And, whereas he refers
to what he found in Christ in Phil 3:7–11 as his reason for
giving up his life under the law, here in Galatians the juxtaposition of his life under the law and Christ's appearance to
him functions as a basis for his reasoning against the Galatians' having themselves circumcised. It is on that basis that
he could refer to the Galatians' desire to become circumcised
as a reversal of the sequence of the law and Christ in his own
experience: "Having begun with the Spirit, you now end up
with the flesh" (3:3b).

Conclusion on the Meaning of Christ for Paul Himself

The single event of the resurrected Christ's appearance to
Paul has different meanings for him in the three main texts
we have discussed above: In Phil 3:2–11, Christ's resurrection
functions as his defense for no longer living in accordance

with the law. Christ's resurrection for the Christian means to be found in Christ, to know him and the power of his resurrection, which requires Paul to abandon everything he had achieved as an exemplary Jew under the law.

In 1 Cor 15:8–11 Christ's appearance to Paul is not part of his reasoning, but a parenthesis to which he was led when he rounded off the list of persons to whom Christ appeared. In this text Paul experiences Christ's appearance to him as an embarrassment, out of which he tries to extract himself by claiming to have achieved more than the others.

In Gal 1:13–16 Christ's appearance functions as part of Paul's proof that "the gospel" he proclaims is not the product of his own intentions, but what he has been commanded to do by God. In this case Christ's appearance has an implied second meaning as well. As in Phil 3:2–11, it makes clear that Christ's appearance made it necessary for him to give up his subservience to the law, which he makes explicit later in 2:19, but which he then expresses in terms of participation in Christ's crucifixion. In the larger context of Paul's reasoning in Galatians, this second meaning functions to give expression to a third meaning as well, as an argument against the Galatians' considering having themselves circumcised. Doing so would mean "Having begun with the Spirit, you now end up with the flesh" (3:3b).

The Meaning of Christ for the Believer

Introduction: Levels of the Meaning of Christ

As we have seen, these three texts — Phil 3; 1 Cor 15; and Gal 1 — express how Paul presented the meaning of Christ's resurrection for himself. Belief in the resurrected Christ's appearance is the foundation of that meaning; Paul does not appeal to the facts of Christ's death, resurrection, and Parousia themselves. In the texts in which he expresses the

meaning of Christ for the believer, those events are what constitute the foundations of his reasoning. Although Christ's
appearance to Paul already had a certain meaning in itself as
Paul's call, demanding a specific response from him, the facts
of Christ's death, resurrection, and Parousia are multivalent:
they have multiple meanings. Paul himself expresses awareness that Christ's death was multivalent. In 1 Cor 1:23–24 he
acknowledges that it is "a scandal for the Jews, and foolishness for the Gentiles, but for us, the elect, Jews as well as
Gentiles, Christ, the power of God and the wisdom of God."

Although Christ's appearance to Paul was already a meaningful event to begin with, he always brought to expression
what meaning Christ had for his readers, which was multivalent in a different sense as well. Here we do not have
alternative meanings, as in 1 Cor 1:23–24, but levels of meaning. Thus, 1 Thess 5:1–11 displays the levels of meaning of
Christ's death:

> [1]Concerning times and periods, brothers [and sisters], I do not
> need to write to you, [2]for you know very well that the day of the
> Lord comes like a thief in the night. [3]When they say, Peace and
> tranquility, then suddenly destruction is upon them like labor
> pains on a pregnant woman, and they will not escape. [4]But you,
> brothers [and sisters], are not in the dark, that the day catch you
> like a thief, [5]for you are children of the light and children of
> the day. We are not of the night or of darkness. [6]Therefore, do
> not sleep like the rest, but be alert and sober. [7]Those who are
> asleep sleep in the night, and those who are drunk get drunk at
> night: [8]But we, being of the day, should be sober, putting on the
> breastplate of faith and love and as a helmet hope of salvation
> [vv. 1–8].
>
> > [9]For God did not apportion us to wrath but to the acqui-
> > sition of salvation [9a–b] through our Lord Jesus Christ,
> > [10]who died for us [9c–10a] in order that whether we are
> > alert or sleeping we should live with him [10b–c].
>
> [11]Therefore encourage each other, and sustain each other, as
> indeed you do [11].

I cannot go into the details of the analysis of this passage,
leading up to the identification of the levels of the meaning of

Christ's death. It must suffice here to summarize those levels. What should be clear is that Paul's purpose in the passage is not to provide an interpretation of the meaning of Christ's death: his purpose is clearly exhortatory, and Christ's death functions as the ultimate foundation for Paul's persuasion.

The event of Christ's death is displayed at the right on the diagram, representing the most fundamental, but least specific meaning. From there the levels become increasingly more specific to the left. The most specific level of meaning is at the left margin.

For Paul, the event of Christ's death evokes five levels of meaning:

1. At the most fundamental level there is the bare fact of Christ's death: "Christ who died" (v. 10a).

2. At a second level, Paul interprets the meaning of Christ's death as having been "for us" (still 10a), restricting its meaning in a general way to beneficence for his readers.

3. At a further level of meaning, Paul specifies that beneficence: "For God did not apportion us to wrath but to the acquisition of salvation" (9ab).

4. At the fourth level, Paul engages his readers more fully in the meaning of Christ's death: Christ died "in order that whether we are alert or sleeping we should live with him" (10b–c).

5. Finally, the exhortatory context in which Paul expresses how he expects his readers to live their lives in Christ in the face of the coming end (1–8 and 11) makes clear what function the christological statements in verses 9–10 fulfill in Paul's reasoning in the passage.

Paul does not present Christ's death as a fact and then interpret its meaning for his readers, as a theologian might do, but as a pastor he admonishes his readers to the appropriate behavior in the face of Christ's expected imminent Parousia (vv. 1–8 and 11). Then he appeals to Christ's death and what it means to his readers at three intermediate levels (vv. 9–10) to provide a foundation for his admonition.

We can use this model of the five levels of meaning in our investigation of the two texts in which Paul bases his reasoning on the meaning of Christ's resurrection for his readers: 1 Cor 15:1–8, 12–23 (we have already seen that verses 9–11 are parenthetic, concerning Paul himself, personally); and Rom 6:1–14.

1 Cor 15:1–8, 12–23

I recall for you, brothers [and sisters], the gospel we preached to you, which you also received, in which you also stand, through which you also live, with which words we proclaimed to you, if you remember, unless you believed in vain. For I handed over to you in the first place what I also received [1–3b],

> that Christ died in accordance with the Scriptures [3c–d] for our sins [3c] and that he was buried and that he was resurrected on the third day according to the Scriptures, and that he appeared to Peter, then to the Twelve. Then he appeared to more than five hundred brothers at one time, of whom the most remain to this day, but some have died. Then he appeared to James, then to all the apostles. Last of all he appeared to me as to one untimely born [4–8].

Thus, whether I or they, so we proclaimed and so you believed [11]. If, then, Christ is proclaimed to have been raised from the dead, how do some among you say that there is not a resurrection from the dead [12]?

> If there is no resurrection from the dead [13a], Christ also was not raised. And if Christ was not raised [13b–14a], empty would our proclamation be, and empty your faith. We would be found false witnesses of God, because we witnessed against God that God raised Christ [14b–15c], whom he did not raise [15d], that is, if the dead are not raised. For if the dead are not raised [15e–16a], Christ was also not raised. And if Christ was not raised [16b–17a], your faith is madness; you are still in your sins [17b–c]; and so those who have died in Christ would be lost [18]. If it is only in this life that we hope in Christ, we are the most miserable of human beings [19].
> But now, Christ was raised from the dead [20a], the firstfruits of those who have died. For if death

came through a man, resurrection from the dead is also through a man. For as in Adam all died, so also in Christ all are made alive. But each in one's own order [20b–23a]: As the firstfruits Christ [23b], then those who belong to Christ at his Parousia [23c].

The two parts 1 Cor 15:1–8 and 11–22 belong together, separated by the parenthesis in verses 9–10, which concerns Paul personally. There are a number of connecting links between the two parts. In verse 11, "whether I or they, so we proclaimed and so you believed," Paul refers back to those represented in the tradition in verses 3c–7 as witnesses to Christ's resurrection, including himself in verse 8, and to his readers' acceptance of the tradition.

The proclamation to which Paul refers in verse 11 is the tradition he quotes in verses 3c–7. This referral is clear from the way in which he introduces it: "I recall for you, brothers [and sisters], the gospel we preached to you, which you also received, in which you also stand, through which you also live" (vv. 1–2a). Paul makes his reference to the tradition explicit when he writes in verse 2b, "with which words we proclaimed to you." Uncharacteristically, he acknowledges that it is a tradition he received: "I handed over to you in the first place what I also received" (3a–b). Thus he prepares for the unity between himself and the others to whom he refers in verse 11: "Whether I or they, so we proclaimed and so you believed."

In his introduction of the tradition, Paul prepares for another statement in the second part of his discourse: "(with which words we proclaimed to you,) if you remember, unless you believed in vain" (v. 2c–d). With that statement he anticipates a central point in his reasoning in verses 12–22: "For if the dead are not raised, . . . your faith is madness; you are still in your sins" (vv. 15–17).

These connections reveal Paul's purpose with the reference to his earlier proclamation, which comes to focus in the tradition he quotes in verses 3c–7; he wants to provide a basis for his reasoning in verses 12–22. Verse 12 marks a clear transition from the proclamation that he established in verses 1–8 and 11, to the reasoning that follows in verses 13–22. First he points backward to the earlier proclamation: "If, then, Christ is proclaimed to have been raised from the dead" (12a–b). Then he points forward to the central point in the discussion that follows in verses 13–22: "How do some among you say that there is not a resurrection from the dead?" (12c–d).

Nowhere does the freedom with which Paul adapts material for the purpose of his reasoning become clearer than in the way in which he makes use of the tradition recorded in verses 3c–7 to serve what he wants to say in verses 12–22. All he needs from the confession is the fact that Christ was raised from the dead, which the list of resurrection appearances are intended to establish unequivocally. Verse 12 clarifies that the purpose of the tradition is to refute the view that "there is not a resurrection from the dead" (12d), for which Christ's resurrection is Paul's key argument: "If there is no resurrection from the dead, Christ also was not raised" (v. 13; cf. 16).

Furthermore, he makes use of a statement in the tradition, "Christ died . . . for our sins" (v. 3c), as an argument in his reasoning in verses 11–22, not, however, in connection with Christ's death, as in the tradition, but in connection with Christ's resurrection: "And if Christ was not raised, . . . you are still in your sins" (v. 17). Indeed, if he had formulated the statement in terms of Christ's death, it would have been counterproductive: If Christ's death itself guaranteed his readers' redemption from sin, as in the tradition, they would not have been left in their sins, even if Christ had not been raised from the dead, as in Paul's reasoning.

It may appear as if there is a contradiction in Paul's use of these two statements. Actually, they reveal the degree to which, in his mind, Christ's death and resurrection are integral to each other. The Christ who had appeared to him was the Christ who had been crucified. That is what makes it possible for him, in his own reasoning, to take the traditional statement that Christ died for our sins and reformulate it in terms of Christ's resurrection.

From the relationships between the tradition Paul quotes in verses 3c–7 and his own reasoning in verses 12–22, we may conclude that he established the fundamental facts for his reasoning by quoting the tradition and then interpreting what it means in verses 12–22. Verse 11 constitutes the transition from those facts to the interpretation of their meaning. It is not an interpretation of what the tradition itself means, but of what Paul means by quoting it. He signals his intended meaning already by the way in which he introduces the tradition: "the gospel we preached to you, which you also received, in which you also stand, through which you also live, with which words we proclaimed to you, if you remember, unless you believed in vain" (vv. 1b–2). In that way he signals his purpose for using the tradition as the basis for his reasoning that is to follow in verses 12–22.

The tradition itself provides no indication of what it means, except as the listing of facts. Only once is there a move from the level of the facts to what they mean. In verse 3c the meaning of Christ's death is interpreted as "for our sins," at a third level of meaning according to our model from 1 Thess 5:1–11. This interpretation of the meaning of Christ's death is uncharacteristic of the tradition, which otherwise merely states the salvific facts without interpreting their meanings. It is possible that Paul himself could have inserted the phrase. The tradition would read fine without it; but there also is no way of knowing whether that is the case. It is the only constituent of the tradition as quoted by Paul, in addition to establishment of the fact of Christ's resurrection, of which he makes use in his reasoning in verse 17, in the negative argument: "If Christ was not raised, . . . you are still in your sins." As we have recognized, Paul does not make direct use of the meaning of the phrase about Christ's death as expressed in the tradition, but adapts it to express the meaning of Christ's resurrection.

As we turn to the levels of meaning of Christ's death, we may perceive that Paul uses the tradition to establish, at the first level of meaning, the fundamental fact on which he bases his reasoning: Christ's resurrection from the dead. He states it negatively three times as the implication of a denial of the resurrection of the dead: In identical form in verses 13b and 16b, "(If there is no resurrection from the dead,) Christ was also not raised," and in between, in verse 15d, "whom [God] did not raise, (that is, if the dead are not raised)." And then as his conclusion, he says positively, "But now, Christ was raised from the dead" (20a). From there he goes on to discuss the implications of Christ's resurrection for believers, leading him to a discussion of Christ's Parousia and its effects.

Paul does not interpret what Christ's resurrection means at the second, general level of meaning. Where he uses "for us" in verse 3c of the tradition, it is already more specific, at the third level of meaning, as we have seen: "for our sins" interprets the meaning of Christ's death.

At a third level, Paul expresses what Christ's resurrection means by placing it in opposition to the denial of the resurrection of the dead in verse 13: "If there is no resurrection from the dead, Christ was also not raised"; and in verse 16, "If the dead are not raised, Christ was also not raised." With these statements Paul is at the heart of what the resurrection of Christ means in the passage. Denial of a general resurrection of the dead contradicts the indisputably established fact of Christ's resurrection. This is a fact for Paul because the resurrected Christ had appeared to him.

At the fourth level of meaning, Paul contrasts his and the other apostles' proclamation of Christ's resurrection, as well as his readers' acceptance of it, with the view of those who deny it by implication: "Thus, whether I or they, so we proclaimed and so you believed. If, then, Christ is proclaimed to have been raised from the dead, how do some among you say that there is not a resurrection from the dead?" (vv. 11–12). And then, inversely, he clarifies what the negation of

Christ's resurrection, implied by a denial of the resurrection of the dead, would mean for his and the other apostles' proclamation and for his readers: "Empty would our proclamation be, and empty your faith. We would be found false witnesses of God, because we witnessed against God that God raised Christ" (14b–15c). "Your faith would be madness; you would still be in your sins; and so those who have died in Christ would be lost" (17b–18). Paul's use of these fourth-level meanings is not to interpret what Christ's resurrection means to him, to the other apostles, or to his readers; they instead are arguments that reinforce his refutation of a denial of the resurrection of the dead.

Only in a single case does Paul reach the fifth level of what Christ's resurrection from the dead means for himself and his readers, once more negatively, by implication, in verse 19: "If it is only in this life that we hope in Christ, we would be the most miserable of human beings." Unlike in 1 Thess 5:1–11, however, this fifth-level statement is not the purpose of Paul's appeal to the reality of Christ's resurrection. It too, like the fourth-level meanings, functions in Paul's reasoning as an argument reinforcing his refutation of a denial of a general resurrection of the dead at the more theoretical third level of meaning: "How do some among you say that there is not a resurrection from the dead?" (12c–d). That does not diminish the significance of the statement. Even though the thrust of Paul's reasoning is at the theoretical third level of the resurrection of the dead, the statement in verse 19 probably expresses one of the most important reasons why Paul engaged in the issue.

In verse 20a Paul makes his conclusive statement about the issue: "But now, Christ was raised from the dead." His argument is complete. Nothing more needs to be said. He continues at a theoretical level to declare the results that emerge from Christ's resurrection, which he clarifies in terms of Christ's Parousia. Christ is "the firstfruits" of those who have died (v. 23b). In the rest of the chapter, Paul no longer discusses Christ's resurrection, but what follows from it:

Christ's Parousia and the Jewish belief in the resurrection of the dead, which he now assumes to be established beyond further doubt.

Romans 6:1–14

The table on page 129 illustrates the relationships between the resurrection and the life of the believer. These relationships will be developed in the following pages. Compared with 1 Cor 15:1–8; 12–23, the way Paul expresses the meaning of Christ's death in Rom 6:1–14 could hardly be more different. In 1 Cor 15 it does not become clear what Paul means with his quotation of the tradition in verses 3c–7, including the reference to Christ's appearance to himself in verse 8, until he states in verse 12, "If, then, Christ is proclaimed to have been raised from the dead, how do some among you say that there is not a resurrection from the dead?" In contrast, the agenda for Paul's entire reasoning in Rom 6 is set by the two rhetorical questions in verses 1–2: "Shall we remain in sin in order that graciousness may abound? By no means! We who died to sin, how can we still live in it?"

The christological statements in verses 4c–d and 9b–10 play a crucial role in Paul's reasoning:

> Christ was raised from the dead through the glory of the Father; . . . Christ, raised from the dead, will no longer die; death no longer reigns over him. For the one who died, died once for all to sin; the one who lives, lives for God. —

Nevertheless, these statements have no independent meanings. Their meanings are determined by the way they function in Paul's reasoning. The close correlation between the christological statements and what they mean to Paul and his readers is revealed by the way they are embedded in statements that express their meanings.

The first christological statement, "Christ was raised from the dead through the glory of the Father" (v. 4cd), is embedded on the one side in the preceding reference to dying with

¹What then shall we say? Shall we remain in *sin* [6:1a–b]

  in order that graciousness may abound? ²By no means! We who died to *sin* [6:1c–2b],

how can we still live in it [6:2c]? ⌉ A

  ³Or do you not realize that we who were baptized into Christ Jesus were baptized into his death? ⁴Thus, we have been co-buried with him through the baptism into his death, *so that, as* [6:3–4b]

    Christ was raised from the dead through the glory of the Father [6:4c–d], ⌉ B

  so also we might walk in the newness of life [6:4e].

  ⁵For if we became co-physical in the similarity of his death [6:5a], ⌉ C

  we will also be of his resurrection [6:5b].

    ⁶Knowing this: Our old self is co-crucified [6:6a–b] ⌉ D

  in order that the body of *sin* may be destroyed [6:6c],

so that we no longer slave for *sin* [6:6d]. ⌉ E

    ⁷For the one who died [6:7a] ⌉ D′

  is justified from *sin* [6:7b].

    ⁸If we died with Christ [6:8a], ⌉ C′

  we believe that we will also live with him, ⁹*knowing that* [6:8b–9a]

    Christ, raised from the dead, will no longer die; death no longer reigns over him. ¹⁰For the one who died, died once for all to *sin*; the one who lives, lives for God [6:9b–10]. ⌉ B′

  ¹¹*So also* we consider ourselves dead to *sin*, living for God in Christ Jesus [6:11].

¹²Thus, do not let *sin* reign in your mortal bodies to be obedient to its lusts, ¹³nor put your members at the disposal of *sin* as weapons of evil, but place yourselves at the disposal of God as living from death, and your members as weapons of justice for God [6:12–13]. ⌉ A′

  ¹⁴For *sin* will not rule over you [6:14a];

    for you are not subject to the law, but depend on graciousness [6:14b].

Christ through baptism, for which it (the first christological statement) provides a basis: "We who have been baptized into Christ Jesus were baptized into his death? Thus, we were co-buried with him through the baptism into his death, *so that, as . . .*" (vv. 3b–4b). Paul is moving toward a conclusion: "*so also* we might walk in the newness of life" (v. 4e). The christological statement is embedded syntactically between verses 3b–4b and 4e by means of "so that, as . . . so also." The conjunction "so that" signals that what follows in verse 4c–e carries further what was said in the preceding statement about baptism in verses 3b–4b.

The second christological statement, "Christ, raised from the dead, will no longer die; death no longer reigns over him. For the one who died, died once for all to sin; the one who lives, lives for God" (vv. 9b–10), is also embedded in statements concerning what it means for Paul and his readers. In the first instance we confront Paul's statement concerning dying with Christ and living with him. This first christological statement is conditioned by what it means for Paul and his readers. On the one hand, the christological statement provides support for the statement concerning dying with Christ and living with him: "If we died with Christ, we believe that we will also live with him, *knowing that . . .*" (vv. 8–9a). On the other hand, the christological statement lays the ground for the conclusion for Paul and his readers: "*So also* we consider ourselves dead to sin, living for God in Christ Jesus" (v. 11).

As in the case of the syntactic links established by means of "so that, as . . . so also" between the first christological statement (v. 4c–d) and what it means for Paul's readers (vv. 3b–4b and 4e), so here too syntactic links are established by means of "knowing that . . . , so also" between the second christological statement (vv. 9b–10) and what it means for Paul's readers (vv. 8 and 11).

Paul's purpose with the statement about baptism in verses 3–4b is not to provide his readers with information concerning baptism as such. By drawing on baptism as an accepted reality, he brings to the fore those features that are relevant and what the statement means for his readers: "Christ was raised from the dead through the glory of the Father" (v. 4c–d). Paul includes that statement to mean for his readers, "so also we might walk in the newness of life" (v. 4e), the newness of the life in Christ to which they are called.

There is no reference to Christ's death in the first christological statement, only to his resurrection. Christ's death is, of course, present as part of the context provided by the preceding statement about baptism as participation in Christ's death in verses 3–4b. Yet Paul begins his reasoning by not focusing on Christ's death as the liberation from sin, but on Christ's resurrection as the foundation of the new life into which Paul and his readers are called (vv. 4e–5). Participation in Christ's death is the basis on which this new life is made possible, but Christ's death is not in the forefront in this part of Paul's reasoning.

Coordinate with Paul's focus on Christ's resurrection is the absence of any reference to sin before verse 6, in which it becomes dominant all the way to the end of his reasoning. Apart from the two references in verses 1–2, from verse 6 onward, Paul refers to sin eight more times between verses 6 and 14 (in italics above). What Paul is aiming at, also in the first part of his reasoning, is liberation from sin, the issue raised by the rhetorical questions in verses 1–2.

Paul's main reasoning in the passage takes place between the two christological statements, each followed by a fourth-level meaning, introduced with the identical "so also we":

> so also we might walk in the newness of life [v. 4e],

> so also we consider ourselves dead to sin, living for God in Christ Jesus [v. 11].

These verses begin with two sets of third-level statements, followed by fourth-level ones, C and D on the diagram of the text:

> For if we became co-physical in the similarity of his death, we will also be of his resurrection [v. 5],

> Knowing this: Our old self is co-crucified in order that the body
> of sin may be destroyed [6a–c].

Paul then concludes with a single fifth-level statement, E on
the diagram of the text: "So that we no longer slave for sin"
(v. 6d).

Even though this concluding statement coordinates well
with the second clause of Paul's negation of the first rhetorical
question, "How can we still live in [sin]?" (v. 2), and could
have concluded his reasoning as a whole, he was evidently
not satisfied. Hence, he continues the discussion with two
more sets of third-level statements, followed by fourth-level
ones (D' and C' on the diagram of the text):

> For the one who died is justified from sin [v. 7].

> If we died with Christ, we believe that we will also live with
> him [v. 8].

These statements lead up to the second christological statement (vv. 9–10).

At first sight, the statements in the two halves of Paul's
reasoning in verses 5–6c and 7–8 appear repetitive, without
significant development. In reality, they are well structured
in a chiasmus that begins and ends with the semantically
parallel statements in verses 5 and 8, which are C and C' on
the diagram of the text:

> For if we became co-physical in the similarity of his death, we
> will also be of his resurrection.

> If we died with Christ, we believe that we will also live
> with him.

With these parallel statements, Paul picks up the thoughts
about participation in Christ's death through baptism in
verses 3–4, and expands them with statements about participation in Christ's resurrection as well. This is in agreement
with the application of the first christological statement to
Paul himself and his readers in verse 4e: "So also we might
walk in the newness of life."

Death is a critical element in Paul's negation of the first rhetorical question, but it is death in a qualified sense, death to sin (v. 2b), which is what is missing in the parallel statements in verses 5 and 8, the topic on which Paul focuses at the center of the chiasmus. Two semantically parallel statements, D and D′ on the diagram of the text, show this:

> Knowing this: Our old self is co-crucified in order that the body of sin may be destroyed [v. 6a–c].

> For the one who died is justified from sin [v. 7].

These statements frame the chiastic center (E on the diagram of the text), "so that we no longer slave for sin" (v. 6d).

With the focus on dying to sin, Paul returns to the central issue that he raised in the rhetorical questions in verses 1–2: living in sin or dying to it. With the central statement in verse 6d, Paul is back at the heart of the matter. He negates the erroneous suggestion, "Shall we remain in sin in order that graciousness may abound?" (v. 1bc) with the second rhetorical question: "We who died to sin, how can we still live in it?" (v. 2b–c). Now the negation is no longer in the form of a rhetorical question; it becomes a firm statement.

The chiastic structure of verses 5–8 reveals Paul's ability to focus his thoughts sharply. It is not necessary to assume that he consciously structured his thoughts formally in a chiasmus. The chiasmus appears rather to be the result of the way his thoughts move forward toward his goal. Paul's aim is to reinforce his negation of the mistaken view expressed in the first rhetorical question, a point he appears to have reached in verse 6d, "so that we no longer slave for sin," at the center of his chiasmus. But he is evidently not satisfied. His thoughts move on, resulting in the chiastic parallelism between, respectively, verses 5–6c and 7–8. Even with that, Paul has not yet reached his goal; he moves on to a new christological statement: "Christ, raised from the dead, will no longer die; death no longer reigns over him. For the one who died, died once for all to sin; the one who lives, lives for God" (vv. 9b–10). Although, in a way, Paul already says all he needs to say at the center of the chiasmus in verses 6–7, it is possible for him to establish an excess of meaning in the second christological statement, compared with everything that precedes: Christ died to sin and lives for God. "For the one who died, died once for all to sin; the one who lives, lives for God" (v. 10). In that way Paul grounds the statement in verse 7 in Christ's death and applies it to himself and his readers: "For the one who died is justified from sin." This is the foundation of his statement at the center of the chiasmus in verse 6d: "So that we no longer slave for sin."

Paul formulates the second christological statement specifically with what it means for his readers, as he makes explicit in verse 11: "So also we consider ourselves dead to sin, living for God in Christ Jesus." The expression in verse 11 has features that are parallel to the earlier expression in verse 4e, both introduced with "so also we," as we have already observed: "So also we might walk in the newness of life" (v. 4e). "So also we consider ourselves dead to sin, living for God in Christ Jesus" (v. 11). Here we should recognize an important difference: In addition to the newness of life in Christ in the first statement, the second includes the crucial element of a death to sin as well.

It now becomes clear that we may also consider verses 4c–e and 9b–11 as parallel parts of the chiasmus:

> So that, as Christ was raised from the dead through the glory of the Father, so also we might walk in the newness of life [v. 4c–e]. . . .

> Christ, raised from the dead, will no longer die; death no longer reigns over him. For the one who died, died once for all to sin; the one who lives, lives for God. So also we consider ourselves dead to sin, living for God in Christ Jesus [vv. 9b–11].

We should perceive the difference between these two statements. The presence of dying to sin is present only in the second and reveals Paul's intention. The structure of his discourse has two steps, each with its own focus: First, the new life in Christ (vv. 3–5); and then, dying to sin (vv. 6–11). The latter conception was clearly Paul's goal when he formulated what had been at issue in the two rhetorical questions: Remaining in sin (v. 1b) and living in it (v. 2c), over against dying to sin (v. 2b). The function of the two christological statements in Rom 6:1–11 are not exhortatory as, for example, in 1 Thess 5:1–11. But they concern a more theoretical issue stated in the beginning, in the two rhetorical questions in verses 1 and 2: Can reliance on God's graciousness be considered a motivation to sin? Nevertheless, as a pastor, Paul cannot refrain from bringing the discussion to an exhortatory conclusion in verses 12–13:

> Thus, do not let sin reign in your mortal bodies to be obedient to its lusts, nor put your members at the disposal of sin as weapons of evil, but place yourselves at the disposal of God as living from death, and your members as weapons of justice for God.

Paul's primary concern in the passage as a whole is not exhortation. He returns to a theoretical level of the liberation from sin with a concluding statement: "For sin will not rule over you" (14a). Now the statement has a different basis: "For you are not subject to the law, but depend on graciousness" (v. 14b). This final statement leads Paul back to the original issue: "What then shall we say? Shall we remain in sin in order that graciousness may abound?" (v. 1). Paul has formulated the issue differently: "What then, shall we sin because we are not under the law, but under graciousness?" (v. 15).

This passage is complicated. Let us now see if we can follow Paul's reasoning. He begins by stating the issue by means of two rhetorical questions (vv. 1–2). Then, after establishing the believer's dying with Christ through baptism, he is moved by the second part of the second rhetorical question to the first christological statement affirming Christ's resurrection (v. 4c–d) and the believers' participation in it (v. 4e). At this point Paul's focus is on Christ's resurrection, momentarily surrendering his death and what it means for the believer. In verse 5, he reaffirms the believer's participation in Christ's resurrection. The real issue, however, is not the new life in

Christ as such, but that the new life in Christ is a death to sin. That is the issue to which Paul returns in verse 6, not to slave for sin (v. 6d), with which he ends the first part of his reasoning.

The argument does not leave Paul satisfied. He moves back up the chiastic ladder to the second christological statement, with parallel statements to those that lead from the first christological statement to the central point of the chiasmus in verse 6d, including the first half of the second christological statement. The second half of that statement provides the foundation for the point he wants to make about Christ's death to sin and his life for God (v. 10).

On that basis Paul can now say, in parallel to verse 4e, "We might walk in the newness of life." We now live for God: "living for God in Christ Jesus" (v. 11b). Paul adds: "We consider ourselves dead to sin" (v. 11a); this is the basis on which believers can live for God.

The meaning of Christ's resurrection for Paul in Rom 6:1–14 is that "we might walk in the newness of life" (v. 4e), and that his readers can consider themselves "living for God in Christ Jesus" (v. 11b). At the same time, in contrast with what Paul wrote in 1 Cor 15:17, "If Christ was not raised, you are still in your sins," it is not through Christ's resurrection, but through his death that he defeated the power of sin: "The one who died, died once for all to *sin*" (v. 10ab). Rom 6:1–14, apart from expressing what Christ's resurrection meant, that through it "we might walk in the newness of life" (6:4e), makes clear that it is through Christ's death that believers are liberated from sin.

One might argue that if Christ had not been raised from the dead, his death would have been ineffective. There is reason to believe that Paul himself would have understood that to be true. Christ's death and resurrection cannot be separated as unrelated events in his thought. Christ's resurrection established the effectiveness of his death as the event of salvation, certainly for Paul, for whom the encounter with the resurrected Christ was what changed his life. *The unity of Christ's death and resurrection as a single complex event of salvation* was so complete in his thought that he was able to write in 1 Cor 2:2, "I decided not to know anything among you except Christ Jesus, and him crucified," even though he was also able to write in 1 Cor 15:17, "And if Christ was not raised, your faith is madness; you are still in your sins," without contradicting himself. In his mind the Christ who had been crucified was the resurrected Christ who had appeared to him, and inversely, the Christ who appeared to him was the Christ who liberated him from sin.

Chapter 6

Resurrection:
The Dead Sea Scrolls
and the New Testament

James H. Charlesworth

Driving down from Jerusalem to the coastal plain awakened in me thoughts about the Maccabean Revolt, especially as I passed the signs to Modiin. It was during the time of the Maccabees and the final editorial work on the book of Daniel that the concept of resurrection finally makes a clear and unmistakable impact on the biblical books. I turned northward toward Haifa because my work that day took me to a place just north of Tel Aviv. After parking the car, I took the elevator to the top penthouse floor of an impressive high-rise hotel. Then I walked to a most elegant door and rang the bell. The owner opened, and a longtime friendship was rekindled. I looked at the owner's collection of antiquities and thought how the Vatican and other museums had failed to obtain what he treasured. I was in my element, with priceless antiquities all around and the sea spreading out beyond my view to the west.

We talked and conversed for hours. The phone rang, and as my host was preoccupied, I sauntered out past the twenty-foot ceilings to look down to the gently pounding surf below. The sun was warm, and the Mediterranean Sea looked so inviting. I thanked the sustaining Creator for life and health. Then I looked off into the distance toward Princeton, which I had not seen for almost a year, and Florida, where I grew up in the 1940s and 1950s.

Returning to the spacious living room with walls of glass, my host and I pondered the meaning of life and death. He affirmed that God is the one whom we yearn to know more about. Somewhat more realistically than mystically, he said that the Hebrew word for God, *Ēl,* is actually grounded on the preposition, *el,* which means "toward." Thus, he confided God is the one (*Ēl*) to whom (*el*) we pour forth our yearning, dedication, and constant praying. I felt that he had hit on something that might have been said near his spacious home over three thousand years ago.

The conversation turned to the question of an afterlife. "No way," he affirmed. He stressed that God had created this world. God does not make mistakes or duplicate his work. "Why should God make two worlds?" he asked. This world is the only world we know. This world is the one into which we were born. There is only one world. There is no resurrection into another world; the present and this world are what God has given us. We must not yearn for a future. We dare not miss the gift of the present in search of dreams.

I was impressed. Here was a brilliant mind who did not quote others. Here was a mind that had learned from life. Although he was given an honorary degree, some years later, he was well taught by life's experiences. Here was one who had the Bible (the Hebrew Bible) memorized in Hebrew, and even in English. I had some problems with what he had said, and I told him that while I agreed with much of what he had said so insightfully, finally I would have to reject his claim that God made only one world and that there is no resurrection. The concept of two worlds does not demand the concept of God making a mistake. The concept of two worlds, or two ages, was an ancient one, antedating the destruction of the Temple in Jerusalem by the Romans in 70 CE.

Driving back to the chill of Jerusalem, I thought about the pleasant warmth of the coastal town north of Tel Aviv. I pondered the insights obtained from the stimulating discussion. My host had awakened my interest in a future task: speaking on the concept of resurrection at a symposium at Florida Southern College. Then and there I decided to rework my reflections and presentation.

In my view, theological reflection leads to two insights. First, it makes sense that God does not need to create two worlds, and any reflection on the possibility of "two worlds" must not develop so that this world is perceived to be evil. That was the metaphysical mistake made by the Gnostics. Second, it seems obvious that while God is active and present in the present world, God also transcends everything we may and can know about this world.

Do these insights mean we should explore the use of other words for pondering "another" world? Perhaps there is one big world, and we know only part of it, the part we inadvertently call "this world." We need to rethink our nomenclature as well as our perceptions. Certainly, the Hebrew concept of *sāmayîm,* or "heavens," ceases to be sufficient. For example, the early Russian cosmonauts announced from space that there was no God because they could look down on the clouds and could clearly see that there was no old man sitting on them. This claim only showed how much Jewish and Christian theology was miscast and misperceived. No theologian was concerned by such nonsense; in fact, we were amused and not offended. Jettisoning "God" into heaven or another world is possible only when one fails to grasp biblical theology and the narrative claim that "the Lord God" dwelled among us and we beheld his glory (John 1:14).

A Being that is localized only in heaven is not a concept present when Jews in synagogues and Christians in churches pray, "Our Father who is in heaven." God, the Creator, does not live in some unknown space above us. We need to perceive that when we pray "Our Father who is in heaven" we do not intend to conceptualize one who is a *deus absconditus* — an absent God. We know that God is all around us and within us. God is not categorized or delimited by the present world, as we are.

Perhaps, then, we should find a better word to represent what we mean when we refer to "heaven." Should we explore other terminology and concepts? Should we think about a parallel universe? Or should we contemplate another dimension?

Scientists skilled in subatomic physics or astrophysics have given us fresh insights and models for thinking about God and the so-called other world. Should we add to the search for the infinite particle, perhaps a fluctuating wave, the concept of God's being? If so, is "God" an appropriate noun for what we strive toward?

After World War I Paul Tillich was commissioned to find theological language that was not stained and myopic. During one of his public lectures, a learned man on the front row advised Tillich not to replace the noun "God." This scholar, Martin Buber, and Paul Tillich thence commenced a life of friendship in which "I-Thou" language helped shape the perception of the Ground of All Being — Tillich's way of referring to God without replacing that name. If we keep the noun "God," we would do well not to forget that, as Philo of Alexandria taught us, God is not a category we can comprehend; God is a supracategorical term. Virtually all of us call out, with the author of Isa 26:8, "We long for the name by which You are called" (TANACH).

If there is a "big bang" with which creation commenced, what or who created it and guided the dispersion of matter? Who and where then is the Creator? Such thoughts are enlightening and offer freedom from preset agendas. Such reflections also lift us above the quagmire of stultifying dogmatics.

Thinking about the Awesome One, thus, does not prove that this one created only one world. We know so little about this world as to be lost in wonder about the extent of the present world or universe. Is there one universe? Perhaps the black holes are windows into other universes. In summation, belief in a resurrection from the dead does not rise or fall from contemplating "another world."

Essentially, what I told my host in the palatial abode north of Tel Aviv is that I fundamentally believe in the concept of a postmortem resurrection because of my own experiences. That is, my source of theological insight comes as much from intensive reading and studying as it does from introspection and reflection on my own experiences that now cover over sixty years and twenty nations. Over these years and in these places, I have experienced the presence of the Creator and sought to understand how and in what ways this Being has been part of my experiences. Thus, I am led to confess (Is that the proper word?) and contend that my life has been enriched by experiences that would be defined as glimpses into immortality. And for me, the means was some form of resurrection faith.

What am I trying to convey? Perhaps I am seeking ways to express my dissatisfaction with something we have all inherited from the thinkers during the time of the Enlightenment. We have been taught that knowledge comes to us from thinking, willing, or feeling. Thought, will, and feeling are the three means of obtaining wisdom. That tends to trifurcate our being. I frankly do not know how I obtained some insights, and I do not want to spend time sorting them out into three circumscribed categories. For me, it is the totality of these three human activities — their relatedness and also experience — that has been our great teacher. Thus, I have no doubt that Michael Jordan, Tiger Woods, and other phenomenally successful athletes were able to master the knowledge of a particular sphere of meaning not primarily through categories of thought, will, and feeling. They learned it from feeling an environment with a well-defined space, from willing themselves toward a focused goal, and notably from practically experiencing how one achieves the goal. Such knowledge has to be learned from doing and living in a world with a defined set of values and rules. It thus becomes automatic and spontaneous. Reflection thus becomes replaced by reaction; and knowledge is the experience of repetition.

In summation, I have experienced something not easily articulated; somehow I am led to believe that life is not terminated and defined by death. Somehow I not only believe but know, from experience, that there is a resurrection after death. Why? It is part of my experience, and that entails living within the world that produced Jesus of Nazareth and also within a culture in which Jesus continues to be a living presence because the Lord raised him from the dead.

As a scholar who is a Christian and who specializes in the world that produced Jesus and his earliest followers, I have certain guiding assumptions that shape my theology. The most important assumption is that Christian theology must be based on what was experienced and perceived within Jesus' Judaism and within the Judaism of his followers. The Twelve were unperceptive of Jesus' intentions and parabolic teachings, according to the evangelists. The thinking of Jesus' followers developed with the conviction that he was not a failure but one whom the creating Creator raised from the dead. New Testament theology, thus, is founded on the thoughts and memories of those who experienced Jesus through resurrection faith.

Skeptics will demand proof of what I mean by experience and "knowledge" of resurrection belief. They should not influence our thinking or force us to attempt answers that are shaped by logic and reasoning. Resurrection thought is not shaped by or evolved from categories shaped by logic or reason. Resurrection belief is not merely mysticism; but it also transcends concepts and categories in which reflective thought can be proved or disproved. Furthermore, when we work with apocalyptic writings, in which resurrection belief first appears within Judaism, we at best can obtain only probability, not proof.

How and why should we ground our belief in Jesus' resurrection on a balanced and nuanced perception of the thoughts and lives of those who lived in the first century CE and also upon our own experiences? Let me turn to the Dead Sea Scrolls, related Jewish literature, and the New Testament to explore ways to answer this question.

Studying Ancient Texts

We should study ancient texts within the gamut of experiencing the struggle and context of their authors. We should imagine and interpret them within their original contexts.

My comments now, obviously, must be highly selective. There are dozens of books on my shelves that are concentrated on one or more of the areas I have chosen now to explore. In this brief essay, it would be foolish to attempt to replicate the discussions and research found in them. Thus, my focus will be limited to the Jewish matrix of Jesus and the birth of what eventually will be called Christianity.

I shall begin with the Dead Sea Scrolls. How shall I organize and present my report from exploring these texts? That is always a daunting issue. I have decided to employ some thoughts read when I visited the Tel Aviv Museum of Art. There in late winter of 1998, I studied the artwork of a distinguished Israeli artist named Avigdor Arikha, who was born on April 28, 1929. His artwork was riveting in its language, and even more impressive was Arikha's chosen words to explain his masterpieces.

Arikha explained that his "drawings organize themselves differently thanks to the edges." By these words he meant: "For me everything begins at the edges and advances towards the center." Scanning the Jewish literature that antedates the demise of ancient Israel under Bar Kokhba in 135 or 136, we can readily see the appearance of the Jewish concept of a resurrection after death. It appears sometime before the middle of the second century BCE and then develops. One is impressed with the diversity of early Jewish thought on the edges and throughout Second Temple Judaism. These early Jews show no clear tendency to move toward a central idea or a set of core ideas. Yet, within the fascinating world of contrasting opinions of what God's Torah means for them, some early Jew developed a belief in postmortem life and indeed a resurrection to a fuller life, which is eternal.[1] With these preliminary comments, we can begin by studying the concept of resurrection in light of the Dead Sea Scrolls.

Dead Sea Scrolls

From the time the Dead Sea Scrolls were first discovered in 1947 until relatively recently, most experts concluded that these early Jewish writings did not contain the concept of a resurrection of the dead. The Qumranites apparently thought that as Sons of Light, they could purify themselves, and with the transformation possible through the Holy Spirit, would ascend to something like angelic status. Qumran anthropology ascends to angelology; thus, there is no need for a resurrection after death. The Qumranite could experience both immortality and oneness with the Lord in the House of Holiness, the Community, thanks to the presence and assistance of the Holy Spirit.

This consensus has been shaken by three developments. Unlike other early Jews, the Qumranites were buried north-to-south. Perhaps this alignment was caused by the belief that paradise was in the north, since a document found at Qumran, *1 Enoch,* situates paradise in the north (*1 En.* 77). If this reasoning is correct, the Qumranite would be resurrected facing north and paradise, the abode of the righteous after death. Second, two texts found in Cave 4 contain the belief in a resurrection from the dead. The texts are *On Resurrection*

(4Q521) and *Pseudo-Ezekiel* (4Q385). If these texts represent Qumran thought, then the Qumranites, or some of them, believed in the resurrection of the dead. Third, a distinguished Qumran expert, E. Puech, has published a massive work that refocuses on some well-known scrolls. He concludes that the Qumranites thought there was a resurrection from the dead.

Let us begin an examination of the Dead Sea Scrolls to see if they contain clearly and without qualification a belief in the resurrection of the dead (that is, category 15, as explained in ch. 1, above).

Some preliminary perceptions assist an exegesis of the relevant passages. First, we should distinguish between resurrection faith and the *raising of a group from disenfranchisement* (category 2; see ch. 1). The Qumranites had been banished from the Temple (even though they claim to have left; cf. 4QMMT), hence some of the passages in the *Thanksgiving Hymns* (or *Hodayot*) may allude to this disenfranchisement and establishment at Qumran.

A similar thought is found in *1 En.* 25, a document also found in the Qumran Caves. This passage states "they shall be glad and rejoice in gladness" (25:6). This thought most likely is a reference to the establishment of the righteous, who have been persecuted, because "as the fathers" they will have "long life" *on earth.* At that time the righteous shall enjoy the life that is usually typical of paradise or the afterlife: "torments, plagues, and sufferings shall not touch them" (25:6).[2] This idea is not a form of the belief in a resurrection of the dead to immortal life; it is a resurrection from disenfranchisement to authority here on earth, after which the individuals will die.

Second, we must distinguish between resurrection faith and the *raising of the individual from personal embarrassment* (category 4). This category is found, most likely, in the Qumran *Thanksgiving Hymns.* The author is probably the Righteous Teacher, the religious genius who most significantly shaped early Qumran thought. He is probably the author of some passages in the *Thanksgiving Hymns,* since his personality seems apparent in the self-consciousness and self-understanding that he is the Lord's interpreter (cf. 1QpHab 7).[3] He states that he has been embarrassed but that the Lord raised him up him from such disgrace. Here are the major lines:

> And you made me an object of shame and derision for traitors,...
> But (then) you made me a banner for the elect of righteousness,
> And the interpreter of knowledge concerning marvelous mysteries,
>   to test [the men of] truth
>   and to try those who love instruction.
>
> (1QH^a 10 [= olim 2].9–14)

The author celebrates how he has been resurrected from being an object of shame to being the interpreter of knowledge. He later adds that though his enemies cast him down toward the pit, he has not died; the Creator has appointed — and in that sense elevated — him to be the incomparable interpreter.

Third, we must distinguish between resurrection faith and the *raising of the individual from inactivity to do the Creator's will* (category 6). As Émile Puech, the distinguished and gifted French scholar living in the École Biblique in Jerusalem, points out, 1QH^a 14 (= olim 6).29–30, is difficult to understand. No one can point with insight to a full context, since the many holes (lacunae) in the manuscript undermine a contextual study of the passage.[4] Initially, one might obtain the impression that the author has referred to a belief in the resurrection of the dead.[5] Here is the passage:

> And at the time of judgment God's sword shall hasten,
> And all his sons of tr[ut]h shall be awakened to [destroy] the
>   sons of ungodliness.
> And all the sons of transgression shall be no more.
>
> (1QH^a 14 [= olim 6].29–30)

The verb "shall be awakened" and the connection with "the time of judgment" tend to suggest that the author may be thinking about a resurrection after death (cf. Dan 12:1–3).

The verb form, however, means not only "to be awakened," but also "to be incited," or "to be roused." Thus, the verb may not suggest the meaning of being raised from the dead.[6] In my judgment, the passage probably does not portray a resurrection of the righteous from the dead. The lines most likely refer to the energizing of the righteous so that they can perform the Creator's deeds at the end of time. Of course, some Qumanites and other Jews might well have interpreted this passage to denote a belief in postmortem resurrection.

A following line (34) of the hymn refers to those "who lie in the dust." Does not this comment prove that this hymn in the *Thanksgiving Hymns* refers to a resurrection belief? As pointed out earlier (in ch. 1), a reference to "dust" in Biblical Hebrew may be a euphemism for humility (1 Sam 2:8; Ps 44:26 [25 ET]).

The passage in 1QH^a 14, then, seems to predict the raising up of the righteous ones, probably the Holy Ones of the Community who are aligned with the Holy Ones in heaven (cf. the *Angelic Liturgy*), at the time of judgment, the end of time. The Holy Ones do not need to die to rise up. They have entered into the Community of the end time and have transcended the usual categorization of time into past and future. They are now, in the present, preparing for the final eschatological battle. This time is not postmortem, as becomes clear from a study of the *War Scroll* (1QM). The raising up of the Qumranites inaugurates the final days and the judgment, after which comes the time of bliss, when there is no more evil and Belial (Satan) is defeated.

The passage seems to be a metaphor. The author uses language sometimes associated with death to depict the rising up of the righteous on earth to withstand Belial, or Satan, in "the battles of wickedness" (1QH^a 14.29; cf. the *War Scroll*). Puech thinks that the author of 1QH^a 14.29–30 is the Righteous Teacher.[7] In light of the use of the first-person singular pronouns in this hymn in 1QH^a I would agree.[8]

Fourth, we should distinguish between resurrection faith and the *raising of the individual from meaninglessness in this world to a realizing eschatology* (category 9). At Qumran the dualism espoused in the *Rule of the Community* (1QS cols. 3–4) began to break down. The human is not categorically distinct from the divine; angels are (imagined) present during worship services. It is impossible to know if the Hebrew *'elîm* mentioned in some Qumran Scrolls denotes divine beings or members of the *Yaḥad* who are very advanced, "the Most Holy of Holy Ones." Time was not bifurcated or trifurcated; the future was breaking into the present. The cosmos was not divided into heaven and earth; heaven was perceived as touching earth in the Community. When one became a full member of the Community, he moved into a new world full of meaning; he entered into an eternal Community that was an antechamber of heaven.

What was scripturally and traditionally preserved for Jews after their resurrection was now transferred to the Qumranites in the present age and world. Two examples of this category are 1QH[a] 11 (= olim 3).20 and 1Q[b] 5.23. In the *Thanksgiving Hymns* we find the following Praise to the Lord:

> I thank you, O God, for you have redeemed my soul from
>   the pit;
> And from the Sheol of Abaddon.
> You have *raised me up* to an eternal height,
> So that I may walk about in uprightness without limit.
> And I know that there is hope for the one whom you have
>   fashioned from dust for the eternal council.
>   (1QH 11 [= olim 3].19–21;[9] italics mine)

Along with other scholars,[10] I am persuaded that this passage does not contain a belief in post-mortem resurrection. The issue in interpretation pertains to the meaning of "the pit; / And from the Sheol of Abaddon." Is this prepositional phrase a metaphor, or does it refer to the resurrection from Sheol of one who is dead? I am convinced that 1QH[a] 11 does not present the idea of a resurrection from the dead, and that the author had no reason to need such a view, since he was living in the *Yaḥad,* the Community. Furthermore, "the eternal council" is not a postmortem realm; it denotes the organization of this Community.

Nevertheless, it is conceivable that some Qumranites may well have imagined that the passage did contain resurrection beliefs. We must ever be on the alert that we do not limit the boundaries for interpretation at Qumran, not only over three centuries but also at the same time, and indeed in the same Jew.

Let me stress some basic points in interpreting a section of the *Thanksgiving Hymns* and other Qumran Scrolls. Here are seven helpful perceptions:

- The Qumranite did not consider the "future" as far off. He also did not divide time into past, present, and future (using French, English, Greek, or Latin verbal systems). At Qumran the "future" was being experienced in the present.

- The Qumranite seems at times to imagine that the end time is already being realized. The most advanced Qumranites were not clearly distinct categorically from angels.[11]

- At Qumran "the Most Holy Ones" did not have to wait until the future to participate in the assembly of angels; they do so already (cf. 1QS 2.25).[12]

- The Qumranites imagined that the *Yaḥad* was the *axis mundi,* or center of the earth, and that their Community was where the Holy Ones, angels, and the Holy Spirit could be found *on the earth.*

- The Holy Ones of Qumran did not only hope to share the abode of the angels; they also claimed to be experiencing it already in the *Yaḥad* (Community).[13]

- Most important, references to "pit," "Sheol," and "Abaddon" are sometimes clearly implored metaphorically prior to and at Qumran, especially in the Psalms.

- It is conceivable that when the author composed the passage in question, the concept of resurrection had not yet made its impact on Qumran theology or on his own theology.

Fifth, we ought to clarify what is clearly resurrection faith: it is the *raising of the individual from death to eternal life.* The only clear passage in the Hebrew Bible (Old Testament) of this category is found in Daniel: "Many of those who sleep in the dust of the earth shall awake, some to everlasting life, and some to shame and everlasting contempt" (12:2 NRSV).[14]

Thanks to the recent publication of fragments of scrolls available since the 1950s, it is now clear that a hope and belief in a postmortem resurrection is explicit in at least two Qumran Scrolls. *On Resurrection* is the name of a text found in Cave 4 (4Q521). Here is my translation:[15]

1 [The hea]vens and the earth will obey his Messiah

2 [th]at (is) in them. He will not turn back from the commandments of the Holy Ones.

3 Be strong, (all)[16] you who seek the Lord, in his (marvelous) work.

4 Will you not find in this the Lord, all those who wait (for him with hope) in their hearts?

5 Surely the Lord will seek the Pious Ones, and he will call the Righteous Ones by name.

6 And over the Poor Ones his spirit will hover and (to) those believing in his might he will renew (their strength).

7 [. . .] he will glorify the Pious Ones upon the crown of the eternal kingdom.

8 He will free the captives, open the eyes of the blind ones, (and) straighten those be[nt over].

9 For[ev]er I will hold fast [to him with al]l [those who] finish and I [will trust] in his loyalty,

10 and [his] go[odness . . .]. *The Holy One* will not linger [to come].

11 And the glorious things which are not the work of *the Lord, when he shall [come]*,

12 then he *will* heal those defiled and *give life (to) those dead,* (and) bear joyful news to the Poor Ones.

13 [. . .] *'sh*[. . . the holy] ones he will lead, he shall feed [th]em, he shall work

14 [. . .] and all of it *k*[. . .].

This Qumran fragment clearly refers to the belief in a resurrection of the dead. Observe the presence of two criteria necessary to be certain that this passage concerns the resurrection of the dead. First, obviously, it is necessary to have a noun that means or represents those who once lived but now are dead. Second, a verb meaning "to give life again" or "to resurrect" must be linked grammatically with the noun just mentioned. Lines 11 and 12 supply these criteria, as the italicized words in the translation help clarify: "The Lord, when he shall [come], . . . will . . . give life (to) those dead."

One cannot be certain that this text was composed at Qumran. Despite the claims of some established scholars, the mere presence of a text in a Qumran Cave does not provide any information for its original provenience. The presence of the technical term "the Poor Ones," frequently a self-designation of those living at Qumran, does suggest that this text may have been composed at Qumran.

A second Qumran document contains a belief in the resurrection of the dead. It is *Pseudo-Ezekiel*, which like *On Resurrection* was a text found in Qumran Cave 4 (4Q385 frg. 2). The author perceives "the bones" mentioned in Ezek 37 as belonging to "a large crowd of men" who "will rise and bless the Lord of Hosts who causes them to live." The text may not have been composed at Qumran.

A third Qumran document also may refer to a belief in the resurrection of the dead. This text may have been composed by the sect, perhaps early in its history and maybe before they settled at Qumran. The reference in this text to a resurrection belief is not so clear as in *On Resurrection*. Here is my translation of lines from this text, *Sapiential Work A* (4Q416 frg. 2 3.6–8):

a If <God> commits <you> to die in your poverty,

b entrust yourself to him and do not rebel against him in your spirit.

c Then you will rest in the truth,

d And in your death your remembrance will blosso[m for eve]r,

e And in the end you will inherit joy.

In lines *a* and *d* it is clear that those who are dead are the subject of the poem. It seems likely that the author is thinking about the ones who die without any reward for their commitment to (trust in) "God." The thought seems to progress from dying in poverty (line *a*), through resting in the truth (line *c*), to inheriting joy in the end (line *e*). The requisite noun is "you who die," and the necessary verb may be "inherit joy." The phrase "in the end" may denote the judgment day at the end of time. Understanding this fragment as referring to the resurrection of the dead seems supported by another fragment of *Sapiential Work A:* "the seekers of truth will wake up to the judgment[of God (?)" (4Q418 frg. 69 line 7).

The Old Testament Pseudepigrapha and the Eighteen Benedictions

The early Jewish documents in the Old Testament Pseudepigrapha sometimes contain clear and unmistakable references to a belief in the resurrection of the individual after death. As I stated in the introduction to the *Old Testament Pseudepigrapha*, the belief in the resurrection of the dead is found significantly in the *Testament of Job*, the *Psalms of Solomon*, *4 Maccabees*, *Pseudo-Phocylides*, *2 Baruch*, and *2 Enoch*. The author of *2 Baruch* even describes the resurrected body in a long section (*2 Bar.* 49–52). For the present brief summary, I shall quote only some portions of this long section of *2 Baruch:*

> For *the earth will surely give back the dead* at that time,...not changing anything in their form....And as I have delivered them to it so *it will raise them.* For then it will be necessary to show those who live that *the dead are living again,*...then my judgment will be strong;...both the shape of those who are found to be guilty as also the glory of those who have proved to be righteous will be changed. For the shape of those who now act wickedly will be made more evil than it is (now) so that they shall suffer torment. Also, as for the glory of those who proved to be righteous on account of my law,...their splendor will then be glorified by transformations, and the shape of their face will be changed into the light of their beauty so that they may acquire and *receive the undying world* which is promised to them....Then both these and those will be changed, these into the splendor of angels and those into startling visions and horrible shapes; and they will waste away even more....Those who are saved because of their works and for whom the Law is now a

hope, ... time will no longer make them older. For they shall see
that world, ... and they will be like the angels and be equal to
the stars. And they will be changed into any shape which they
wished, from beauty to loveliness, and from light to the splendor of glory. For the extents of Paradise will be spread out for
them.... And the excellence of the righteous will then be greater
than that of the angels. (50:2–51:12; *OTP* 2.638; italics mine)

The belief in the resurrection of the dead is also a common aspect of Jewish liturgy today. Most likely, in some form,
the belief found in the *Eighteen Benedictions* predates 70 CE.
Here is the old Palestinian version of the *Eighteen Benedictions,*
benediction 2:

> Thou art mighty — humbling the haughty,
> Powerful — calling to judgment the arrogant,
> Eternal — preserving the dead;
> Causing the wind to blow and the dew to fall,
> Sustaining the living, resurrecting the dead.[17]

This confession most likely was recited in ancient Palestine
during the time of Jesus and his earliest followers. There is
no reason to doubt that he and they knew and recited words
somewhat similar to what has been quoted.

As we turn again to the Jewish artist, Arikha, we can learn
from his comment that "everything begins at the edges and
advances toward the center." The diversity of early Jewish
thought does not represent a chaotic worldview. The chaos
among the Jews erupted in the First Revolt that began in 66
CE; before that date there was a greater degree of coherence.
In many ways, Jewish thought is united by a belief in One
Being, who has been known in biblical history; by a belief
that this Being has given Torah or Law to an elect nation, Israel; and by a belief that the promises made in Scripture are
trustworthy. For some Jews, perhaps the belief in a resurrection helped solve questions raised by beliefs in a Benevolent
Being and the hardships caused by the seeming disproof of
any special status in the world. Most of the Jewish groups,
with the exception of the Sadducees, affirmed that the Lord
was the one who raised the dead.

It now is abundantly clear that the concept of a resurrection of the dead was well known in the Judaism of the time of Jesus. It was not only on the edges or fringes of so-called mainstream Judaism; it was also espoused by many groups within Second Temple Judaism. Once scholars erred and assumed that the *Psalms of Solomon* was a Pharisaic composition. Judaism was misperceived from a naive assumption that the New Testament writers faithfully portrayed the theology of Second Temple Judaism, and that only the Pharisees believed in resurrection. Hence, the *Psalms of Solomon* was declared a Pharisaic composition because of such passages as the following:

> The destruction of the sinner is forever,
>   and he will not be remembered when (God) looks after the
>   righteous.
> This is the share of sinners forever,
>   but those who fear the Lord *shall rise up to eternal life,*
>   *and their life* shall be in the Lord's light, and it
>   *shall never end.*   (3:11–12; *OTP* 2.655; italics mine)

Now, we know that other Jews beside the Pharisees believed that after death the righteous, and sometimes also the unrighteous, were raised by the Creator. This belief is found clearly in the latest book in the Hebrew Bible, notably in Dan 12, and perhaps in later interpolations, as in Isa 26 (esp. vv. 19–21); thus, resurrection belief is found within groups that have given us the Scriptures. It appears again, later, in *On Resurrection* and perhaps *Sapiential Work A*; and while these documents may have been composed elsewhere, they were certainly influential at Qumran. Resurrection belief was espoused by a variety of early Jewish groups, including those who have given us the corpus known as *1 Enoch*, as well as the considerably different groups that are behind the shaping of such works as the *Testament of Job, 4 Maccabees, Pseudo-Phocylides*, *2 Baruch*, and *2 Enoch*. We must by no means assume that resurrection belief was only an aspect of sectarian Judaism; it appears clearly in Scripture and in the *Eighteen*

Benedictions. To use the words of Arikha, the belief in post-mortem resurrection to eternal life "advances towards the center" of early Jewish thought.

Resurrection belief was part of the Judaism Jesus knew. He is reputed to have taught that "the Father raises the dead and gives them life" (John 5:21 NRSV). One of his followers is reported to have confessed to Jesus that she knew her brother "will rise again in the resurrection on the last day" (John 11:24 NRSV).

With this clarifying insight, we may now more insightfully examine the major passages containing this belief in the New Testament. At the outset, I must stress that the reason for resurrection belief in this collection of early Jewish writings has shifted. Resurrection belief is no longer a hope or an expectation. According to the Jews who composed the New Testament documents, it is a fact of history, because God raised Jesus from the dead. This specificity demarks New Testament theology within, not from, early Jewish theology.

The New Testament

As we move to the New Testament writings, we find that applying Arikha's insight again appears helpful. The diversity of thought and confessions (as well as kerygmata) within the first generation of Jesus' followers is obvious. This discovery distinguishes the last two centuries of scientific research on the New Testament from the previous 1900 years.

The diversity of ideas in the New Testament may seem chaotic. The variety does move from the edges to a center. Recognizing the vast diversity among Matthew, Mark, Luke, John, Paul, Hebrews, and Revelation should also go hand in glove with the perception that each of them affirms that Jesus was raised from the dead by the Lord. Not one author in the early Palestinian Jesus Movement denies or even undermines the claim that Jesus was resurrected from the dead. Resounding within the chorus of New Testament voices is the affirmation that he who was dead is now alive. Thus, using the words of Arikha, we can report that "everything begins at the edges and advances toward the center." There is unity within the diverse New Testament proclamations: it is Jesus' continuing presence because of the resurrection. We can better understand that unity by assessing its eight features:

1. Jesus Raised by the Lord

The New Testament resurrection faith is grounded in the belief — indeed claimed experience — that Jesus *was raised by the Lord*. Too many translations of the New Testament represent the passive verb *egerthe* as "he has risen" (as in Mark 16:6 RSV). The verb is a passive form; it should be translated as a divine passive: "he was raised." What does this mean? It means "he was raised (by the Lord)."

The same reasoning applies to the passive verb *ophthe*. This verb means "he appeared." The Creator's power and action behind the appearance of Jesus is too often lost in exegesis and exposition of this verb. As is well known, this verb appears as an aorist passive in the resurrection narratives (see esp. 1 Cor 15:5–8). When Paul states that Jesus "appeared" to Cephas, the Twelve, James, to others, and finally to himself, he means that the Creator was actively involved in this cosmic event.

Now, what may I, a twenty-first-century Christian, confess without shirking my indebtedness to modern scientific research? Frankly, I do not believe that Jesus was dead and simply rose again three days later. That violates all I know about physics and New Testament Greek.

I do, however, believe that the Creator raised up Jesus from the tomb. That confession makes sense in terms of physics and the biblical view that the Creator can create ex nihilo, something "out of nothing," which is not a "Christian" creative insight, since it appears clearly in 2 Macc 7:28 (God created the heaven and the earth from "things that are not").

The New Testament authors make it clear that *Jesus' resurrection was an act by the ever-creating Creator.* Listen to Paul again: "Christ...was raised on the third day" (1 Cor 15:4 NRSV). The verb is another example of the divine passive. When Paul states that Jesus "was raised," he assumes his reader knows that Jesus was raised by the Creator. The Lord raised him up from the dead.

With his prior Pharisaic faith in a resurrection of the dead, Paul grounds belief in Jesus' resurrection by the Lord: "We testified of God that he raised Christ — whom he did not raise if it is true that the dead are not raised. For if the dead are not raised, then Christ has not been raised" (1 Cor 15:15–16 NRSV). Paul's thoughts remind us of the *Eighteen Benedictions,* which he may have known and probably recited in religious services.

2. The Centrality of Resurrection Faith

While the study of the historical Jesus does not demand belief in a resurrection, the mastery of New Testament theology reveals the centrality of resurrection faith. Christianity, based on the New Testament, is clearly, more than any other religion, a religion of resurrection.[18] For example, Paul opens his message to the Romans by stressing the paradigmatic significance of Jesus' resurrection. Paul begins his most powerful letter by claiming that he is a "servant of Jesus Christ." Notice how he defines this Jesus Christ as "designated Son of God in power according to the Spirit of holiness by his resurrection from the dead" (Rom 1:4 RSV).

Paul inherited this confessional formula from the earliest followers of Jesus. Thus, it is not merely the idiosyncratic thought of Paul. It means that Jesus is "the Son of God" and Lord because of "his resurrection from the dead." This confessional recognition is the foundation of New Testament faith. That faith is realistically built on the crucifixion and resurrection. Hence, the horrible death of Jesus is not the final act in the Jesus story that introduces Friday night. The story continues: there is the Easter Dawn of Sunday morning.

All New Testament authors, with various voices, join a united chorus to proclaim that Jesus is alive again because the Lord raised him from the dead. It is this perspective that made the proclamations (kerygmata) of the earliest followers so focused on sharing the "good news." That good news, the gospel, is the message that He-who-was-to-come has appeared on earth, is alive never to die again, and will come again in glory. The second coming thus presupposes the Easter message.

3. Resurrection Appearances of Jesus

The New Testament authors distinguish between dreams, visions, and resurrection appearances of Jesus. They try to make it clear that the resurrection appearances are neither dreaming nor seeing visions. They claim that Jesus' earliest followers, the disciples and others, experienced a resurrection appearance of Jesus.

The resurrected Lord is the Jesus whom these men and women had known earlier. They had shared life in Galilee and Judea with him. They had heard him teaching. They had seen this resurrected one earlier, performing miraculous healings in Galilee and Jerusalem.

Paul keeps his experience of the resurrected Jesus categorically separate from visions and dreams. He had a startling experience of the resurrected Jesus. The appearance of the resurrected Jesus to Paul is recorded not only in Acts and Galatians but also described categorically in 1 Cor 15: "Last of all, as to one untimely born, he appeared also to me" (1 Cor 15:8 RSV). Paul also had an apocalyptic vision. He alludes to it in 2 Cor 12, but he does not confuse the resurrection experience with "visions." His vision of "Paradise" results from a trip, in the body or out of the body, into the third heaven (cf. *2 En*. 8). The two events are distinct and different categories.

4. Resurrection in Spite of Lost Hope

The resurrection faith of Jesus' earliest followers was not because they let the wish become the father of the thought; not one resurrection text depicts Jesus' followers hoping he would be raised from the dead. Some New Testament experts claim that the hope that Jesus was still alive gave impetus to the confession that he was still alive; in so doing, they miss the message of the New Testament. The resurrected Jesus appears to those who "know" he is still dead.

Jesus appears again not to those who are hoping he will be raised; he appears to those who have lost hope. According to Luke, Cleopas informs a traveling companion, "We had hoped that he would be[19] the one who would redeem Israel" (Luke 24:21). Cleopas and his companion have thus been walking, depressed and dejected, to Emmaus. Their great hope was gone. Jesus has been publicly crucified. Finally, the apparent stranger reveals to them that he is Jesus. Thus, Jesus does not appear to Cleopas and his companion because they have wished or hoped for this event; in their depressed state of losing hope, they suddenly are startled to learn that their companion is identical with the one who had been crucified.

According to Mark, some women go to Jesus' tomb Sunday morning. They have allegedly planned to anoint the corpse of Jesus (16:1). They seemed ill prepared and confused on the way to the tomb, even wondering, "Who will roll away the stone for us from the door of the tomb?" (16:3 RSV). There is no resurrection faith at that moment.

According to John, Mary Magdalene goes to the garden in the early morning hours of Sunday. She meets someone she mistakes as the gardener. She wants to remove Jesus' corpse and place it somewhere else. She tells a man, obviously to her the gardener, "Sir, if you have carried him away, tell me where you have laid him, and I will take him away" (20:15 RSV).

Within the inherited traditions, it is not clear what is going on in the author's mind. Yet, it is obvious that Mary Magdalene is not even contemplating the possibility that Jesus has been raised from the dead. It is also strikingly clear that the empty tomb elicits no resurrection faith. It is merely a given and unclear aspect of the tradition. Peter and the Beloved Disciple run to the open tomb; the Evangelist John makes it clear that they do not believe in Jesus' resurrection by what they see (John 20:1–10). In fact, after these two have reported to the disciples, they all go "back to their homes" (20:10 RSV). There is no hope. At this point there is no belief in the resurrection of Jesus.

The compiler of the traditions in John 21 makes it clear that all the disciples remaining in Jesus' group return to Galilee and take up their previous lives. They follow Peter when he announces: "I am going fishing" (21:3 RSV).

The New Testament presents an amazingly consistent picture: the mission of Jesus was a failure. The hopes in him have been dashed. There are no more wishes that can father the thought that he is alive again. The Jesus Movement is over, finished. After Friday's crucifixion, there is no more to this story: it is ended. Despair characterizes Jesus' followers — if he has any followers remaining.

The point is driven home again in the Johannine narrative. The disciples tell Thomas that they have seen the Lord alive again (John 20:25). He finds them overly enthusiastic and scolds them: "Unless I see in his hands the print of the nails, and place my finger in the mark of the nails, and place my hand in his side, I will not believe" (20:25 RSV). Good for Thomas! He is the model disciple.[20] Thomas makes it clear to his associates and friends that he cannot believe because of others' experiences. He must experience what they have experienced, and he has his objective criteria to protect him from being duped by wishful thinking. Rather than hope, the New Testament resurrection accounts are shaped by a resistance to believe in Jesus' resurrection. Unfortunately, too many New Testament scholars have failed to perceive this most important element in these writings.

For example, the gifted J. Dominic Crossan contends that the belief in Jesus' resurrection was the result of "wishful thinking" by Jesus' earliest followers. Crossan is convinced that such an event as the resurrection never "did or could happen." He adds that no one "at any time brings dead people back to life."[21]

This position, of course, does not derive from New Testament theology. It is crucial to stress that the evangelists, and Paul, make it crystal clear that the disciples do not wish that Jesus would rise from the dead; instead, they are startled by such a belief and tend to resist it.

To grasp this point more fully, we should again turn to the poetic vision of Arikha. He offered the opinion that the "vitality of a good drawing stems from what is not in it, and what the lines define." What is not in New Testament resurrection faith is some dreamlike trance. There is no wishful thinking. In resurrection faith there is no exit from this world into a world of fantasy. Perhaps that is the meaning in Jesus disclosing his wounds to Thomas. It is none other than the crucified one who has been raised. The resurrected Christ is the former Jesus who had died in such a public and disgraceful way.

From the beginning, "Christians" affirm that there is history here in these narratives. Although the narratives are shaped by a mastery of Hellenistic rhetoric, they are not merely rhetorical gems.

5. Jesus Unexpectedly Alive Again

In all New Testament resurrection narratives, Jesus reveals that he is alive again and does so unexpectedly. All of this gloom and doom disperses unexpectedly, without any warning. Jesus simply pops up before the disciples and followers and announces by some means that he is the one they have known as Jesus of Nazareth. To Cleopas and his companion, Jesus makes himself known by interpreting Scripture, and finally in a familiar act of taking, blessing, and breaking the bread (Luke 24:30). How did his words and actions reveal who he was?

All we learn is that, following Jesus' words and actions, Cleopas and his companion immediately recognize that the stranger is none other than Jesus. They do not need to discuss what has happened. They unanimously and spontaneously know that Jesus has been raised from the dead. They instantly decide to rush back to Jerusalem to share this good news with what remains of the Twelve.

According to the compilers and editors of the Gospel of John, Mary Magdalene does not recognize Jesus. She mistakes him for a gardener. It is only when Jesus pronounces her name, and obviously in a familiar way, "Mariam," that her look turns into perception. It is immediate. She does not need to think or contemplate. She responds emphatically and tenderly: "Rabbouni" (John 20:16).

Again, we can learn from Paul. He claims to have experienced a "revelation of Jesus Christ" (Gal 1:12). According to 1 Cor 15, Paul never says Jesus was seen by someone. Paul repeatedly uses the concept of appearing by Jesus: the resurrection faith is initiated by Jesus. Recall Paul's words: "[Christ]...appeared to Cephas, then to the twelve. Then he appeared to more than five hundred" people "at one time.... Then he appeared to James, then to all the apostles. Last of all,...he appeared also to me" (1 Cor 15:5–8 RSV).

Two points seem obvious: Jesus appears to an individual: the individual does not initiate the action. The act is a passive one: Jesus appears to someone. Jesus, not another, is the one who does and can initiate the event. Second, the resurrection appearances end. They are followed by dreams or visions. Paul was the last one to whom Jesus appeared.

6. Controlled Reporting, Not Speculative

The New Testament authors are under careful control when they describe Jesus' resurrection. There is none of the unbridled speculation of the authors of the apocryphal gospels.

The authors of the intracanonical Gospels provide no explanation for the "how" of Jesus' resurrection. Only Matthew slips in the idea that there was an earthquake and that an angel of the Lord descended and rolled back the stone from the tomb (28:2), but he certainly does not elaborate on how Jesus was resurrected from the dead.

In contrast to the intracanonical Gospels, Matthew, Mark, Luke, and John, the extracanonical gospels sometimes present rather absurd details. The best example is found in the *Gospel of Peter*, which certainly was not written by Peter. Here is the account:

> Now in the night in which the Lord's day dawned, when the soldiers were keeping guard, two by two in each watch, there was a loud voice in heaven, and they saw the heavens open and two men come down from there in a great brightness and draw near to the sepulchre. That stone which had been laid against the entrance to the sepulchre started of itself to roll and move sideward, and the sepulchre was opened and both young men entered.
>
> When those soldiers saw this, they awakened the centurion and the elders, for they also were there to mount guard. And while they were narrating what they had seen, they saw three men come out from the sepulchre, two of them supporting the other and a cross following them and the heads of the two reaching to heaven, but that of him who was being led reached beyond the heavens. And they heard a voice out of the heavens crying, "Have you preached to those who sleep?" And from the cross there was heard the answer, "Yes." (9.35–10.42)[22]

Few who hear this account will need to be shown that it is a late legendary accretion to the Gospel tradition. No stone moves by itself. No cross walks and talks. The elevated and unrealistic Christology has Jesus' head protruding into the heavens. This historically absurd narrative is important for the way it helps us perceive the careful constraint of the canonical Gospels. As with Paul, the evangelists do not attempt to explain the inexplicable. In the New Testament we thus are not told how the resurrection of Jesus occurred. It is sufficient to know *that* the Lord raised him from the dead.

7. Resurrection, Not Resuscitation

The New Testament authors make it clear that the concept of resurrection is not resuscitation. Jesus' resurrection is not like the resuscitation of Lazarus and Jarius's daughter (category 14). These two are resuscitated and will have to die again. They are not resurrected. The miracle of resuscitation must not be confused with the cosmic miracle of resurrection. It is imperative to observe a taxonomy of resurrection in which the various types of resurrection are categorized and distinguished (see chapter 1).

8. Raised from Death to Life, beyond the Power of Sin and Death

What then is resurrection faith? How is it different from mere resuscitation? Resurrection faith is the belief that one who had lived but died has been raised from the dead to life again, and that there is no further possibility of experiencing sin or death.

We are not told by the New Testament authors to what place Jesus was resurrected. We should not even seek to discern that he may have been taken to "Paradise," because of Luke's report that Jesus told the penitent thief, "Today you will be with me in Paradise" (Luke 23:43 RSV). These words may not be authentic to Jesus; most likely Luke added them, and they are not supported by other New Testament passages. Again, the New Testament authors have indicated that such questions are sufficiently answered by the recognition that Jesus is now with the Awesome One. And that raises the question of the area in which the Creator and Sustainer is to be found.

As we come to the assessment of New Testament faith, we may learn again from the Israeli artist Arikha. He said that it took him a long time to be able to work with colors: "Eight years past until I could paint from nature in color. . . . It came out simply, because I'd crossed the bridge, in black-and-white, with a paintbrush."

Crossing the bridge is essential but sometimes difficult. Because of resurrection faith, Jesus' followers passed from the stage of confusion to one of enlightenment. They moved from blind faith to a resurrected faith. In the words of the Fourth Evangelist, Peter and the Beloved Disciple did not have a resurrection faith when they saw the empty tomb, because they did not yet "know the scripture, that he must rise from the dead" (20:9 RSV). This knowledge was supplied after the Easter event.

From Mark, Matthew, and Luke we learn about Peter's denial and the scared women who visit the tomb on Easter morning. These accounts make sense only if Jesus' followers after Thursday night were confused and lost in despair. This confusion was wiped away by a proclamation from the tomb: "[Jesus] has been raised" (Mark 16:6 NRSV). According to Luke, Cleopas says that "we had hoped that he was the one . . . " (Luke 24:21 RSV). This lost hope was restored by Jesus as he spoke to them on the way to Emmaus and dramatically in his breaking of the bread. According to Paul, he ceased persecuting Jesus' followers because of their absurd resurrection faith, not because of tradition, or teaching, but "through a revelation of Jesus," who had been raised from the dead (Gal 1:12 RSV). As with Arikha, the bridge from one faith to another was possible by crossing "the bridge." Jesus' early followers had moved from the black-and-white of despair to the color of nature's glory on Easter morning.

The Resurrection and Christian Theology

We have finished a brief review of what resurrection faith means in the New Testament. It becomes obvious that some would want to conclude that the resurrection faith found in the New Testament is the cornerstone of Christian theology.

More than Bishop John Shelby Spong would object. In seeking to be honest to his own conscience and to serve those Christians who find it difficult to believe in Jesus' resurrection, Bishop Spong declared that in this modern world, we must jettison the idea of Jesus' resurrection.

We can admire the integrity and honesty of Bishop Spong. He is also no man's fool. He has carefully and thoughtfully read the primary sources; his *This Hebrew Lord* is challenging and rewarding reading. With him, Christians today should be able to say that they can also find "a Lord" who is the "a center" for our being. Indeed, Christians may continue by affirming with Bishop Spong: "Behind the supernatural framework of the first century, behind the language of myth, magic, and superstition, I discovered a life I wanted to know; a life that possessed a power I wanted to possess; a freedom, a wholeness for which I had yearned for years."[23] I wholly admire his contention that we who live in the modern world "must be free today to seek as openly as they were able to seek; we must be free to comprehend him within the thought forms of our day."[24]

What arrests me is Spong's insistence that the resurrection is part of the supernatural outdated framework of the first century. He even claims that the resurrection faith "assumed a three-tiered universe that died with Copernicus."[25]

Spong has left us with three major ideas to discuss. First, he contends that the New Testament witness was distorted by a three-tiered universe. Is that accurate? Second, he claims that modern science makes resurrection faith no longer believable. Is that what we have learned from the scientists? Third, has Spong accurately understood the New Testament resurrection faith? Let us take a glimpse at each of these three.

Distortion by a Three-Tiered Universe?

First, Bishop Spong's claim that the New Testament witness presupposes a three-tiered universe is shared by many today. The most influential New Testament scholar of the twentieth century, R. Bultmann, stressed that a three-storied universe and the belief in a resurrection connected to it is an outdated cosmic conception.[26] Bultmann contended that modern scientific theory makes such conceptions impossible today.[27] Nothing can precede resurrection faith and prove Jesus' resurrection objectively.[28]

For many erudite individuals, it is difficult, if not impossible, to believe in Jesus' resurrection or any form of resurrection. The reason they usually give is that resurrection belief is wrapped up in an outmoded view of the cosmos. They tell me that resurrection belief demands a triformed universe: heaven above, earth beneath, and hell under the earth. They cite the New Testament to bolster their claim, but their exegesis is based on the publications of New Testament experts who lived in the first half of the twentieth century. The critics assert that there is not a trifurcated universe, and that therefore any belief in a resurrection must be jettisoned by enlightened Christians.

My response to these critics is that resurrection faith did not originate within a Jewish cosmology that was divided into heavens, earth, and the world below the earth. The author of Gen 1 portrays a two-layered universe: "In the beginning God created the heavens and the earth" (1:1 RSV). There is no world beneath the earth.

In the Hebrew Scriptures, or Old Testament, "under the earth" usually means beneath the surface of the earth. The dead are not beneath the earth; they are under the surface of the earth: "rewards and punishments *under the earth*" (*Ant.* 18.14). Josephus is probably thinking about "under" the surface of the earth and envisioning a three-tiered universe.

Today, in and near Jerusalem, one can descend beneath the surface of the earth and see where the ancients buried their dead. The Jews did not take their dead to a cosmic region separated from the earth and beneath it. They took their dead relatives to a place on the earth but beneath its surface. This insight derives from archaeological excavations in ancient Palestine. As Elledge points out (ch. 2), inscriptions on these tombs celebrate the belief that there is life after death.

Many may ask, "Are not the dead now being punished in the afterlife perceived by early Jews as residing beneath the earth?" According to the Jewish apocalyptists, the dead being punished are not placed in a world beneath the earth. They are often placed in one of the heavens. According to *1 En.* 17–21, Enoch is lifted up (17:1, 4) into the heavens, and Uriel shows him the prison house (21:10). In this "terrible place" (21:10) are located the angels who have sinned; now in one of the heavens, they suffer terrible tortures, including "a great fire" (21:7).

Thus, those who developed the concept of a resurrection and a postmortem life did so within a concept of a universe that is not antagonistic to what we are in the process of learning. For the early Jews, there are only two regions: the earth and the heavens above it. It follows, therefore, that modern cosmology does not disprove a postmortem existence. Modern astronomy and subatomic physics do not disprove nor disparage a belief in a resurrection from the dead. Surely, if one can be faithful to the insights and discoveries of scientists and believe in creation ex nihilo, then one can also believe that the creating Creator can revive a person who had been alive only a few hours, or three days, earlier. We can now turn to the second concept shaping Spong's mind.

Resurrection Faith No Longer Believable?

Second, Spong claims that modern science renders resurrection faith no longer believable. He contends that today we must salute modern science for freeing us from a concept of the universe that fosters superstitions like resurrection belief. Has Spong misunderstood modern science?

Scientists have not and cannot prove that there are no miracles and that there are no supernatural acts in our lives.

Scientists need repeatable and quantifiable data; that is not possible with a miracle, which by definition is unique within our world of thought. Surely the resurrection of Jesus, as an unprecedented event in world history, is not open to study via historiography or advanced physics.

Science has not evolved from objective scientific methods. All methods are subjective and evolve out of some unprovable presuppositions. Mathematical and scientific breakthroughs often are the result of qualitative contemplation and not quantitative analysis. Albert Einstein strove to prove that his genius did not lie in mathematical precision but in intellectual and subjective reflection and imagination. Reality is not predictable, as Heizenberg suggested with his indeterminacy principle. Scientists are no longer asking us with them to see a closed universe well ordered and logical; the universe is not shaped by a limited number of laws. The scientists invite us to contemplate the awesomeness of an expanding universe that cannot be reduced to set laws and rules. At the beginning of the twenty-first century, scientists have pointed to (but obviously are incapable of displaying) a universe that is far more mysterious than we had imagined. There are black holes and puzzling oddities that defy human conception. Moreover, the universe is too vast for even quantification by the most advanced computers.

The scientists have not shown us a closed system explained by Euclidian geometry and Newtonian physics. For example, the Clowes Professor of Science at Harvard, R. P. Kirshner, must confess that no one knows what dark energy and dark matter is, although scientists agree: "We live in a mixed dark-matter and dark-energy universe."[29]

There is no closed universe with unalterable laws, as Newton proposed. We all live within a cosmos full of wonder and mystery. The astronomers have helped us imagine a universe shaped by mystery and wonder. The subparticle physicists tell us to comprehend that at the heart of reality are not "atoms" — indivisible particles — but the arena in which our conceptions of waves and subatomic particles coalesce. Scientists do not present us with logical principles, but with a world of astonishing wonder and unfathomable beauty. In such a mysterious universe the resurrection faith is not anathema; it is appropriate and indeed harmonious with recent scientific advances.

In *The God of Hope and the End of the World*,[30] the physicist and Anglican priest, J. Polkinghorne, who has shown considerable interest in the relation between science and theology,[31] points out that advanced scientific research indicates a universe that is destructive and doomed to collapse, as shown by exploding supernovae and crashing meteors. Recognition of galaxy cannibalism seemed to follow such observations as cosmic acceleration (the expanded universe), so that about 13.4 to 13.6 billion years after the Big Bang, type Ia supernovae, five billion light-years away, appear 20 percent fainter. Thus, the resurrection of a *fleshly body* is not consonant with advanced metaphysics. However, Paul's concept of a "spiritual" body of those who are raised from the dead is harmonious with modern science.

One final word must suffice regarding modern scientific theory and the theology of the resurrection. T. F. Torrance has correctly pointed out that Einstein's insight into the dynamic fluidity of the space-time continuum (a needed corrective to Newton and Kant) has opened up a new concept of science for human exploration of the universe.[32] Hence, the postmodern scientific culture is not antithetical to Christian faith; in many ways it is consistent with the Jewish and Christian concept of creation and perspective of life after death.[33] For example, if matter can become energy, as in $E = mc2$, then there is a dynamic relation between matter and energy perhaps suggesting that energy can become matter.[34] If so, then we might have a window through which to comprehend the Christian concept of the incarnation and the belief in postmortem resurrection.

Has Spong Understood the Resurrection Accounts?

Third, has Spong understood the New Testament resurrection narratives? He claims that "Easter is many things to me, but at the very least it is the moment when it finally dawned upon the disciples who Jesus was and what the secret of his power was and is; and when they saw, they experienced the transforming birth of that life-giving power in themselves."[35]

While the sentiment and commitment is beautiful, I must point out that this is not primarily what the New Testament authors reported. They do not present us with something dawning upon the disciples. Jesus' followers do nothing to initiate the experience of the resurrection appearances. As previously indicated, they habitually resist them.

It is also misrepresenting the accounts to talk about what "they saw" — they did not see Jesus as if it was something they did. Jesus appeared to them. The resurrection is what the Creator did for Jesus and what Jesus shared with his followers. The resurrection narratives are not categorized by a statement such as "when they knew the affirmation that was in him."[36] Jesus' resurrection is not to be reduced to something in the disciples or something they did.

New Testament resurrection faith is not the "explanatory packaging" that is no longer "relevant to our day."[37] The resurrection accounts reveal the inexplicable act of the Creator upon the life of one who had been alive and now can appear again to his disciples. That demands faith. But it is not a faith that demands "the unearthly vocabulary of the first century."[38] It is a faith that resounds with the mystery disclosed by the latest scientific explorations.

Again, we need to perceive that those who reported their resurrection faith did not appeal to the study of Scripture or to prophecy. Their claim was grounded in *experience*. They did not couch the proclamation of the resurrection in the hope that Jesus was alive again. They reported the failure of a great mission and dream: "We had wished that he was the One."

Paul's faith was resurrection faith. It was grounded in his experience. He distinguished his experience of the resurrected Lord from dreams and visions (as recognized above). All the others about whom we have reported use the same cognitive means of conveying the belief that they had seen the resurrected Lord: Jesus had come to them — and the narratives indicate that the resurrected one intrudes into their lives almost as one uninvited. Thus, the earliest followers of Jesus claimed to have experienced Jesus as the risen Lord. The story of New Testament resurrection faith is one of surprising confrontation by the One who has been raised by the Creator from the dead.

Finally, Spong argues that we must understand Jesus and the faith of his followers "in a Hebrew context."[39] He is absolutely correct; but precisely here Spong has misunderstood the context of the resurrection texts. Not only Spong but also others, including New Testament experts, conclude that the belief in Jesus' resurrection is "a form of expression" so "conditioned by its environment" that "we shall not be able to regard as binding on us."[40] This may make sense for those who now are announcing it, but they should not seek to force their contentions on others.

I disagree with Spong's assessment of the context in which the resurrection faith took form. It was not within a context influenced by Adonis, Isis, or the emperor Augustus — all of whom had followers who believed that they had been resurrected from the dead. Fine, but that is not the context of Jesus' followers. They lived in a different world. They lived within the world of Second Temple Judaism; and it was in this context that the resurrection texts and the Christian belief in Jesus' resurrection were conceived and developed. Jesus and his earliest followers were not Romans; they were not even Christians. They were Jews. Thus, their thoughts and presuppositions should be weighed and assessed within the world of Second Temple Judaism.

In fact, we have much to learn from Jews living today. For example, Pinchas Lapide has been led to believe that Jesus

was raised from the dead by the Creator because of the Jewish context of this idea. Lapide develops his perspective in *The
Resurrection of Jesus: A Jewish Perspective.* As we have endeavored to clarify at the outset of this chapter, Lapide tried to
show that the Jewish context of New Testament resurrection
belief makes sense. First, Lapide rightly points out that

> the New Testament designates this resurrection of the Nazarene
> explicitly as a deed of God as both Paul and Peter declare unan-
> imously, "whom he [God] raised from the dead" (1 Thess. 1:10)
> and "but God raised him up" (Acts 2:24). Jewish Christianity
> was, in good Jewish fashion, convinced that its Messiah did *not*
> rise by his own power but was revived by the Lord of all life.[41]

Earlier we have seen that the New Testament authors do stress
that the Creator was the one who raised Jesus from the dead.
This indeed is a belief developed by Jews living in ancient
Palestine when the Temple was still standing.

Lapide adds: "According to my opinion, the resurrection
belongs to the category of the truly real and effective oc-
currences, for without a fact of history there is no act of
true faith." His following words deserve reporting fully. The
resurrection of Jesus by the Creator is a

> fact which indeed is withheld from objective science, photogra-
> phy, and a conceptual proof, but not from the believing scrutiny
> of history which more frequently leads to deeper insights.
>   In other words: Without the Sinai experience — no Judaism;
> without the Easter experience — no Christianity. Both were Jew-
> ish faith experiences whose radiating power, in a different way,
> was meant for the world of nations.[42]

Listening to the words of Lapide, thinking about the appearance of resurrection faith within Second Temple Judaism,
and then imagining the origins of the New Testament resurrection narratives — all this brings us in touch with Jewish
history. We enter into the world of pre-70 Judaism, and it
is certainly obvious that the belief in Jesus' resurrection
appeared almost immediately after his crucifixion.[43]

New Testament resurrection faith was not something that evolved after centuries or even decades. It appeared in the thirties, within a decade of Jesus' death.

While faith must not wait for the judgment of a historian, we must disagree with Barth that we should remove the resurrection faith from historical investigation.[44] To do so would mean that we ultimately ignore and undermine the historicity of Jesus' resurrection by the Lord Creator. The claim that Jesus was raised by God, and that this event occurred in history, is part of the scandalous nature of Christian faith. If New Testament resurrection faith is not grounded in secular history, then it is pious imagination. And that runs against what we have observed being reported in the New Testament documents.

Trust must not follow knowledge. Faith-knowledge, or *fides*, must be a prelude to *fiducia*, or trust. *Fiducia*, trust, is thus grounded in some form of *fides*, knowledge.[45] The earliest followers of Jesus could trust in their belief that the Lord had raised Jesus from the dead because of their experienced knowledge, *fides*, that he had appeared to them unexpectedly and to an extent unwanted. The disciples were totally unprepared for an appearance of Jesus, but their knowledge, *fides*, of him and their experience with him earlier, for perhaps three years, enabled them to trust their own experiences of his resurrection, exercising *fiducia*. There thus is a cognitive basis for the disciples' resurrection faith. As Pheme Perkins states, "Only those who are convinced that a special revelation of God occurred in the life and teaching of Jesus of Nazareth can be persuaded that God raised Jesus of Nazareth from the dead."[46]

That means that the historical Jesus is not a presupposition of New Testament theology (*pace* Bultmann). The historical Jesus is alive in resurrection faith.

Not only Spong, as we have stated, but also some influential New Testament scholars advise us to dismiss the concept of resurrection. They want us to believe that resurrection faith is an outmoded and old-fashioned concept that does not fit the modern world's metaphysics. They sometimes suggest that the origins of resurrection faith may be discovered in the visions of Peter, who was remorseful after denying Jesus.

We may wonder and ponder what happened to the body of Jesus — whether it decayed two thousand years ago in ancient Palestine or was somehow transformed. If so, we should acknowledge that such pursuits are not central to New Testament resurrection faith. In the first and second centuries, documents like the *Gospel of Thomas* imply a spiritual resurrection of Jesus; other documents, including the Gospel of John, affirm a bodily resurrection of Jesus.[47] Such imaginations are on the edges. What is central is Jesus' resurrection by the Creator's action.

Furthermore, we must recognize that Jesus' resurrection was proclaimed by Jews within the thought world of Second Temple Judaism. Hence, some form of bodily resurrection is inherent in the proclamation that the Creator raised Jesus from the dead. The impression that they were thinking of a resurrection without a body flies in the face of those who have given us the intracanonical Gospels and Epistles. As Wright states:

> The common idea that, when the early Christians said "Jesus was raised from the dead," they meant something like "He is alive in a spiritual, non-bodily sense, and we give him our allegiance as our lord" is historically impossible.[48]

So much is not explained about resurrection faith. We need to distinguish between what is on the edge and what is central.

What is essential? Resurrection faith discloses that Jesus is not only a man of the past. As the resurrected Lord; he is the one who has gone on into the future, who is preparing a way for us. That is possible because the Creator Lord called him back from the dead.

Can the Creator do that? Of course, but only one who has experienced the resurrected Lord may be able to comprehend that this is a legitimate commitment that makes sense not only within the first century but also within any century. I think that my interlocutor with whom I discussed *El* on the shores of the Mediterranean and in Israel would agree with me on that point, even if my concluding comments will probably not satisfy his inquisitive mind.

Cui Bono?

Who benefits? What difference then does it make whether Jesus was raised by the Creator or not? Is it not odd that today some Christians reject the belief that the Lord raised Jesus from the dead and some Jews affirm it? Does not this observation force us to confront the issue of what difference does it really make if the Creator raised Jesus from the dead?

Obviously, one can claim to continue to be a Christian and deny the resurrection of Jesus. Does it make any difference? That a Christian bishop denies it and a Jew affirms it forces upon us to reflect what difference belief in Jesus' resurrection makes. Allow me, now, in some concluding personal reflections, to offer some initial reflections on this piercing question. I do not think we should simply quote Paul or some other religious genius of the past. We need to struggle afresh with the focused question.

First, New Testament resurrection faith tends to affirm that Jesus was the bearer of wisdom. The resurrection seems to be a "Yes" to Jesus' way of living and thinking. It does significantly prove Jesus' importance and the truthfulness of his message.

A British New Testament theologian helps us at this point. James D. G. Dunn of Durham University rightly states that belief in Jesus' being raised by the Lord implies that Jesus' earthly life was faithful to the one whom he called Father, which implies that Jesus was full of the Creator's grace.[49]

Second, to affirm that the Lord raised Jesus from the dead does tend to verify Jesus' uniqueness. The Essenes did not think that the Righteous Teacher had been raised by the Creator. The followers of Hillel did not affirm that he had been raised from the dead by the Lord. But, all of Jesus' earliest followers (as far as we know) and all of those whose writings are in the New Testament did claim that the Lord raised Jesus from the dead. This recognition indicates the uniqueness of Jesus. He is the first indication of the truth in Jewish resurrection beliefs.

Third, New Testament resurrection faith helps to demonstrate the revelatory genius of Jewish theology during the time of Jesus. The "Christian" belief that the Lord raised Jesus from the dead derives from the Jewish belief in a Lord who has been Creator and continues to create anew. The belief in the resurrection of the dead was developed within pre-70 Palestinian Judaism. The acknowledgment of a Jewish male, Jesus, who was raised places Jesus squarely within Judaism. Thus, Judaism is at the heart of Christian theology, since all these three aspects are Jewish: the concept of the Lord, resurrection, and the Jewish man Jesus.

Fourth, affirming the resurrection of Jesus is a wonderful basis for affirming that our own death is not the final curtain of our own lives. Does that mean we will again see our loved ones who have departed? I think the New Testament witness is a resounding "yes," and that is especially clear in 1 Thess 4.

Fifth, belief in Jesus' resurrection helps us understand the most confusing concept in our lives: time. What is time? Why do we get lost in schedules and times? Surely, Jesus' resurrection helps us stand on the edges of eternity and perhaps helps affirm our own value in the economy of salvation. Those words were certainly on the lips of the earliest followers of Jesus who chanted in the *Odes of Solomon:*

> Death has been destroyed before my face,
> And Sheol has been vanquished by my word.
>
> And eternal life has arisen in the Lord's land,
> And it has become known to his faithful ones,
> And been given without limit to all that trust in him.
>
> (15:9–10)

Sixth, the belief that the Lord raised Jesus from the dead indicates the dawning of a new world perspective and the dismissal of the fear of death having the last disturbing laugh. In the process, the importance of life is affirmed.

As Christian theologians, we need to explore what is meant by "resurrection" — to where? Where is the resurrected Jesus? We have only the New Testament record that he went up into the sky or into heaven. Are these concepts in need of rethinking and reformulating? Should we explore the possibility of a "parallel universe," as suggested at the outset? And what would that mean? Should we contemplate the existence of another dimension, especially in light of Einstein's demonstration that "time" is a dimension? And then, what do we mean by "dimension"?

When Christians sing "He lives within my heart" or claim that the Creator is within their hearts, they do not intend to denote that the Creator is only within their hearts. The Awesome One is within and without each of us, but what does it mean to say that the Creator is outside us? Where then is this Infinite One? Is there a special place or dimension in which this One is allowed to be fully present? The ancient Jewish visionaries and apocalyptic seers place the Creator in a remote heaven; surely we cannot merely turn to them for all our answers. What is meant by "heaven"? Surely our initial questioning has not been left behind.

Seventh, the belief that the Lord raised Jesus from the dead implies that the Creator does raise the dead to a new life. That is either a wonderful dream or a fantastic reality. New Testament theology indicates the latter. Such "reality" evolves out of the perception that the New Testament authors show that the resurrection belief is not grounded in hope. It is rooted in despair and lost hope. In a closed room, hiding from the authorities who might whisk them off to a horrible death, the disciples huddled fearfully, and in their moment of fear Jesus is reported to have appeared to them. Thus, New Testament resurrection faith evolved out of claims to a specific experience.

Eighth, to claim that the Creator raised only Jesus from the dead implies something about their relationship. Some New Testament authors suggest that Jesus was the only human who at all times and in all places willed to do only the will of the Father, who sent him into the world (cf. John 5:30; 7:16–18). Was the uniting of one divine will the reason the Lord raised Jesus?

The same author, the Fourth Evangelist, or the final editor of his masterpiece, under the influence of resurrection faith confessed that Jesus should be portrayed as the Word that was with the Creator in the beginning (John 1:1). Rather than trying to remove the tension between these two thoughts, preserved in John 5 and 1, it is best to perceive that such tension, and internal contradiction, is essential to the dynamics and dialectics of resurrection faith.[50]

Ultimately, of course, belief in Jesus' resurrection entails asking about his nature. Was there something pure and divine about Jesus' nature that led the Creator to raise him from the dead? That conclusion seems to be behind the confession that Jesus was born of a virgin, developed in the early chapters of Matthew and Luke, and the claim that Jesus is the One from above (John 1:1; Phil 2:5–11). If we proceed too far along the road of exploring a divine nature in Jesus, we risk distorting Christian theology. First, we risk moving New Testament thought out of its matrix within Judaism and into third-century Greek philosophy, as became evident when Constantine made Christianity the religion of the empire. Second, we risk falling into the perennial and most dangerous Christian heresy: the Docetic belief that Jesus was not fully human, a false teaching already combated within the New Testament (cf. 1 John).

Ninth, the belief that Jesus was raised from the dead by the Lord displays a living continuity between us alive today and those who lived in the first century. Jesus is not dead; he is alive. This point was driven home to me many years ago in Jerusalem. A well-meaning American Jew told a large assembly of Christians that if "Jesus were alive today he would be thrilled." A resounding still and condemning silence ebbed from the evangelical Christians who subsequently and energetically asserted that they experience Jesus alive and present in their midst.

Because of resurrection faith, Christians can appeal to a living Lord and not merely cling hopelessly to a crucified corpse. For Christians, the Easter hymns are appropriate each and every Sunday. Each day is an Easter for the Christian. Christians are not antiquarians; they are tied to One who has gone on before them, to use the words of the author of Hebrews. And in the words of some who have written on Jesus, he is the Modern Man, the Man of the Future.[51] This affirmation is possible only because of Jesus' resurrection by the continuing Creator.

This affirmation is the heart of the New Testament kerygma (proclamation). It is in continuity with another perspective. The Jews who wrote the many documents cited in this essay are also alive; they come to life when we hear their words.[52]

Conclusion

Not too long ago, the citizens of the United States watched as the impeachment trial of Clinton turned to airing the sworn testimonies recorded on video tape. The solemn session opened with the senate chaplain reporting that the senate clerk, Scott Bates, had been killed in a traffic accident. In the prayer the chaplain declared that "he now lives with you, God." He added that this affirmation is confirmed in the assurance of the resurrection and eternal life. This prayer was bipartisan, interconfessional, and interreligious: the belief in the resurrection of the dead can be declared publicly on television in the senate, and it unites Democrats and Republicans, Protestants and Roman Catholics, and even Christians and Jews. It is impressive to me how Jewish theology and New Testament theology can appear as a uniting force within such a divided body of legislators.

My rapid survey has attempted to show that resurrection faith developed significantly first within Palestinian Judaism and sharply divided the Pharisees and many other groups or sects from the Sadducees, who argued "that there is no resurrection" (Matt 22:23–33 RSV). Jesus and his earliest followers were nurtured by resurrection belief. In fact, the belief in the resurrection of the dead to a better and eternal life is what allowed the followers of Jesus to proclaim, using the words ascribed to the Eleven by Luke, "The Lord has been raised [by God] and has appeared to Simon!" (Luke 24:34).[53]

The texts for Christian resurrection faith are the New Testament documents themselves. The proper method for studying these texts is in their original contexts. The authors of the New Testament documents unite together to affirm that the Lord raised Jesus from the dead. Their text was not the Hebrew Scriptures, or Old Testament. Their text was not the Jewish writings contemporaneous with them. Their text was their unexpected confrontation with a living Jesus — a resurrected Lord. As the ten disciples told Thomas, who is about to have a marvelous experience: "We have seen the Lord." (John 20:25 RSV).

Notes

1. As N. T. Wright points out, the ancients imagined resurrection to be a "two-step story. Resurrection itself would be preceded (and was preceded even in the case of Jesus) by an interim period of death-as-a-state." See Wright, *The Resurrection of the Son of God* (Christian Origins and the Question of God 3; Minneapolis: Fortress, 2003), 31.

2. These words are preserved only in the Greek and in two Ethiopic manuscripts (Princeton Ethiopic 3 of the eighteenth or nineteenth century, and EMML 2080 of the fourteenth century). For the Greek edition of *1 Enoch*, see M. Black, ed., *Apocalypsis Henochi Graece* (PVTG 3; Leiden: Brill, 1970), 35.

3. See A. Dupont-Sommer, *Les écrits Esséniens découverts près de la mer Morte* (8th ed.; Paris: Payot, 1980), 221n1. Also see G. Jeremias, *Der Lehrer der Gerechtigkeit* (SUNT 2; Göttingen: Vandenhoeck & Ruprecht, 1963), 192–201.

4. This comment seems odd. Lines 29 and following of this column in 1QH[a] are in a section of the *Thanksgiving Hymns* that is better preserved than most. I have benefited from the photographs in the Princeton Theological Seminary Dead Sea Scrolls laboratory.

5. E. Puech, *La croyance des esséniens en la vie future: Immortalité, résurrection, vie éternelle? Histoire d'une croyance dans le Judaïsme ancien* (2 vols.; ÉBib, NS, 21; Paris: Gabalda, 1993), 2:356–63.

6. As D. Dimant states, "Nowhere in the scrolls is there a clear formulation of these beliefs (i.e., resurrection of the dead), and some passages in 1QH[a] (6 [now 14]:29–34; 11 [now 19]:12) interpreted to this effect may be otherwise explained" (542). Dimant, "Qumran Sectarian Literature," in *Jewish Writings of the Second Temple Period* (ed. M. E. Stone; CRINT 2.2; Assen: Van Gorcum, 1984), 483–550.

7. Puech, *La croyance*, 2:356.

8. Jeremias also attributes this hymn to the Righteous Teacher. Jeremias, *Der Lehrer der Gerechtigkeit*, 226–44. Most commentators have rightly concluded that 1QH[a] 14 (= olim 6).29–30 does not contain a belief in resurrection from the dead (namely, Rowley, Licht, Vogt, Laurin, Carmignac, Mayer-Reuss, Sutcliffe, Maier, G. Jeremias, Buitkamp, Braun, Nickelsburg, Le Moyne, Bailey, Rosso Ubigli, and Dimant).

9. Unless otherwise indicated, all translations are mine.

10. B. P. Kittel, *The Hymns of Qumran: Translation and Commentary* (SBLDS 50; Chico, CA: Scholars Press, 1975), 80.

11. Hence, in the PTSDSS Project we translate *'elîm* as "divine beings," leaving it open if Qumranites or angels are intended by an author.

12. See J. A. Fitzmyer's insight published many years ago and now readily available again: "A Feature of Qumran Angelology and the Angels of 1 Cor 11:10," in *Paul and the Dead Sea Scrolls* (ed. J. Murphy-O'Connor and J. H. Charlesworth; Christian Origins Library; New York: Crossroad, 1990), 31–47.

13. For further reflection, see J. H. Charlesworth, "The Portrayal of the Righteous as an Angel," in *Ideal Figures in Ancient Judaism* (ed. J. Collins and G. W. E. Nickelsburg; SBL Septuagint and Cognate Studies 12; Chico, CA: Scholars Press, 1980), 135–51.

14. See the judicious insights of Prendergast in *ABD* 5:682–83.

15. I wish to thank the Israel Antiquities Authority for allowing me to study 4Q521 and for clear photographs of all fragments.

16. Since the verbs are plural, I have added "all." This reconstruction is supported by the *kôl* in line 4.

17. The translation is taken from J. Heinemann, *Prayer in the Talmud* (Studia Judaica 9; Berlin: de Gruyter, 1977), 26.

18. For further thoughts on this point, see C. F. Evans, *Resurrection and the New Testament* (Studies in New Testament Theology, 2d Series, 12; London: SCM, 1970).

19. The Greek verb is present tense: "is." Codex D and most Old Latin MSS read "was."

20. For further reflections, see J. H. Charlesworth, *The Beloved Disciple* (Valley Forge, PA: Trinity Press International, 1995).

21. J. D. Crossan, *Jesus: a Revolutionary Biography* (San Francisco: HarperSanFrancisco, 1994), 94. Also, see this volume's ch. 7, by W. W. Willis.

22. For the full translation, see J. K. Elliott, *The Apocryphal New Testament* (Oxford: Clarendon, 1993), 156–57.

23. J. S. Spong, *This Hebrew Lord* (San Francisco: HarperSanFrancisco, 1993), 13–14.

24. Ibid., 4.

25. Ibid., 166.

26. R. Bultmann thought that Jesus' sayings that predicted his resurrection were added by the "Hellenistic Church." Bultmann, *Theology of the New Testament* (trans. K. Grobel; 2 vols.; New York: Charles Scribner's Sons, 1951), 1:30.

27. R. Bultmann, *Kerygma and Myth: A Theological Debate* (trans. R. H. Fuller; ed. H. W. Bartsch; 2d ed.; vol. 1; New York: Harper & Row, 1961), 2–5. Also, see the discussion by W. W. Willis (ch. 7).

28. Bultmann wrote, "Nothing preceding the faith which acknowledges the risen Christ can give insight into the reality of *Christ's resurrection*. The resurrection cannot — in spite of 1 Cor. 15:3–8 — be demonstrated or made plausible as an objectively ascertainable fact on the basis of which one could believe." *Theology of the New Testament*, 1:305.

29. R. P. Kirshner, *The Extravagant Universe* (Princeton: Princeton University Press, 2002), 270, then 263.

30. J. Polkinghorne, *The God of Hope and the End of the World* (New Haven, CT: Yale University Press, 2003). Also, see C. D. Elledge's comments in ch. 2, above.

31. See esp. J. Polkinghorne, *Reason and Reality: The Relationship between Science and Theology* (Philadelphia: Trinity Press International, 1991).

32. T. F. Torrance, *Space, Time and Incarnation* (London: Oxford University Press, 1969).

33. Although M. Jammer does not discuss the concept of a resurrection, his book on *Einstein and Religion: Physics and Theology* (Princeton: Princeton University Press, 1999) is full of insights that have helped me develop the perspective imagined above.

34. See esp. F. D. Schubert, "Thomas F. Torrance: The Case for a Theological Science," *Encounter* 45 (1984), 123–37, and esp. 133: "A God of pure energy, then, could well become 'matter' in an Incarnation." Reflections on such a new paradigm for comprehending a unified field theory can lead to insights regarding the resurrection of one now dead who had been alive.

35. Spong, *This Hebrew Lord*, 179.

36. Ibid., 180.

37. Ibid.

38. Ibid.

39. Ibid., 13.

40. H. Braun, *Jesus of Nazareth: The Man and His Time* (trans. E. R. Kalin; Philadelphia: Fortress, 1971), 122–23.

41. Pinchas Lapide, *The Resurrection of Jesus: A Jewish Perspective* (trans. W. C. Linss; Minneapolis: Augsburg, 1983), 91.

42. Ibid., 92.

43. See the excellent comments by Gerald O'Collins, SJ, in *The Resurrection of Jesus Christ: Some Contemporary Issues* (Milwaukee, WI: Marquette University Press, 1993), 5.

44. At this point I am in full agreement with G. Lüdemann in his work entitled *The Resurrection of Jesus* (trans. J. Bowden; London: SCM, 1994), 4. A more popular version, by idem with A. Özen, appears under the title *What Really Happened to Jesus* (London: SCM, 1995).

45. I am indebted to the reflections of P. Carnley in his *The Structure of Resurrection Faith* (Oxford: Clarendon, 1987), 223ff.

46. P. Perkins, "The Resurrection of Jesus of Nazareth," in *Studying the Historical Jesus* (ed. B. Chilton and C. A. Evans; New Testament Tools and Studies 19; Leiden: Brill, 1994), 423–42; quotation from 442.

47. G. J. Riley concludes that the Gospel of John was written to combat the ideas contained in the *Gospel of Thomas;* see his *Resurrection Reconsidered: Thomas and John in Controversy* (Minneapolis: Fortress, 1995). I doubt that *Thomas* antedates the Gospel of John.

48. Wright, *The Resurrection of the Son of God*, 718.

49. Dunn is referring to the exaltation language of Phil 2:6–8, and thus it pertains to Paul's resurrection faith. See J. D. G. Dunn, *Christology in the Making* (Philadelphia: Westminster, 1980), 121.

50. See J. E. Loder, *The Transforming Moment: Understanding Convictional Experiences* (Colorado Springs: Helmers & Howard, 1989); and P. N. Anderson, *The Christology of the Fourth Gospel* (Valley Forge, PA: Trinity Press International, 1996), 148.

51. See J. Middleton Murray, "The Man of the Future," in *Jesus* (ed. H. Anderson; Englewood Cliffs, NJ: Prentice-Hall, 1967), 148–51. For Middleton Murray, however, it was not the resurrection that made

Jesus the Man of the Future; it was his "unparalleled imagination" to die in Jerusalem at Passover as the sacrificial lamb.

52. For a development of this thought, which is the foundation of hermeneutics (in my opinion), see J. H. Charlesworth, "Polanyi, Merleau-Ponty, Arendt, and the Foundation of Biblical Hermeneutics," in *Interpretation of the Bible* (ed. J. Krasovec; Ljubljana: Slovenska akademija znanosti in umetnosti; Sheffield: Sheffield Academic Press, 1998), 1531–56.

53. The bracketed addition is mine; it brings out the actor of the passive verb, which is a divine passive.

Chapter 7

A Theology of Resurrection: Its Meaning for Jesus, Us, and God

W. Waite Willis Jr.

The Importance and Problem of the Resurrection

The resurrection of Jesus has been a problem for the Christian faith in modern times. Actually, it has not been a problem for the faith for most Christians. At least in my experience in churches and in the classroom, Christians have no problem with the resurrection. In fact, according to a 1994 Harris poll, 87 percent of the American population believes in the resurrection. It is salutary for theologians to realize that, while they struggle with the actuality and meaning of resurrection, most American Christians, at least, believe with certainty that God could and did raise Jesus from the dead; and consequently, they trust that God will do the same for them. When congregations sing "Christ the Lord is Risen Today" or "Lord, I Lift Your Name on High" on Easter Sunday, they really mean it. A careful observer might conclude that, while scholars today are debating the meaning of a post-modern existence, the people in the pews have not yet entered what scholars refer to as the modern era, a time when all traditional beliefs must be criticized and possibly rejected. Lay Christians easily believe what academic types were taught that modern people could not believe. The resurrection of Jesus, then, is not a problem for the Christian faith but rather an issue for biblical exegetes, theologians, philosophers, and a few other disquieted spirits.

Theologians have been compelled to struggle with resurrection as they have confronted the philosophical critiques of the Enlightenment, which rejected special revelation or special acts of God that interrupt the normal working of the world. The Enlightenment philosopher David Hume, for instance, mercilessly attacked the epistemological foundation of religious belief. While Hume did not want to deny categorically the possibility that there might be an occurrence that does not conform to the usual course of nature, he did assert that such an occurrence is so unlikely that "no human testimony can have such force as to prove a miracle and make it a just foundation for any such system of religion."[1] In a transparent allusion to Christianity, Hume speaks of an imaginary resurrection of Queen Elizabeth:

> Suppose that all the historians who treat of England should agree that on the first of January 1600, Queen Elizabeth died; that both before and after her death she was seen by her physicians and the whole court...; and that, after being interred for a month, she appeared again, resumed the throne and governed England for three years — I must confess that I should be surprised at the concurrence of so many odd circumstances but should not have the least inclination to believe so miraculous an event.... I should only assert it to have been pretended, and that it neither was, nor possibly could be, real.[2]

It is in response to attitudes of this type, which have permeated the intellectual milieu of the modern era, that theologians have debated whether or not the resurrection can be accepted and if it can be, in what way one should believe it and what it would mean.

Many Christian scholars have accepted the Enlightenment's critique and disposed of the resurrection or at least crucial elements of resurrection belief. Harold DeWolf of the Boston University School of Theology told this story of the early days of the gatherings of the American Theological Society, in which only a few such as DeWolf, Reinhold Niebuhr, H. Richard Niebuhr, Paul Schilling, and Paul Tillich participated.[3] In one meeting, after Tillich had elucidated the meaning of his notion of New Being in Christ, Reinhold Niebuhr asked, "But Paulus, when one dies, is there any conscious existence for the person?" Tillich answered, "No, No." Niebuhr responded to the group, "We now know what many of us have long suspected, that in Paul Tillich we have a great Christian heretic." A few years ago, I was speaking to a much-loved and respected New Testament scholar and preacher of international repute. I mentioned the centrality of the resurrection. My conversation partner said, "No, we can no longer put our faith in the resurrection of Jesus." When I pushed him on this issue, he called over to one of the other scholars, one who had actually been my professor in graduate school and from whom I had learned about the centrality of the resurrection in the New Testament. The question was, "Do you have to believe in the resurrection of Jesus to be a Christian?" The answer was "no."

These declarations from Christian scholars that narrow the meaning of or dispense with the resurrection stand over against the long history of the Christian faith. If a theology is going to align itself with both the biblical witness and the tradition of the church's proclamation, it cannot easily eliminate or reduce the significance of the resurrection of Jesus. From the apostolic age to the medieval Church to the Reformation to important contemporary theological voices, the resurrection has stood at the center as a sine qua non of the Christian faith. Around 400 CE, Augustine preached that "the resurrection of the Lord Jesus Christ is the distinctive mark of the Christian faith"[4] and that "faith in His resurrection saves and justifies us."[5] Twelve centuries later, Martin Luther declared:

> When one wants to preach the Gospel, one must treat only of
> the resurrection of Christ. For this is the chief article of our
> faith.... For if there were no resurrection, we would have no
> consolation or hope, and everything else Christ did or suffered
> would be futile.[6]

Four centuries beyond Luther, Karl Barth claimed, "To
know Him (Christ) is identical with knowing the power of
His resurrection (Phil 3). The confession that He is the Lord
is based on the faith that God has raised Him from the dead
(Rom. 10:9)."[7] And a decade later Jürgen Moltmann put it suc-
cinctly: "Christianity stands or falls with the reality of the
raising of Jesus from the dead by God.... A Christian faith
that is not resurrection faith can therefore be called neither
Christian nor faith."[8]

This tradition of understanding resurrection as central to
the Christian faith is grounded upon the biblical witness, for
the resurrection of Jesus is a presupposition of the writers of
the New Testament. Unlike other features of the New Testament — for instance, the story of the virginal conception of
Jesus, found in only two books (Matthew and Luke) and only
in the first two chapters of each — the proclamation of almost
every author in the New Testament is permeated by the resurrection faith. The primary example of the centrality of belief
in the resurrection in the witness of the New Testament is
Paul's statement in 1 Cor 15:14–19:

> If Christ has not been raised, then our preaching is in vain and
> your faith is in vain. We are even found to be misrepresenting
> God, because we testified of God that he raised Christ.... If
> Christ has not been raised, your faith is futile and you are still
> in your sins. Then those also who have fallen asleep in Christ
> have perished. If for this life only we have hoped in Christ, we
> are of all men most to be pitied. (RSV)

This passage from Paul claims that the resurrection is foundational for understanding the work of Jesus, who God is,
and for what we human beings can hope. However we may
struggle with it, however it may challenge modern presuppositions, however it may disturb our comfortable faith —

resurrection still stands as an essential element of the biblical and historical witness of the Christian community. Without the resurrection, Jesus is not the living Lord but a dead person held in memory.[9] Without the resurrection, God is not the God of the living, not the one who has the power to conquer death. Without the resurrection, humankind has no ultimate hope, for the "last enemy," death, wins.

Resurrection, Empty Tomb, and Appearances

To make the claim that the resurrection of Jesus is essential to the Christian faith does not yet clarify what one should believe in when holding this doctrine. For many Christians the first image that comes to mind is the drama of the empty tomb, as it is portrayed in the Gospels. Easter sermons regularly stress the reality of Jesus' resurrection by appealing to the empty tomb and the appearance stories that follow. In fact, scholars also have written, and continue to write, volumes, subjecting the resurrection accounts in the Gospels to the razor of historical criticism. Even after these critiques, and while realizing that the Gospel stories contain historical problems, many New Testament scholars and theologians claim that there is at least a historical core in the empty-tomb traditions. At an academic conference called the "Resurrection Summit," held in New York over the Easter weekend in 1996, the Jesuit scholar Gerald O'Collins bristled at the idea that New Testament scholars had given up on the empty tomb. He listed thirty-eight New Testament scholars who at least "maintain a historical nucleus in the empty tomb tradition."[10]

Other scholars have gone far beyond the claim of the probability of a historical empty tomb to the use of the empty tomb as part of an apologetic strategy in support of the actuality of the resurrection itself, which in turn provides a foundation for the faith.[11] Traditional Roman Catholic fundamental theology, responding to the enlightenment critiques,

tried to prove the resurrection as a historical fact by show-
ing philosophically the possibility of such an event and then
demonstrating the historicity of the New Testament accounts
of Jesus' resurrection. This theology argued that the Old
Testament prophecies, as well as the prophecies of Jesus,
predicted the resurrection. Along with these predictions, it
said, the factuality of Jesus' miracles provided the basis upon
which to accept the miracle of the resurrection. Then historical arguments for the empty tomb and appearances of
the risen Lord, which, it was claimed, could not have been
preached in Jerusalem "unless the tomb had in fact been
empty,"[12] were given to prove the factuality of the resurrection. According to this theology, the resurrection was not
itself an article of faith but a demonstrable fact that provided
the apologetic basis for the faith.

Francis Schüssler Fiorenza has argued that this traditional
fundamental theology has been criticized and that its structure has collapsed.[13] Roman Catholic theology has moved in
other directions when explicating the resurrection. However,
the same cannot be said for Protestant evangelical theology,
which continues to do apologetics by arguing for the factuality of the empty tomb as evidence for the resurrection.
For instance, William Craig, in arguing against the views of
John Dominic Crossan, supports the empty-tomb tradition
by giving evidence for the historical accuracy of Joseph of
Arimathea's burial of Jesus. He writes:

> For if the burial story is basically accurate, the site of Jesus'
> tomb would have been known to Jew and Christian alike. But in
> that case, it would have been impossible for resurrection faith to
> survive in the face of a tomb containing the corpse of Jesus. The
> disciples could not have adhered to the resurrection; scarcely
> any one else would have believed them, even if they had; and
> their Jewish opponents could have exposed the whole affair by
> pointing to the occupied tomb.[14]

In recent decades one of the most respected theologians
in the world, Wolfhart Pannenberg, who while not a conservative evangelical (in the American sense of the word

"evangelical"), believes as well that evidence can be given to support the historical actuality of Jesus' resurrection. According to Pannenberg, faith is trust, not risk; therefore, one of the tasks of theology is to establish as certainly as possible the basis of faith in the resurrection.[15] While we cannot know precisely what happened to Jesus, and while ultimate verification of the resurrection will only occur eschatologically with the general resurrection, we can gain provisional but reliable evidence that supports the resurrection.[16]

To support the resurrection Pannenberg gives evidence for both the appearances of Jesus and the empty-tomb tradition. For instance, in 1 Cor 15:1–11, when Paul lists appearances of the resurrected Lord to Peter, the Twelve, James, and the five hundred, "most of whom are still alive" (RSV), Pannenberg asserts (as did Bultmann) that Paul is arguing for the factuality of the resurrection, because the persons on the list could have been interrogated.[17] For the historicity of the empty tomb, Pannenberg uses some common arguments, such as the claim that the Jerusalem Christians could not have proclaimed Jesus' resurrection without an empty tomb; for without it the claim that Jesus had been resurrected could have been refuted by inspecting the place of burial.[18] Furthermore, according to Pannenberg, the best evidence for the empty tomb is that early Jewish polemic against Christianity "does not offer any suggestion that Jesus' grave had remained untouched." Rather, "it shared the conviction with its Christian opponents that Jesus' grave was empty."[19]

This attempt by Christian scholars to support the belief in the resurrection of Jesus by giving historical arguments for the factuality of the empty tomb and appearance traditions is replete with problems and places Christian theology in a tenuous position. While we can understand and applaud the motives of these theologians to make belief in the resurrection, and therefore the faith, more acceptable, their method is limited and might well produce the opposite of the intended consequence.

In terms of the empty-tomb stories, the most obvious limitation of this method is the fact that an empty tomb does not prove a resurrection. It is a theological cliché, but nevertheless true, to assert that an empty tomb is not the same thing as a resurrection. It is possible to have an empty tomb without a resurrection. Perhaps, as the guards in the Gospel of Matthew were told to say or as the critic Hermann Samuel Reimarus concluded, the disciples stole the body. Perhaps, as H. E. G. Paulus and Friedrich Schleiermacher suggested, Jesus didn't really die. Perhaps, as Mary thought in the Gospel of John, a gardener moved the body. The point is that an empty tomb is not the same as resurrection and cannot ground belief in it.

Moreover, if one does ground a belief in the resurrection partially on the historicity of the empty tomb, then that belief would be reduced to the degree that the factuality of the empty-tomb stories was called into question. In this case, the attempted apologetic would end up producing a lack of faith. Indeed, many New Testament scholars and theologians have questioned even the historical nucleus of the empty-tomb tradition. After a review of the issues in the Gospels, Hans Küng asserts: It is "scarcely possible therefore to refute the assumption that the stories of the tomb *are legendary elaborations of the message of the resurrection.*"[20] New Testament scholar Norman Perrin wrote that scholars were increasingly "coming to the conclusion that the empty tomb tradition is an interpretation of the event . . . rather than a description of an aspect of the event itself."[21] John Dominic Crossan — with his suggestion that Joseph of Arimathea's burial is the creation of Mark and that Jesus' body, like those of other executed criminals, was probably placed in a shallow grave and, subsequently, eaten by dogs — is also among those who reject any historical element in the empty-tomb traditions.[22]

It is, however, the New Testament witness itself that ultimately keeps us from relying too heavily on the empty-tomb stories or equating them with resurrection. While it is the case that every writer of the New Testament proclaims the resurrection, it is also true that this proclamation is accomplished in various ways. Some passages focus upon appearances of the resurrected Jesus. Others stress resurrection as Jesus' exaltation to heaven. It is only the Gospels that use the empty-tomb stories. The earliest account of the resurrection is not found in the Gospels, however, but in the letters of Paul, who wrote his Epistles in the decade of the fifties, some eleven to sixteen years before the earliest Gospel, Mark. In 1 Cor 15, written around 54 CE, Paul gives an account of the resurrection. Paul, who did not know Jesus during Jesus' lifetime, was not converted until a few years after Jesus' death.[23] Paul claims that he is passing on what he himself had also received from those who were believers before him. New Testament scholars affirm that Paul (at least in verses 3–4) is transmitting an early creedal statement, perhaps the earliest Christian creed:

> For I delivered to you as of first importance what I also received, that Christ died for our sins in accordance with the scriptures, that he was buried, that he was raised on the third day in accordance with the scriptures.... (RSV)

Paul then goes on to a list of those to whom the resurrected Jesus had appeared:

> ...and that he appeared to Cephas, then to the twelve. Then he appeared to more than five hundred brethren at one time, most of whom are still alive, though some have fallen asleep. Then he appeared to James, then to all the apostles. Last of all, as to one untimely born, he appeared also to me. (1 Cor 15:5–7 RSV)

In this passage, *Paul stresses the appearances of the resurrected Jesus as the basis for knowing that he was resurrected.* Although some scholars today are still trying to determine the nature of these appearances — whether they were generally visible to anyone who would have been there, whether they were spiritual or in some sense physical, or whether they were entirely subjective — Paul himself gives no details of what kind of encounters they were.[24] Beyond this, it is important to recognize that neither here in 1 Cor 15, which deals exclusively with the resurrection, nor anywhere else in any of his letters does Paul mention the empty tomb. Either he did not know the tomb traditions, or he knew them and did not use them when writing about the resurrection. In either case, it is apparent that in the New Testament traditions it is possible to speak of the resurrection of Jesus without reference to the empty tomb. *The empty tomb, therefore, is not a necessary element in the proclamation of the resurrection.*

Furthermore, in response to those scholars mentioned above who assert that the claim of resurrection could not stand if there had not been an empty tomb in Jerusalem, one might appeal to Paul. Paul declares that "flesh and blood cannot inherit the kingdom of God" (1 Cor 15:50 RSV). He also claims that the resurrected one no longer has a physical body but a spiritual body: "What is sown is perishable, what is raised is imperishable.... It is sown a physical body, it is raised a spiritual body. If there is a physical body, there is also a spiritual body" (1 Cor 15:42–44 RSV). For Paul, the resurrection involves a transformation of the whole person, including the body; but the new, transformed body is not the old flesh, which would still be subject to decay, disease, and death.

Although not defining what a spiritual body might be, Paul can use images in which the new body is not contingent upon the old body. In 2 Cor 5:1, he writes, "For we know that if the earthly tent we live in is destroyed, we have a building from God, a house not made with hands, eternal in the heavens." Without pressing these images too far, it is possible to conceive of a resurrection even with the remains of the old "flesh and blood" still in the tomb.[25] To put it in contemporary terms, God's resurrecting activity does not depend upon the molecules that make up the physical body. While there can be an empty tomb without a resurrection, *it is possible as well to think of a resurrection without an empty tomb.*

Another aspect of Paul's account of the resurrection appearances is his claim that, although his encounter with the resurrected Jesus was "as to one untimely born," it was the same type that Peter, the Twelve, James, and the others had experienced. This is a very different understanding from the Gospel accounts, particularly Luke-Acts and John, in which Jesus appears in a physical form for a few days, and after that no one has an encounter with the resurrected Jesus. According to Acts 9, for instance, Paul has a visionary experience of Jesus, but not an encounter, as the disciples had witnessed in Luke, with the resurrected Jesus who was bodily present. However, Paul's understanding that a few years later he could still have a resurrection appearance fits well with another way in which the New Testament writers at times envision Jesus' resurrection. They frequently view his resurrection as his exaltation to heaven and his enthronement and empowerment in the heavenly sphere (Rom 1:3–4; Phil 2:5–11; 1 Thess 1:9–10; Col 2:12–15).[26] In this case, resurrection and ascension become a single process, and the resurrection appearances of Jesus are made from heaven. This means that whether they occurred right after the resurrection or several years later would make no difference.

Peter's Pentecost speech in Acts 2 contains an example of resurrection, which is primarily conceived as exaltation to heaven and Jesus' enthronement in heaven as the Messiah. In explaining the manifestation of the Spirit to critics, Peter says:

> This Jesus God raised up, and of that we all are witnesses. Being therefore exalted at the right hand of God, and having received from the Father the promise of the Holy Spirit, he has poured out this which you see and hear. For David did not ascend into the heavens; but he himself says, "The Lord said to my Lord, Sit at my right hand, till I make thy enemies a stool for thy feet." Let all the house of Israel therefore know assuredly that God has made him both Lord and Christ, this Jesus whom you crucified. (Acts 2:32–36 RSV)

If we had only this passage, we might be led to believe that Jesus became the Messiah only in being resurrected, which included his exaltation to God and enthronement in heaven. It is from this heavenly position that the exalted Jesus later appears to Paul. Notice that in Peter's speech there is no mention of the empty tomb. In fact, while the author of Luke-Acts

certainly knows empty-tomb stories, they are never mentioned in Acts when the early Christians are speaking about
the resurrection. Once again we see that the authors of the
New Testament writings have ways other than the empty
tomb to proclaim the resurrection.

Only the Gospels use the empty-tomb stories when speaking about the resurrection. And yet, when these stories are
examined, they generate further questions. Although the four
Gospels have certain features in common, such as the discovery of the empty tomb by the women, the details of their
tomb stories are irreconcilably different. The list of women
who find the tomb is different in each of the Gospels, from
a group of women in Luke to Mary Magdalene by herself
in John. In Mark, Luke, and John the tomb is open when
the women get there. But Matthew has the tomb closed as
the women arrive and then, during an earthquake, has an
angel roll the stone away. Only Matthew has guards around
the tomb. Mark has one man at the tomb; Matthew has one
angel. Luke has two men, while John has two angels. In Mark
the women are told to go and tell the disciples to meet Jesus
in Galilee, but they do not do it. So, the disciples are still
waiting to hear about the resurrection, and Jesus is still waiting for them to come to Galilee. In Matthew, the women are
given the same instructions, but in this case they do tell the
disciples. The disciples, apparently believing the women, go
and meet Jesus in Galilee. In Luke, even though the women
are not directed to tell the disciples anything, the women tell
them about the tomb; however, the disciples do not believe
the women and think the report is an "idle tale." In Luke
there is nothing about going to Galilee, but later the disciples are told to stay in Jerusalem until they are "clothed with
power from on high" (24:49 RSV), which happens on Pentecost, fifty days later, when they receive the Holy Spirit. In
Luke the resurrection appearances take place not in Galilee
but in and around Jerusalem. In John 20 the resurrection appearances are in Jerusalem, but there is no waiting for the
Spirit, which is given on Easter day. No Gospel shares an

appearance story with another Gospel, and which person is first to encounter the resurrected Jesus is different in each Gospel. Mark recounts no appearances. Matthew has the two Marys as the first to encounter Jesus, while for Luke the first are the two on the road to Emmaus, Cleopas and one who is unnamed. For John the first to encounter the resurrected Jesus is Mary Magdalene alone.

Though there have been attempts to harmonize these accounts, particularly by biblical inerrantists, the details remain irreconcilable. When it is realized that neither empty tomb nor the narratives of the appearances — in which, for instance, Jesus actually shows his physical wounds from crucifixion and eats a piece of fish (Luke 24:39–43; John 20:20, 26–29) — are mentioned in the earliest material in the New Testament, and when it is discovered that the details of the empty-tomb stories and the appearance narratives are widely contradictory, it is no wonder that scholars generally view these stories as later, theologically determined expansions of the earliest preaching of the resurrection.[27] These stories cannot be used as factually accurate accounts that can help ground the faith historically, because they are themselves not so much history as they are already the expressions of faith.[28] They must, therefore, primarily be read theologically rather than historically.

Those who are trained academically are familiar with and used to this sort of analysis. We theologians and other scholars and pastors involved with congregations, however, have not been very effective in teaching laypersons the critical issues in reading the Bible. This means that many would be upset by the problematic character of the resurrection stories. (Recall the agitated letters to the editor a few years ago when the results of the Jesus Seminar hit the papers with the headline that declared, "Scholars say the resurrection didn't really happen.") It is important, therefore, to make it clear that *calling into question the empty-tomb tradition does not mean discarding belief in the resurrection.*

Actually, reading the New Testament stories carefully should prevent anyone from being disturbed. For the writers of the Gospels narrate the resurrection stories themselves in such a way that the empty tomb cannot be mistaken for the resurrection. First, there is a certain modesty in the stories. No one sees the resurrection take place. No one, therefore, knows what happened in the tomb. Unlike the account in the apocryphal *Gospel of Peter,* no one even sees Jesus emerge from the tomb. Even in Matthew, where the stone is still sealing the tomb when the women arrive, Jesus is already gone when the tomb is opened. That is, *the whole process of resurrection takes place in mystery behind the narrative of the empty tomb.* As Ignatius stated about other Christian doctrines in his *Letter to the Ephesians* (19.1), the resurrection is "wrought in silence by God."

In addition to their modesty, another aspect of the tomb stories that might ameliorate the reaction of some people to a scholarly analysis is the manner in which the stories point away from the tomb itself. Even in the stories that focus on the tomb, the tomb does not produce faith. No one in these stories comes to belief by viewing or hearing about the empty tomb. According to Mark, the women find the empty tomb and are even told by the young man that Jesus is risen. But they go out in fear and say nothing to anyone. According to Luke, the disciples think it is an "idle tale" (24:11) when the women tell them about the empty tomb. According to John, Mary Magdalene sees the tomb and assumes that the gardener has removed Jesus' corpse. Remarkably, in the stories that stress the empty tomb, the empty tomb is not sufficient to produce faith. In these stories, *only one thing definitely brings faith in the resurrected Jesus, and that is an encounter with the resurrected Lord.*

The unbelieving disciples in Luke believe only after Jesus appears to Simon and then to the rest of them. According to John, Thomas comes to belief only in the encounter with the resurrected Jesus. And before him, Mary Magdalene, who has seen the tomb and the angels without coming to belief, talks to the supposed gardener (Jesus), and in the encounter, when he calls her name, she comes to know that Jesus is alive. In the stories, it is only the encounters with the resurrected Lord, not the tomb, that bring faith in him as the living Lord.

This analysis is instructive for theology today, for, on the one hand, it calls into question the efficacy of using historical research apologetically to establish certain facts upon which to ground belief in the resurrection. It is not only the resurrection event but also the supposed facts themselves that remain illusive. On the other hand, the analysis demonstrates that it is not the facts of the empty tomb or the details of the appearance narratives that are either necessary or sufficient for believing in the resurrection. *Belief in the resurrection is based only on an encounter with the living Lord, who is known only as one comes to faith.* The question then may be asked, Is belief in the resurrection really only something that happens in the faith of the believer?

The Subjective Understanding of the Resurrection

Many scholars who have investigated the biblical record have come to the conclusion that it is impossible to say anything objective about what happened to Jesus in the resurrection. Others, adding to their biblical research a modern understanding about what is and is not possible, have taken the position that resurrection, at least as it makes claims that something happened to Jesus after he died, simply cannot be believed by reasonable people. Many of these theologians have developed an alternate apologetic strategy to make the faith more accepted to modern people, not by attempting to find some factual way of supporting the resurrection, but either by suppressing the importance of the resurrection or by reinterpreting it as a subjective event in the believers.

Some theologians have tried to establish a ground for faith without dependence on the resurrection at all. The great nineteenth-century theologian Friedrich Schleiermacher, for instance, rejected the importance of the resurrection (even speculating that Jesus might not have really died) and instead based belief in Jesus on the mode and impact of his existence during his earthly life. Schleiermacher asserted that the defining element in all religion was the "feeling of absolute dependence."[29] The degree to which a person informs every other aspect of life by the feeling of absolute dependence determines the degree to which that person is religious or, as Schleiermacher also states it, has developed a God-consciousness.[30] Now human beings sin: we fail to develop our God-consciousnesses, even though we and the world are made in such a way that this development is possible.[31]

Unlike everyone else, however, Jesus had a fully developed, unwavering God-consciousness; his feeling of absolute dependence always determined his relationship to everything at every moment.[32] He redeems believers, therefore, by assuming them "into the power of His God-consciousness," so that the feeling of absolute dependence in him becomes active in them.[33] Believers are empowered by his God-consciousness to develop their own. According to Schleiermacher, this redeeming activity of Jesus takes place before and even without resurrection, for the "disciples recognized in Him the Son of God without having the faintest premonition of His resurrection."[34] We could, Schleiermacher states, "accept Him as Redeemer or recognize the being of God in Him, (even) if we did not know that He had risen from the dead."[35] This means, according to Schleiermacher, that resurrection is not a constituent element of Christology or a necessary part of faith, but belongs rather to the doctrine of Scripture and is to be believed only insofar as it seems adequately attested.[36]

Schleiermacher, however, is not only moving away from the position of the New Testament, which stresses the centrality of the resurrection. He is also on tenuous historical and biblical ground in claiming that the disciples recognized the saving significance of Jesus before the cross and resurrection. Furthermore, Schleiermacher's attempt to form a theology based on the feeling of absolute dependence means that he is able to eliminate from his theology any troublesome elements of the New Testament story that he does not view as related to the feeling of absolute dependence — elements such as the cross and resurrection.

Other scholars, instead of eliminating Jesus' resurrection as an element in faith, have tried to interpret the resurrection as something that happened within the subjectivity of Jesus' followers rather than as something that happened objectively to Jesus. The accounts of the empty tomb, appearances, and exaltation are various ways of expressing what were really subjective experiences of one type or another. John Dominic Crossan, for instance, claims that the resurrection was the result of "wishful thinking" on the part of the early Christians and that events like this never "did or could happen." He writes, "I do not think that anyone, anywhere, at any time brings dead people back to life."[37] The resurrection is, rather, the symbolic expression of Jesus' "continuing presence in a continuing community."[38]

Likewise, Willi Marxsen claims that resurrection does not mean a new transformed existence for Jesus but that "the cause of Jesus continues" in the lives of the disciples.[39] John Hick attempts to explain the resurrection experience of the early Christians in naturalistic terms. The resurrection has to do with the disciples' experience, which might have been "waking versions" of near-death experiences or bereavement reactions, in which a recently dead person is experienced as present to those loved ones who are mourning.[40] Sallie McFague also does not speak of anything actually happening to Jesus in the resurrection. According to her, what really happened was "the awareness of his continuing presence and empowerment. . . . The resurrection is a way of speaking about an awareness that the presence of God in Jesus is a permanent presence in our midst." Through this presence, the disciples are continuously empowered.[41]

Perhaps the most powerful treatment of resurrection as a subjective experience of the disciples is still Rudolf Bultmann's existentialist interpretation. Bultmann does not think that modern people can or should accept the mythological worldview found in the New Testament — a worldview that includes miracles, Satan, demons, angels, a three-storied universe, as well as apocalyptic ideas, including resurrection. On the one hand, the knowledge of the world that we now possess does not permit it.[42] On the other hand, the New Testament itself demands that we should not accept ancient myths literally, because the real purpose of myth is not to communicate objective information about the structures of the world or facts about the persons in the stories. The real purpose of the myth is to give an expression of a life transformed by an encounter with what God has done in Jesus. The New Testament myths show the authentic existence of those whose self-understandings had been transformed by the realization of the meaning of Jesus' death. "Hence the importance of the New Testament mythology," Bultmann states, "lies not in its imagery but in the understanding of existence which it enshrines."[43]

This understanding of existence also confronts us and challenges us to decide for this authentic mode of existence. For Bultmann, then, the resurrection "is not an event of past history" that is open to historical research.[44] It is not believing a fact about something that happened to Jesus after he died. "*Faith in the resurrection,*" he asserts, "*is really the same thing as faith in the saving efficacy of the cross.*"[45] The resurrection occurred not when Jesus came out of a tomb or in some literal appearance, but when the disciples came to faith in the meaning of the cross: when they realized that in Jesus they were confronted by an authentic existence that was not determined by a fleeing from death, and accepted that existence for themselves. For Bultmann, then, the cross and resurrection "form an inseparable unity," "a single, indivisible cosmic event."[46] Good Friday and Easter occur on the same day. Jesus died on the cross but was raised in the faith of the disciples. And the cross and resurrection occur again and again, anytime anyone comes to faith by making the cross of Christ her or his own.[47]

The power of these interpretations, particularly Bultmann's, cannot be denied. They attempt to uncover how one might understand the claim of resurrection in the context of modern knowledge and the scientific worldview. They attempt to speak about the importance of Jesus to people in this time. These interpretations also stress an important element of belief in the resurrection, the transformation of the believer. In the New Testament, Jesus' resurrection is not a general experience, open to all. It cannot be discovered by getting all of the objective facts straight. It comes to those who simultaneously come to faith. The resurrected Lord is never known without this faith, without a transformation of the self, actually a transformation broader than Bultmann imagined, that goes beyond the self and involves the promise of the transformation of the world, and a call to mission for that transformation. For example, out of an encounter with the resurrected one, Paul, the persecutor of the gospel, becomes the proclaimer of the gospel and a martyr in the mission for the gospel. Bultmann was correct: accepting Jesus' resurrection does involve a new self-understanding.

These theologies that focus upon a subjective change in the believer, however, offer a truncated, one-sided version of what the New Testament declares about the resurrection of Jesus. Even though the New Testament does not even attempt to give access to the hidden process of resurrection, even though the tomb and appearance traditions in the Gospels are of questionable historical value, and even though Paul gives no details about what the appearances that he mentions were — nevertheless, all of the accounts have a common claim. Though these accounts may express that claim by referring to appearances, exaltation and enthronement, or empty tomb, the resurrection traditions presuppose, indeed proclaim, that something happened to Jesus. And that something was this: God gave Jesus new life.

While this is never known except by those who come to faith, according to that faith *what happened to Jesus is not reducible to the appearance of faith in the believers.* The texts of the New Testament are clear that something involving objectivity happened to Jesus, which was prior to, independent of, and the basis for the transformation of the believers. The earliest formula-like statements about the resurrection in the New Testament say it clearly: "God has raised Jesus from the dead" (Rom 4:24b; 8:11a and 11b; 2 Cor 4:14; Gal 1:1; Eph 1:20; Col 2:12; 1 Pet 1:21).[48] To turn statements like this one into a statement about only the coming to faith of the disciples violates the meaning of the language of the New Testament and the tradition. *Faith did not cause the resurrection; the resurrection caused faith.*

The belief of the disciples did not merely come from their reflection on the meaning of the cross, as Bultmann claimed, but because something else decisive had happened that drove them to reconsider the cross. God gave Jesus new life, and the disciples' faith was a response to the encounter with the living Lord. If God did not give new life to Jesus, it might be asked, what is the Christian hope for people and for the world? To paraphrase Paul, "If it is for a transformed self-understanding only that we have hoped in Christ, we are of all people most to be pitied."

Toward the Meaning of Resurrection

The attempts to lay a ground for belief in the resurrection by historical research into the empty-tomb stories or the appearance narratives have failed. The historical work is at best ambiguous. Some scholars assert that the evidence suggests at least a historical kernel to the tomb stories, while others reject such an assertion. The New Testament stories themselves resist historical verification because both the empty tomb and appearance traditions are so contradictory and theologically colored. We have no reason to doubt that Paul and the others he mentioned experienced what they believed was the resurrected Lord, but this report cannot establish that Jesus was actually raised.

However, even if someone could decisively establish a high probably for the empty-tomb stories and all the accounts claiming resurrection appearances, there would still be no verification according to the canons of historical research, which demand that events be analogous to other events if they are to be accepted. *An action of God, such as resurrection, as of yet has no analogy and, therefore, is beyond the view of the historian as a historian.* In any case, to claim that historical reason has the means to grasp the resurrection turns faith into an object of historical probability and reduces resurrection from a decisive action of God to just another event in history. Resurrection is an article of faith and for the believer, then, not probably true but absolutely true, although as an act of God in history its explication is open to trivial interpretation.

The attempt to make resurrection understandable to the modern world by reducing resurrection to a subjective experience of the early Christians fails as well. Such an attempt violates the clear message of the New Testament stories, which claim that something happened to Jesus. It turns the resurrection hope for the transformation of the cosmos and the defeat of suffering and death into the hope for an authentic mode of existence — until one dies.

Against the method of attempting to find a historical ground to support the resurrection, the New Testament demonstrates that the resurrection is not an event that is generally available, but is known only in the transformation of faith. Only believers declare it. Against the method of grounding resurrection by interpreting it as a subjective experience of the believers, the New Testament witness claims that something happened to Jesus. God gave Jesus new life. Finally, the questions of exactly what happened and how — Was there really an empty tomb? Do the appearances mean that the disciples actually saw something with their eyes, or did they have subjective visions? — do not matter for the faith. *Ultimately, the important point is this irreducible, dialectical claim: God gave new life to Jesus, and this is the basis of faith, known only as one comes to faith.* We cannot find facts for apologetics to prove this claim, nor can we alter it for apologetic reasons. We can only deny it or submit to it. We cannot get behind or underneath this claim to explain how it happened; what we can do is interpret its meaning. When we do explicate the meaning of resurrection, we find that, as for Paul, it is constitutive of our understanding of Jesus, ourselves, and God.

When the early Jewish Christians came to believe that God had given Jesus new life, they had a word already available in their vocabulary to communicate this experience and belief. The word was "resurrection," a term and concept drawn from the apocalyptic ideas and literature that developed in postexilic Judaism. In the attempt to explain their history in which the righteous had suffered at the hands of unrighteous empires and rulers — even after God had already judged them for their disobedience by sending them into exile — the Jewish community and its writers went beyond the eschatology of the prophets and borrowed ideas from Persian Zoroastrianism, such as Satan, the division of history into different ages, and resurrection.

This new Jewish apocalyptic outlook saw history divided basically into two ages: the present age where demonic forces reign and the new age in which God would reign. With the advent of the new age, according to some accounts, God would send the heavenly Son of Man, defeat Satan and evil, vindicate the righteous, and establish God's reign or kingdom, which would be consummated by the creation of a new heaven and a new earth. Because Judaism did not have a clear notion of life beyond death, an important question was, What happens to the righteous dead? Jewish apocalyptic ideas claimed that the dead too would be vindicated, because in the new age God would resurrect the dead. These ideas form the backdrop for understanding what the early Christians were claiming when they declared the resurrection of Jesus. In this apocalyptic context, the implications of declaring Jesus' resurrection certainly include, but go far beyond, the claim that this one person received new life to touch every area of Christian theology.

The Meaning of Resurrection for Jesus: Christology

First, *resurrection meant something for and about Jesus.* Because many Jews believed that God would raise the dead at the end of the age, resurrection was not an unexpected miracle but an expected eschatological event. What was surprising was whom God had resurrected first, not a legitimate, righteous person but a crucified outcast. Jesus was the first recipient of God's resurrecting activity. It was God who did this; resurrection was a gift from God. After being annihilated by death, Jesus did not and could not resurrect himself. As mentioned before, the earliest traditions express this activity of God and the passivity of Jesus: "God has raised Jesus from the dead" (Rom 4:24b; 8:11a and 11b; 2 Cor 4:14; Gal 1:1; Eph 1:20; Col 2:12; 1 Pet 1:21).

In this new *creatio ex nihilo*, in which God created life out of the nothingness of death, the gift God gave was new life. Jesus did not return to this life. Resurrection is not coming back to life, a resuscitation of a dead corpse, as reflected in the stories of Elijah (1 Kgs 17:17–24) and Elisha (2 Kgs 4:32–37), and in accounts of Jesus bringing Lazarus (John 11), Jairus's daughter (Mark 5:35–43), and the widow's son at Nain (Luke 7:11–17) back to life. These who are brought back to this life will still be subject to disease and decay; they will have to die again. Resurrection life, on the other hand, is a transformed life in which one enters God's kingdom, not life after death, but life through and beyond death — a new creation, a new existence in which God has conquered death.

The accounts in the New Testament make this point. It is the same Jesus who is resurrected, but he is raised in a transformed state. For Paul, it is the resurrection of the whole self, including the body; but as we have seen, it is a transformed, spiritual body. In the Gospels, particularly Luke and John, the continuity of Jesus before and after the resurrection is expressed in the physicality of the resurrected Jesus. He invites his followers to see and even touch his wounds. And yet this same Jesus is transformed. Not only the two on the road to Emmaus but also Mary in the garden do not recognize him. He can also appear in closed rooms. Because God has given him this new life, Jesus is the living Lord and can now be the Lord of the community of faith, indeed, of the whole cosmos. He can be our Lord; he can change us. Karl Barth rightly asserted that the denial of the resurrection is an attempt to escape Christ's presence with us and lordship over us.[49]

Jesus' resurrection is also God's vindication of Jesus. In this act the concealment of who Jesus was is broken open.[50] If he were left only on the cross and in death, we would not have known the meaning of the appearance of Jesus, for the cross was the contradiction of any expected messiah or savior. And because Jesus' message and being were one, the cross would have been the cancellation of both. God's act of raising him vindicates Jesus' message, life and death, and existence with God. Jürgen Moltmann, the premier contemporary theologian of resurrection, asserts that the resurrection leads us to read history backward as well as forward.[51] Reading backward, we see that the light of God's "yes" to Jesus in raising him illuminates who Jesus really was. The one who was crucified is now identified as the expected "one who is to come," Messiah, Lord, Savior. Yet the resurrection also teaches us that these concepts used to describe Jesus must be transformed by the concrete appearance of Jesus; for the way he appeared was different from the original expectation. Beyond this, reading backward from the resurrection reveals Jesus' true relationship to God (Rom 1:4): He was and is the Son of the God, and he chose to call God "Father."[52] God identifies the divine will and essence with the mission and existence of Jesus, who therefore can be called the incarnation of God and God's future kingdom. Jesus is, therefore, the divine one in our midst.

The resurrection also leads us to read history forward, for it is the first act of God's eschatological promises and points to the continuing and future work of Jesus. He is the living Lord. In his ministry, Jesus preached the coming kingdom of God, as he embodied it in his acceptance of sinners, the sick, and the outcasts. The resurrection vindicates this message and reveals that Jesus is the agent of the advent of the kingdom. He is the Son of Man, who came unexpectedly as a suffering one (Mark), but whose glory will be seen in his Parousia.

The Meaning of the Resurrection for Us: Soteriology

If the resurrection meant something for Jesus only, it is difficult to imagine that it would have captured the attention of the early followers of Jesus. *But the resurrection of Jesus also means hope for the believer.* It means that we, too, have a future beyond the power of suffering and death. Thus, Jesus' resurrection is the verification of the expected general resurrection for us. As Paul says in 1 Thess 4:14, "For since we believe that Jesus died and rose again, even so, through Jesus, God will bring with him those who have fallen asleep" (RSV). Jesus is the "firstfruits" of God's resurrecting activity, for "in Christ shall all be made alive" (1 Cor 15:22 RSV). *By raising Jesus, God promises us new life as well.*

This new life, furthermore, is for our whole selves. Resurrection hope is not the immortality of the soul that was characteristic of much Greek philosophy and that was equated with resurrection in the theology of apostolic fathers and apologists and, therefore, subsequent Christian tradition. Immortality leaves the body behind when it envisions salvation. Resurrection, on the other hand, is for the whole self, including the body. It affirms God's care and concern for the body and calls on believers to treat the body with respect as well (1 Cor 6:13b–20). Likewise, resurrection reveals our total dependence on God for any hope beyond death. No evidence from so-called near-death experiences has any bearing on the Christian hope. Judaism did not have a clear idea of an immortal soul but saw the person as a psychosomatic unity;

hence, when death came, the whole person died. No one in the Hebrew Scriptures dies and goes to heaven. The dead go to Sheol, the realm of the dead. This is why resurrection was and is so important. If there is any hope for new life, it cannot be found in the constitution of the person but only in God.

This resurrection hope, however, is not only for us humans but also for the transformation of the whole cosmos. Because resurrection was a component of the apocalyptic hope, which included the re-creation of all things, God's resurrection of Jesus signaled the validity of this promise for the future transformation of the world. At the same time, it revealed that one did not have to wait for the future to claim this transformation. The future kingdom had already begun, because Jesus had been resurrected, and the Spirit that brought new life to Jesus had been poured out on present reality. Both Luke-Acts and John connect Jesus' resurrection and exaltation with the giving of the Spirit to the community. The Christian community, placed between the resurrection of Jesus and the consummation of the kingdom, claims the power of the kingdom already available in faith.

So far, all the meaning of the resurrection that we have drawn soteriologically for us could be established regardless of whom God raised by the mere resurrection of anyone. But the real basis of hope is seen when theology is attentive to precisely who this resurrected one was. *For in raising Jesus, God shows God's identification with him.* The point is this: The one whom God raised was not the representative of the religious or political powers, as we might expect, but the crucified one. Building on insights from Karl Barth, Jürgen Moltmann points out the significant features of the crucified one who was resurrected.[53] Jesus died as one rejected by the religious authorities, condemned by the political system, forsaken by his friends, a sinner against the law, in horrific physical suffering, with a sense of abandonment by God. And yet, this is the one God resurrected. But if God did indeed resurrect this one, then there is hope for all of those who also are rejected, condemned, forsaken, sinful, suffering, dying, even for those who, at times, do not have a sense of God's presence. For these folk know that whatever happens, they are not alone; in Jesus, God has been precisely where they are, not only in the joys of life but in its lowest points as well. Also, by resurrecting this crucified one, God promises that all human pain, suffering, and death will be transformed into glory.

Furthermore, to trust in God's resurrection of Jesus — to identify with the God who did this — simultaneously throws us into mission on behalf of all such people, and draws us, like God, into work to alleviate such conditions. An encounter with the resurrected Jesus follows the pattern of Old Testament stories of encounters with God. The appearance of this divinity in history is never an end in itself. It is never only to give someone a religious experience; instead, as Peter, Paul, and the other earliest Christians learned, it always involves the component of being sent in mission.

What the Resurrection Means for God: Theology

Finally, one must move from soteriology to theology and ask what the resurrection of Jesus means for God. *For in raising Jesus, God is ultimately vindicating God's self.* The resurrection shows that this God is the God of life, who created life at first and who always re-creates it to defeat death and nothingness. The resurrection vindicates God, because it reveals that God indeed vindicates those who have been faithful to God. This God is true to the covenant promises made in the story of Abraham, to be the God of Israel and yet to go beyond Israel as well, to be a blessing to all nations (Gen 12). For the resurrection reveals Jesus as Israel's Messiah; and yet, in raising the crucified one, God universalizes the covenant, opening its promise to those originally beyond it.

This God of the resurrection is also the God of love, who demonstrates in raising Jesus the crucified, forsaken, rejected, sinful, suffering, dying human being that God's love is unconditional and boundless; thus, nothing can separate humankind from the presence of God's love. For by raising Jesus in the power of the Spirit, this God identifies with Jesus, reveals him to be the true Son, and declares that God was and is present in the history of Jesus. If this is the case, however, we can no longer think of God as a closed, static being, only far beyond us, but must conceive of God as an open, dynamic event that includes us in itself.

For God is both God beyond us but, at the same time, fully present and active in Jesus, and therefore, God with us. The relationship between the God beyond us and the God with us is constituted by the Spirit, through whom God resurrected Jesus and who, out of the relationship between the God beyond us and the God with us, has been poured out into the world. That is, even without the development of a complete argument, one can see how faith in the resurrection of Jesus leads theology inexorably in a Trinitarian direction. One can no longer name God without at the same time naming Jesus and the Spirit of love that they share together and that, therefore, unites them. If this Trinitarian view is accepted, the resurrection of this human Jesus means that humanity is given a place in the divine life of God, and that *God is a God who refuses to be God without humanity.*[54] The resurrection of Jesus, therefore, reveals God as one who includes humanity — with all its joy and sorrow, life, and death — in the divine life and thereby gives all humankind an authentic glory and true hope.

Notes

1. D. Hume, *An Enquiry concerning Human Understanding* (ed. Eric Steinberg; Indianapolis: Hackett, 1977), 88.

2. Ibid.

3. Upon his retirement, H. DeWolf moved to Lakeland, Florida, and taught occasional courses in both the religion and sociology departments at Florida Southern College. He told this story while

lecturing on the theology of Paul Tillich in my course "Current Theological Thought."

4. Quoted in M. Shuster, "Preaching the Resurrection," in *The Resurrection* (ed. Stephen Davis et al.; New York: Oxford, 1997), 311.

5. Augustine, *On the Trinity* (trans. A. W. Haddan), in *The Basic Writings of Saint Augustine* (ed. Whitney Oates; New York: Random House, 1948), 721 (2.17.2). Augustine goes on to say: "For even His enemies believe that the flesh died on the cross of His passion, but they do not believe it to have risen again. Which we believing most firmly,...we wait with certain hope for...the redemption of our body."

6. Quoted in Shuster, "Preaching," 311–12.

7. K. Barth, *Church Dogmatics*, vol. IV/1, *The Doctrine of Reconciliation* (trans. G. W. Bromiley; Edinburgh: T & T Clark, 1956), 299.

8. J. Moltmann, *Theology of Hope* (trans. James Leitch; New York: Harper & Row, 1967), 165–66.

9. On the difference that it makes to trust in a living Lord, see L. T. Johnson, *Living Jesus: Learning the Heart of the Gospel* (San Francisco: HarperSanFrancisco, 1999).

10. G. O'Collins, "The Resurrection: The State of the Questions," in Davis, ed., *The Resurrection*, 14.

11. See F. Schüssler Fiorenza, *Foundational Theology: Jesus and the Church* (New York: Crossroad, 1984), 5–55.

12. Ibid., 11.

13. Ibid., 9ff.

14. W. Craig, "John Dominic Crossan and the Resurrection," in Davis, ed., *The Resurrection*, 253. Not only does this passage make an unwarranted distinction between Jews and Christians, since all of these early Christians were Jews; it also begs many questions about the connection between the empty tomb and resurrection and the new, spiritual body and the old, physical body, as well as about whether everyone would have known where Joseph's tomb was or would have necessarily been interested in it. See also the conservative apologetic theology of G. Habermas, "There Is Proof of the Resurrection," *International Christian Digest* 1, no. 3 (April 1987): 15–16.

15. W. Pannenberg, *Jesus — God and Man* (trans. Lewis Wilkins and Duane Priebe; 2d ed.; Philadelphia: Westminster, 1977), 109–10. For an analysis of Pannenberg's view of the resurrection, see E. Frank Tupper, *The Theology of Wolfhart Pannenberg* (Philadelphia: Westminster, 1973), 146–60.

16. Ibid., 108.

17. Ibid., 89ff.

18. Ibid., 100–101.

19. Ibid., 101.

20. H. Küng, *On Being a Christian* (trans. Edward Quinn; New York: Doubleday, 1976), 364.

21. N. Perrin, *The Resurrection Narratives: A New Approach* (London: SCM, 1977), 82.

22. J. D. Crossan, *Who Killed Jesus? Exposing the Roots of Anti-Semitism in the Gospel Story of the Death of Jesus* (San Francisco: HarperSanFrancisco, 1994), ch. 6.

23. G. Bornkamm, *Paul* (trans. D. M. G. Stalker; New York: Harper & Row, 1969), xi, dates Paul's conversion in 32 CE. J. Fitzmyer places it in 36 CE; see *Paul and His Theology* (Englewood Cliffs, NJ: Prentice Hall, 1989), 11.

24. See O'Collins, "The Resurrection," 9–13. See also S. Davis, " 'Seeing' the Risen Jesus," in Davis, ed., *The Resurrection*, 126–47, who claims that the appearances involved ordinary vision and that a person with a camera could have captured the appearances on film.

25. On this possible interpretation, as well as a critique, see R. Fuller, *The Formation of the Resurrection Narratives* (Philadelphia: Fortress, 1980), 20–21. See also, Küng, *On Being a Christian*, 351, 363.

26. On this, see Schüssler Fiorenza, *Foundational Theology*, 34ff.; and Fitzmyer, *Paul and His Theology*, 54ff.

27. See Fuller, *Formation*, 170–72. See also Pannenberg, *Jesus*, 88ff., 99ff.

28. See Küng, *On Being a Christian*, 360.

29. F. Schleiermacher, *The Christian Faith* (ed. H. R. Mackintosh and J. S. Stewart; Philadelphia: Fortress, 1976), 12.

30. Ibid., 22, 17.

31. Ibid., 54–55, 238–56.

32. Ibid., 385–89.

33. Ibid., 425ff.

34. Ibid., 418.

35. Ibid., 420.

36. Ibid.

37. J. D. Crossan, *Jesus: A Revolutionary Biography* (San Francisco: HarperSanFrancisco, 1994), 94.

38. J. D. Crossan, *The Historical Jesus: The Life of a Mediterranean Jewish Peasant* (San Francisco: HarperSanFrancisco, 1991), 404.

39. W. Marxsen, *The Resurrection of Jesus of Nazareth* (Philadelphia: Fortress, 1970), 62–66.

40. On this, see O'Collins, "The Resurrection," 6–10.

41. S. McFague, *Models of God: Theology for an Ecological, Nuclear Age* (Philadelphia: Fortress, 1987), 59.

42. R. Bultmann et al., *Kerygma and Myth: A Theological Debate* (trans. R. H. Fuller; ed. H. W. Bartsch; 2d ed.; vol. 1; New York: Harper & Row, 1961), 1:2–5.

43. Ibid., 11.

44. Ibid., 42.

45. Ibid., 41; the italics are Bultmann's.

46. Ibid., 38.

47. Ibid., 36.

48. On this statement, see Schüssler Fiorenza, *Foundational Theology,* 33ff.

49. Barth, *Church Dogmatics,* IV/1:310–44.

50. On this, see ibid., 306.

51. J. Moltmann, *The Crucified God* (trans. R. A. Wilson and John Bowden; New York: Harper & Row, 1974), 180.

52. Ibid., 182.

53. See K. Barth, *Credo* (New York: Charles Scribner's Sons, 1962), 95. See also K. Barth, *Church Dogmatics,* II/1, *The Doctrine of God* (trans. T. Parker et al.; Edinburgh: T & T Clark, 1957): 386–87; and Moltmann, *Crucified God,* 126–59.

54. See K. Barth, *The Humanity of God* (Richmond: John Knox, 1960), 45ff.

Conclusion:
The Origin and Development
of Resurrection Beliefs

James H. Charlesworth

The concept that the Creator of the cosmos will raise the dead (both the righteous and the unrighteous or only the former) is stunning, and indeed quite shocking. It is clear that resurrected bodies are not present in our communities. The claim that Jesus had been resurrected by God is a unique claim; it has not been accorded to others, including, for example, Gautama, Hillel, and Muḥammad.

Origins of Resurrection Belief

Even though the preceding chapters focus on resurrection belief in the Christian Bible, some word should be added, at the end, to indicate the origins of the belief in resurrection (also see Elledge, ch. 2). When research helps dissipate the fog of over 2,000 years, it is possible to see where resurrection belief may have first originated. The ancient Egyptians certainly believed in an afterlife for the pharaoh, who was proclaimed divine by many of those who helped build the pyramids; but the Egyptians did not originate the concept of resurrection. Many of the ancient inhabitants of India believed that the individual was like the foam of the sea, momentarily separate and then again absorbed in the greater ocean. The thought is found in the Upanishads. In the Rig-Veda the soul of the deceased is taken by the fire-god and "receives a new, more 'subtle' body, and its life is a replica of human life on earth, though freed from all the imperfections that are inseparable from it here."[1] Such concepts shaped Hinduism and then Buddhism.[2] The concept of rebirth, reincarnation, and the transmigration of souls is not to be confused with Semitic ideas and is paradigmatically different from resurrection belief.[3]

The beliefs of the ancient Greeks are difficult to synthesize. Plato,[4] it seems, imagined a God (the supremely good or beautiful), either a "he" or an "it," who was transcendent and not involved in shadowy existence on earth. Pythagoras, Socrates, Plato, and many Greeks believed in the dualism of the body and soul, affirming immortality of only the latter. Another thought also appears in Greek culture: Asclepius (one of the most powerful gods in the first century CE) is sometimes hailed as one who was able to raise the dead to new life (not necessarily to eternal life).[5] Note what Apollodorus the Historian reports in his *Bibliotheca:* When Asclepius, became a surgeon, he carried the art to a new level, so that "he not only prevented some from dying, but even raised up the dead ... " (III.10,3,5–4,1).[6] Surely mythological is the report found in Diodorus' *Bibliotheca Historica,* which was composed between 60 and 30 BCE. In this world history, Diodorus claims that Zeus killed Asclepius with a thunderbolt because Hades was furious that he was reviving so many who had died.

Perhaps Greek culture influenced Judaism with resurrection belief, but the reverse is also true because of the late date of some traditions about Asclepius "resurrecting" a dead person (cf also Justin, *Apol* 54.10). Clearly, the dominant Greek idea was the immortality of the soul.

The two more likely sources for the first appearance of resurrection belief are Ugarit and Iran. The resurrection concepts in both of them clearly antedate the first appearance of the concept within Judaism, but it is in Second Temple Judaism that we can be certain that full-blown resurrection belief (Category 15) is present, since the concept is preserved in manuscripts that predate the first century CE.

Ugarit (or Tell Ras Shamra) is an ancient city that is now part of an artificial mound or Tell that rises sixty feet high and covers about seventy acres on the Mediterranean coast of Syria. In 1928 a peasant hit a stone with his plow. Excavations revealed the ancient city and eventually thousands of tablets in no less than eight languages. On cuneiform tablets dating from circa 1400 BCE are myths and beliefs that are considerably older. The tablets preserve beliefs in immortality and resurrection; in the *Baal-Anat Cycle* Baal is resurrected. M. Dahood was convinced that ancient Israel knew about resurrection beliefs and that these are evident in the Davidic Psalms. Note in particular Dahood's translation and understanding of Psalm 17:15,

> At the vindication
>   I will gaze upon your face,
> At the resurrection
>   I will be saturated with your being.[7]

The present conclusion allows space only to introduce this option, and let others discuss whether this psalm refers to Category 15: "Raising the Individual from Death to Eternal Life" or Category 3: "Raising of the Individual from Social Disenfranchisement."[8] One should also not overlook the possibility that the psalmist is presenting another thought: merely awakening from sleep or a dream. If so, a translation different from Dahood's is demanded (cf. NRSV).

The major development of resurrection belief and most likely the stimulus for Jewish resurrection belief is Iran and Zoroastrianism (Mazdean apocalypticism).[9] Zarathushtra (or Zoroaster) probably lived in the eighth century BCE (perhaps from c. 799 to c. 750),[10] but all the early manuscripts of his teachings are lost. The texts and traditions are difficult to date, ranging from 1000 BCE to the tenth century CE.[11] In one of the oldest texts, at least linguistically, we read that the dead will rise in their lifeless bodies (*Yasna* 54). This belief appears in a text that describes the end of time and the resurrection of the body. In the hymns of Zarathushtra, which date either from the seventh century BCE or more likely sometime before 300 BCE, we may read Zarathushtra's prayer for himself:

> O Wise One, thou who, as the Most Holy Spirit,
> Didst make the ox and waters and plants,
> Give me Immortality and Integrity,
> Strength and endurance with the Good Mind, at the judgment!
> (*Yasna* 43.7)[12]

According to this prayer, the poet-prophet prays for "Immortality" at the time of the judgment, after his resurrection. It is far from certain that this thought can be traced back to the eighth century BCE and to Zarathushtra. E. M. Yamauchi, for example, is convinced that there "is no certain affirmation of a belief in a resurrection by Zoroaster in the Gathas."[13]

Other texts, the *YASHTS,* are not so old, and their traditions are difficult to date because they evolved over time and are not preserved in ancient manuscripts. In Yasht 19 we obtain an undeniable reference to resurrection: The dead will be resurrected, when the Saosyant "who restores life" appears at the end of time and then the living will never die again (stanzas 89–90).[14] In the *Pahlavi Texts,* which often represent traditions that antedate the third century CE,[15] a very long chapter is devoted to a description of the resurrection and eternal life.[16] Ahura Mazda, the supreme god, reports that creating the air and other aspects of creation was "more difficult than causing the resurrection" (*Bundahisn* 30:5).[17] At the general resurrection when all humans who have died are raised, the dead will receive again their bone from the earth, their blood from the water, their hair from plants, and their life from fire (*Bund* 3:6). The good and righteous who have died will be bodily resurrected to eternal life. Thus, in Zoroastrian thought we obtain clear examples of Category 15: "Raising of the Individual from Death to Eternal Life."[18]

There should be no doubt that Zoroastrian ideas influenced Jews before 70 CE, as I argued in the sixties;[19] for example, the concept of paradise — so influential in Judaism and Christianity — comes from Persia, since it is a Persian loanword. Caravans were sometimes larger than villages, and they brought to the West more than silk, spices, linen, and rubies. They also brought men and women who bore living myths and sacred ideas that could be shared around the fires when stars brightened the night. Most likely the concept of resurrection in Judaism was influenced by Zoroastrian ideas, since the concept and terms to express it are similar in both religions and those to the East of Palestine antedate those in Palestine by centuries. In the later Pahlavi texts, we also must allow for influences from Judaism and Christianity. The influence from the East (Babylon and Persia) began significantly in the sixth century BCE, was heightened by the conquests of Alexander the Great, and accelerated with the successes of the Maccabeans and Hasmoneans in the second century BCE; indeed, Gamla in Galilee was populated by Jews who came to (or returned to) "the Land" from Babylon or Persia. In his perspicacious *Life After Death: A History of the Afterlife in Western Religion,* A. F. Segal concludes that Zoroastrian traditions are "the most important and interesting candidate for borrowing by the Hebrews, for resurrection does not truly enter Jewish life until after they have made contact with Persian society."[20]

The Development of Resurrection Beliefs
in Second Temple Judaism

In the history of the theologies of Israel, resurrection belief is clearly found only in very late literature. The patriarchs and those in the monarchy, as well as those who lived in ancient Palestine before the sixth-century BCE Babylonian exile, did not imagine that the dead would be raised (Category 15 of ch. 1, above). They assumed that the dead were in Sheol, which is variously imagined. Some early Israelites imagined it as a place where the dead resided and could not praise Yahweh. This understanding was supported by visits to the underground tombs, where "the fathers were gathered." There the bones of those placed on stone slabs were eventually pushed through a hole to a chamber beneath, which held the bones of relatives who had died earlier. Thus, the bones of the son fell down upon the bones of the father, whose bones were on top of the bones of the grandfather. Other Israelites and then Jews imagined that perhaps there was some kind of shadelike existence in this abode of the deceased (see ch. 3). Thus, from about 960 BCE, the time of the earliest conceivable writing in ancient Israel, to approximately 300 BCE, the earliest date for sections of *1 Enoch*, Israelites then Jews believed that "the Lord our God" defined the life of a human from an infantile scream to a silent whimper: from womb to tomb.

Within the Second Temple Judaism, the concept of a resurrection first appeared about 300 BCE, when the earliest Jewish belief in a resurrection is expressed in the earliest books within *1 Enoch*. It continued as a major belief in Second Temple Judaism until roughly 70 CE, when the Temple and Jerusalem were burned by Titus's Roman troops.

The belief in a postmortem resurrection was affirmed in numerous Jewish groups or sects. It characterizes the books of Enoch (in *1 Enoch*), which are composed by Jews, perhaps in Galilee, from about 300 BCE to maybe 4 BCE (the end of the reign of Herod the Great). In 164 BCE the author or compiler of Daniel, in chapter 12, clearly presents his belief in a resurrection from the dead. Those living at Qumran were influenced not only by the *Books of Enoch* (with the exception of chs. 37–71) and Daniel, since numerous copies of these works were found in the Qumran Caves. The Essenes living at Qumran were also influenced by *On Resurrection* and *Pseudo-Ezekiel,* and these two compositions among the Dead Sea Scrolls clearly espouse resurrection belief; they may have been composed, or edited finally, at Qumran. Not only Qumranites, but also Essenes living elsewhere in Palestine, or Jews similar to them, believed in the resurrection, since this belief shaped the early Jewish sections of the *Testaments of the Twelve Patriarchs* (see ch. 4). Shortly before the reign of Herod the Great (37–4 BCE), a Pharisaic-like group of Jews in Jerusalem composed a new hymnbook, the *Psalms of Solomon.* This hymnbook affirms belief in a resurrection.

Mainstream Judaism also affirmed belief in the resurrection, since this confession shapes the *Amidah,* or *Eighteen Benedictions* (see ch. 6). Of course, the Palestinian Jesus Movement was a sect within Early Judaism; and the Fourth Evangelist records that a belief in a resurrection at the end of time was held by some of Jesus' followers before his crucifixion. There is evidence that perhaps the Samaritans, before 70 CE, also believed in the resurrection of the dead (cf. *b. Sanhedrin* 90b and *Memar Marqa* 2.9), even though the undisputable evidence is found in the eighteenth-century *Yom ha-Din.*[21]

It is clear, then, that expectation of a resurrection, most likely at the end of time, was common coin among many groups or sects of Jews during the Second Temple Period. Even though the only group of Jews who are recorded to be opposed to a belief in the resurrection of the dead are the Sadducees (Matt 22:23–33), many other Jews might have also been skeptical.

Something new, however, did emerge within Second Temple Judaism, and it occurred shortly after Jesus' crucifixion.

Although the Palestinian Jesus Movement antedates Jesus' crucifixion, a new proclamation appeared in that movement within Judaism. A sect of Jews began to claim that the crucified Jesus has been raised by God and has appeared to his followers. The proclamation (kerygma) that the crucified one has been raised by God and has appeared to his disciples and followers, especially Mary Magdalene, Peter, and Jesus' brother James, was sensational — in both the good and negative senses. Why should those outside the Jesus sect believe it when we have numerous sources that clarify that those within the sect found it impossible to believe?

The Jesus group was a sect, since it was recognized as distinct and outside mainstream Judaism, and the leading priests and authorities in Jerusalem (the sacerdotal aristocracy) actively persecuted members of the Jesus Movement. They chose a man named Saul to arrest the Jews who held the belief that Jesus was the Christ (Messiah) and was resurrected. This Pharisee, whose name was changed to Paul, while on the way to persecute "the idiots" who held these beliefs, was confronted by this resurrected Jesus, according to his own account and according to a secondary source (Acts). Paul even stressed that the sine qua non of the new faith (or "Way," as in Acts) was the belief in the resurrection of the crucified one.

Distinguished humanists have stressed that Jesus appeared, in a resurrected form, only to those who had followed him and believed in him. They thus claim that the faith of Jesus' followers generated belief in Jesus' resurrection. These thinkers miss a major narrative, and a study of it indicates either that they have not read carefully or that their emphasis is foolish and false. Saul, who was vehemently opposed to the new sect, saw the foundations of his former assurance shattered. On the way to arrest believers in Damascus, as he had done in Jerusalem, Saul believed that these Jews have blasphemed and undermined the uniqueness of Yahweh. This belief is transformed into the belief that Jesus has been raised by God. In Gal 1 and 1 Cor 15, Paul asserts that the resurrected

Jesus has appeared to him. Thus, a nonbeliever — indeed, the staunch opponent of the Palestinian Jesus Movement — claims that the resurrected Jesus has appeared to him, and during the time when he did not believe in Jesus' resurrection.

Paul is the parade example of a "nonbeliever" believing in Jesus' resurrection. Is it not axiomatic that if the resurrected Jesus appeared so unexpectedly — as he did according to the New Testament narratives — that resistance to belief in his resurrection would dissipate as quickly as an iceberg nearing the subtropics?

Resurrection Belief and Modern Science

The preceding pages report that some authorities in the church reject belief in Jesus' resurrection because it is against the discoveries of modern science. Such ecclesiastical thinkers present four claims. First, they argue that those who are dead, like Jesus, can never raise themselves. That is certainly true, both in terms of science, commonsense experience, and the biblical record. In the preceding chapters (esp. ch. 6), it was demonstrated that the earliest proclamation was not that Jesus raised himself from the dead. According to the New Testament authors, Peter, Paul, and other Jews claimed that God, the Creator, raised Jesus up from the dead.

Second, some Christian leaders claim that resurrection faith can no longer be affirmed because it is based on a trifold universe. They are correct in pointing out that this cosmology has certainly been disproved by astronomers. It is also clear (see ch. 6) that Peter and Paul, and the other early Jews, did not imagine a cosmos that was trifurcated. In Jesus' culture, Jews and even the apocalyptists contended that there were two realms: the heavens and the earth (cf., e.g., Gen 1:1; *1 Enoch, Apocalypse of Abraham, 4 Ezra* [= 2 Esdras], *2 Baruch*).

Third, the Christians who argue that we should jettison belief in a resurrection point out that the cosmos is closed and follows set laws; hence, they claim, miracles are impossible.

The preceding pages have demonstrated that, beginning with Heisenberg, Hubble, and Einstein and continuing through such minds as Stephen Hawking, luminaries in the world of science have been observing an open and expanding universe, with indeterminacy as a major factor. Thus, it cannot be claimed that miracles are impossible; in fact, if every birth is a miracle, cannot death be similarly understood? Early thinkers in the church pointed out that nature presents us with transformations (or transmogrifications) of forms; for example, Athenagoras (second century CE) in his *On the Resurrection of the Dead* defended resurrection belief by pointing out that resurrection is harmonious with other aspects of nature, as in the transformation of a moth into a butterfly.

Fourth, some erudite and influential Christians — presently J. D. Crossan and G. Lüdemann — have claimed that the wish became the father of the thought: that the followers of Jesus wished he were still alive, felt that he was still alive in their community, and thence claimed that he was risen in their midst. It was demonstrated in chapter 6 (above) that the authors of the New Testament documents do not record any evidence of such a wish. In fact, they independently, and in diverse ways, stressed that the followers of Jesus resisted such a belief. Cleopas had lost hope after the crucifixion (Luke). Mary Magdalene goes to the tomb, sees the empty tomb, and asks a man she assumes is a gardener where he has placed Jesus' corpse (John 20). Peter gives up on Jesus and announces that he is going fishing; and the others, including the sons of Zebedee and the Beloved Disciple, follow him, taking up their previous occupations. Even Thomas resists the enthusiastic claims of men who had been hiding behind closed doors.

Contemplating the concept of resurrection generally, and Jesus' resurrection specifically, allows fresh questions to arise. Here are some that become conspicuous as I read and edit the preceding chapters: Will reflections on the origins of the concept of resurrection help remove the greatest of Christian heresies, anti-Semitism, which is really anti-Judaism? Will the genuinely Jewish dimension of Christian proclamation be recognized? What is the future of theological reflection on the resurrection? Will resurrection faith continue, as in Paul's Epistles, to stand at the center of Christian theological inquiry? Should it, and if so, Why? Will the wonder that attends peering far out into the cosmos or deep within molecular structure help contemplation on postmortem resurrection?

Summary

In summation, the scholars who have contributed to this collection of studies have demonstrated that the concept of resurrection was developed by Jews living within Palestine after the Babylonian exile (although it is clear that resurrection belief was not limited to Palestine, since the author of *2 Maccabees* sent his letter to Jews living in the Diaspora, encouraging them to observe Hanukkah). Resurrection belief was not limited to apocalyptic theology. Within Early Judaism, it probably appeared first within apocalyptic circles and was expressed in apocalypses (*1 Enoch*, Daniel). Obviously, belief in the resurrection at the end of time was held by more than the Pharisees. It was a hope expressed, as we have seen, by many groups or sects, including the Enoch groups, the Essenes, and members of Jesus' group before his crucifixion.

As many Christians, and some Jews, have recently stressed, belief in a general resurrection and also in the resurrection of Jesus by God are concepts held by intelligent persons who are highly skilled, well trained, and knowledgeable about advances made by Einstein and Hocking and many other luminaries in the world of science. Creation from nothing (ex nihilo) is a concept affirmed by Jews, developed by Christians, and observed in the big bang and the appearances of far-off galaxies. Wonder attends reflecting on the creating Creator and on life itself in a complex universe that is only partially visible to the Hubble telescope.

Obviously, the present book raises many unanswered questions. These are perennial. Some may be suggested: Is life possible only on this tiny blue planet? Is life extinguished by death? Is there some form of postmortem existence for each of us who are devoted to the Creator? What lives beyond our graves? If Mother Nature recycles matter and energy, then what is the future of our life-forms?

Belief in a postmortem resurrection is one characteristic of Second Temple Judaism. It defined Jesus' group. The proclamation that "God raised Jesus from the dead" rang out in Jerusalem and Capernaum, and eventually in Rome and throughout the world. There and also where we live, such a scandalous claim was and is rejected as foolishness. More than one of those who have devoted their time and genius by contributing to this symposium have pointed out that such self-assured "savants" correctly perceive the scandalous nature of the claim. Those who have held it cannot point to objective proofs. The belief makes sense only to those who live within the crucible of faith in which Jesus' resurrection is a living reality.

The empty tomb did not answer the questions left by Jesus' demise. It raised the question "Where is Jesus' corpse?" The astonishment of Jesus' followers in seeing the risen Lord is palpable. Eventually, the famous Pharisee, Paul, claimed "assuredly Christ has been raised from the dead, the firstfruits of those who have fallen asleep" (1 Cor 15:20). According to our Scriptures, his claim was founded not only on faith but also on experience.

Notes

1. R. C. Zaehner, *Hinduism* (London: Oxford University Press, 1962), 75.

2. Tibetan Buddhism develops the concept of the afterlife. See esp. W. G. Oxtoby, *World Religions: Eastern Traditions* (2d ed.; Oxford: Oxford University Press, 2002), 257.

3. Resurrection belief appears frequently in the Quran. God informs Mary that her son, Jesus, will "revive the dead with God's

permission" (*The House of Imran* III:3:49. As a child in a cradle, Jesus states, "Peace be on the day I was born, and the day I shall die and the day I am raised to life again!" (*Mary* XVI:19:33). For the Arabic text and translation, see T. B. Irving, *The Noble Qur'an* (Brattle-boro, VT: Amana Books, 1992). G. Parrinder rightly clarifies that the "'resurrection of the flesh' of all men has been held by Muslims and Christians down to modern times." Parrinder, *Jesus in The Qur'an* (Oxford: Oneworld Publications, 1995), 123.

4. See esp. *Phaedo, Apology of Socrates.*

5. This concept is developed in J. H. Charlesworth, *The Serpent: A Good or Evil Symbol* (Anchor Bible Reference Library; New York: Doubleday, 2006).

6. For the Greek and English translation, see E. J. Edelstein and L. Edelstein, *Asclepius* (Baltimore and London: Johns Hopkins University Press, 1945, 1998), 1:8. Apollodorus of Athens lived in the second century BCE, but the extant *Bibliotheca* dates from the first or second century CE.

7. M. Dahood, *Psalms I* (Anchor Bible; Garden City, NJ: Doubleday, 1965, 1966), 93.

8. W. F. Albright heralded Dahood's work on the Psalter enthusiastically; others, especially Y. Avishur were more restrained. Yet, resurrection belief is apparent in Ugaritic. Albright, "Some Excavation Reports and Syntheses," *Bulletin of the American Schools of Oriental Research* 186 (1967): 53–54. Y. Avishur, *Studies in Hebrew and Ugaritic Psalms* (Jerusalem: Magness Press, 1994), 23.

9. I am not suggesting that most Jews believed in some form of resurrection belief. The Sadducees, for example, are known for arguing against it.

10. Zoroaster is his Greek name; his Persian name is Zarathushtra (such traditions influenced Nietzsche).

11. See A. Hultgård, "Persian Apocalypticism," in *The Encyclopedia of Apocalypticism* (ed. J. J. Collins; New York: Continuum, 1999), 1:39–83. Also see Hultgård, "Persian Apocalypticism," in *The Continuum History of Apocalypticism* (ed. B. McGinn, J. Collins, and S. Stein; New York: Continuum, 2003), 30–63. Most of the Pahlavi texts were edited in the ninth century CE, but they have an Avestan background. See Hultgård's contribution (and those by S. S. Hartman and G. Widengren) in *Apocalypticism in the Mediterranean World and the Near East* (2d ed.; ed. D. Hellholm; Tübingen: Mohr Siebeck, 1989). Ancient Iranian religion can be traced back to approximately the third millennium BCE; see W. W. Malandra, *An Introduction to Ancient Iranian Religion* (Minneapolis: University of Minnesota Press, 1983), 4.

12. J. Duchesne-Guillemin, *The Hymns of Zarathustra* (trans. M. Henning; London: John Murray, 1952), 143.

13. See the discussion by E. M. Yamauchi and the works he cites in *Persia and the Bible* (Grand Rapids, Michigan: Baker, 1996), 456.

14. Hultgård, "Persian Apocalypticism," 69.

15. Plutarch knew some of these traditions (cf. *De Iside et Osiride*, chs. 46–47), and he most likely was working from the fourth-century BCE writings of Theopompos. In Pahlavi the general resurrection or the "raising of the dead" is *ristaxez*.

16. By the third century CE we must allow for Christian (and perhaps Jewish) influences on Persian thought.

17. Translated by E. W. West, *Pahlavi Texts* (Delhi: Motilal Banarsidass, 1962 [originally published at the Clarendon Press in 1880), 5:122.

18. See also J. Duchesne-Guillemin, *Symbols and Values in Zoroastrianism* (New York: Harper and Row, 1966), 4.

19. J. H. Charlesworth, "A Critical Comparison of the Dualism in 1QS 3:13–4:26 and the 'Dualism' Contained in the Gospel of John," *New Testament Studies* 15 (1968–1969): 389–418.

20. A. F. Segal, *Life After Death: A History of the Afterlife in the Religions of the West* (Anchor Bible Reference Library; New York: Doubleday, 2004), 183. R. C. Zaehner also concluded that "a bodily resurrection at the end of time was probably original to Zoroastrianism," developing his thought that "from the moment that the Jews first made contact with the Iranians they took over the typical Zoroastrian doctrine of an individual afterlife in which rewards are to be enjoyed and punishments endured" (58). Zaehner, *The Dawn and Twilight of Zoroastrianism* (New York: Putnam's Sons, 1961).

21. For a discussion of the debate regarding the date of the earliest evidence of Samaritan belief in a resurrection, see F. Dexinger in *The Samaritans* (ed. A. D. Crown; Tübingen: Mohr [Siebeck], 1989), 282–84.

Contemporary Studies on Resurrection: An Annotated Bibliography

C. D. Elledge

Bailey, Lloyd R. *Biblical Perspectives on Death.* Overtures to Biblical Theology. Philadelphia: Fortress, 1979. A theological study of the biblical authors' exploration of death and its relationship to the Deity, including resurrection of the dead and other visions of the afterlife.

De Boers, Martinus. *The Defeat of Death: Apocalyptic Eschatology in 1 Corinthians 15 and Romans 8.* Journal for the Study of the New Testament Supplement Series 22. Sheffield: Academic, 1998. A comprehensive study of resurrection and its role in Paul's apocalyptic theology, containing an especially careful exposition of 1 Cor 15, the problem of Corinthian understandings about the resurrection, and Paul's typology of the first and last Adam.

Brown, Raymond E. *The Virginal Conception and Bodily Resurrection of Jesus.* New York: Paulist Press, 1975. A theological and textual study of two of the great mysteries of Christian faith from a Catholic perspective. An especially careful analysis of the Gospel resurrection narratives is undertaken in the latter half of the book.

Bultmann, Rudolf. *New Testament and Mythology and Other Basic Writings.* Edited and translated by S. Ogden. Philadelphia: Fortress, 1989. Essays by the epoch-making New Testament scholar and theologian who rejected understanding the resurrection of Jesus as the resuscitation of a dead corpse and reinterpreted the Church's resurrection faith as a living affirmation that the saving power of the cross remains accessible today for all who believe the good news. See also *Kerygma and Myth: A Theological Debate.* Vol. 1. Translated by R. H. Fuller. Edited by H. W. Bartsch. 2d ed. New York: Harper & Row, 1961.

Bynum, Caroline Walker. *The Resurrection of the Body in Western Christianity, 200–1336.* Lectures on the History of Religions, new series, 15. New York: Columbia University Press, 1995. A profound study of how Christianity continued to struggle with the "resurrection body" long after the writings of the New Testament.

Cavallin, Hans C. C. *Life after Death: Paul's Argument for the Resurrection of the Dead in 1 Cor 15.* Lund: Gleerup, 1974. One of the most complete assessments of resurrection of the dead in early Jewish and Christian literature, originally proposed as the "historical background" to a two-volume study of Paul.

Charles, R. H. *A Critical History of the Doctrine of a Future Life in Israel, in Judaism, and in Christianity.* London: Black, 1913. This masterful study provided a complete statement of what could be known about the present topic at the beginning of the twentieth century. Although it is now clearly outdated by more recent discoveries, it remains of value due to its careful exegesis of particular texts, especially in the Pseudepigrapha.

Collins, John J. "Apocalyptic Eschatology as the Transcendence of Death." *Catholic Biblical Quarterly* 36 (1974): 21–43. An important statement about the role of the resurrection within apocalyptic theology, especially in the book of Daniel. Collins's other works on this topic provide a good example of the "minimalist" position on resurrection in the Hebrew Scriptures (e.g., resurrection is first found in Daniel). On Qumran, see pages 110–29 in *Apocalypticism and the Dead Sea Scrolls.* Literature of the Dead Sea Scrolls. New York: Routledge, 1997.

Craig, William Lane. *The Son Rises: The Historical Evidence for the Resurrection of Jesus.* Eugene, OR: Wipf, 2001. An aggressive apology for the historicity of the empty-tomb traditions and the resurrection of Jesus.

Crossan, John Dominic. *Who Killed Jesus? Exposing the Roots of Anti-Semitism in the Gospel Story of the Death of Jesus.* San Francisco: HarperSanFrancisco, 1994. Chapter 6 of this work contains Crossan's highly provocative assessment that Jesus was not buried, but rather cast into a shallow grave, where his body was possibly consumed by dogs.

Cullmann, Oscar. *Immortality of the Soul or Resurrection of the Dead? The Witness of the New Testament.* London: Epworth, 1960. This perceptive work clarified the centrality of resurrection for New Testament theology and helped to clarify what "resurrection" originally meant in Early Christianity, as distinct from immortality.

Dahood, Mitchell. *Psalms.* 3 vols. Anchor Bible. New York: Doubleday, 1965–70. This three-volume commentary on the Psalms often sees poetic and mythical imagery as evidence of genuine resurrection hope. It provides a good example of maximalist readings of the resurrection in the Hebrew Scriptures.

Davies, W. D. *Paul and Rabbinic Judaism: Some Rabbinic Elements in Pauline Theology.* 2d ed. London: SPCK, 1958. In this classic study, Davies restores Paul's theology to the world of Early Judaism. Throughout the study, especially in its final chapter, Paul's resurrection theology plays a prominent role.

Davis, Stephen T., Daniel Kendall, and Gerald O'Collins, eds. *The Resurrection: An Interdisciplinary Symposium on the Resurrection of Jesus.* New York: Oxford University Press, 1997. The proceedings of an impressive symposium of biblical scholars, theologians, and historians, dedicated to the resurrection of Jesus.

Dimant, Devorah. "Resurrection, Restoration and Time-Curtailing in Qumran, Early Judaism and Christianity." *Revue de Qumran* 19 (1999–2000): 527–48. A careful and accessible reading of *Pseudo-Ezekiel* and its concept of the resurrection.

Evans, C. F. *Resurrection in the New Testament.* Studies in New Testament Theology, Second Series 12. London: SCM, 1970. A detailed study of the resurrection narratives in the New Testament. Evans illustrates the apologetical and theological differences among the four New Testament Gospels.

Fuller, Reginald H. *The Formation of the Resurrection Narratives.* Philadelphia: Fortress, 1980. Among the foremost biblical studies that have cast doubt upon the historical veracity of the empty tomb and appearance narratives in the Gospels. The author views the empty-tomb narratives in the Gospels as full of discrepancies and highly conditioned by redaction. They present theological explorations of the Church's proclamation; not history.

Greenspoon, Leonard J. "The Origin of the Idea of Resurrection." Pages 189–240 in *Traditions in Transformation: Turning Points in Biblical Faith.* Edited by B. Halpern and J. Levenson. Winona Lake, IL: Eisenbrauns, 1981. Contains a study of ancient Israelite mythological traditions that may have inspired Jewish faith in the resurrection hope.

Habermas, Gary R., and Anthony G. N. Flew. *Did Jesus Rise from the Dead? The Resurrection Debate.* Edited by T. Miethe. San Francisco: Harper & Row, 1987. A lively and honest debate over the resurrection of Jesus, between a contemporary Christian apologist (Habermas) and a philosopher who denies the possibility of miracles (Flew). The debate reveals the opposing values and philosophical presuppositions of two contrary views on the resurrection of Jesus.

Hanson, Paul D. *The Dawn of Apocalyptic.* Philadelphia: Fortress, 1975. Contains Hanson's argument that the origins of apocalyptic theology can be traced to social conflicts, during the time of Israel's restoration (c. 538–500 BCE). The work further envisions apocalyptic theology as an intensification of mythological and poetic imagery already found in Israel's prophetic writings.

Heinemann, Joseph. *Prayer in the Talmud.* Studia Judaica 9. Berlin, New York: de Gruyter, 1977. This treatment of liturgical writings in rabbinic Judaism includes a careful treatment of the Amidah (or Eighteen Benedictions), which contain reference to the resurrection.

Hengel, Martin. *Judaism and Hellenism: Studies in Their Encounter in Palestine during the Early Hellenistic Period.* 2 vols. Translated by J. Bowden. London: SCM, 1974. Hengel's magisterial study of Hellenization in early Jewish society contains a careful and insightful treatment of ancient resurrection hope (see 1:196ff.). It is especially valuable for helping us realize the relationships between astral immortalization in Hellenism and in Judaism.

Horst, Pieter van der. *Ancient Jewish Epitaphs: An Introductory Survey of a Millennium of Jewish Funerary Epigraphy (300 BCE–700 CE).* Contributions to Biblical Exegesis and Theology 2. Kampen: Pharos, 1991. Early Jewish attitudes toward death and the afterlife can be studied through the inscriptions left upon burial sites. This book provides an excellent survey of the epigraphic evidence on this question.

Kittel, Bonnie P. *The Hymns of Qumran: Translation and Commentary.* SBLDS 50. Chico, CA: Scholars, 1981. This commentary on the *Thanksgiving Hymns* (thesis, Graduate Theological Union, 1975) provides valuable notes for assessing the possibility of resurrection hope within this document.

Lapide, Pinchas. *The Resurrection of Jesus: A Jewish Perspective.* Translated by W. C. Linss. Minneapolis: Augsburg, 1983. As captivating and controversial today as it was when it first appeared some twenty years ago, Lapide's study of the resurrection led him to believe that Jesus was raised by God in conformity with ancient Jewish beliefs about the resurrection.

Martin-Achard, Robert. *From Death to Life: A Study of the Development of the Doctrine of the Resurrection in the Old Testament.* Translated by J. Smith. Edinburgh: Oliver & Boyd, 1960. A comprehensive study of possible passages in the Hebrew Scriptures that contain reference to resurrection. Martin-Achard remains among the maximalists who see the resurrection in numerous passages of the Hebrew Bible, even as early as Hosea.

Marxsen, Willi. *The Resurrection of Jesus of Nazareth.* Philadelphia: Fortress, 1970. Marxsen ranks among the most important post-Bultmannian interpreters of Jesus' resurrection. He approaches the resurrection, not as a historical event, but as the abiding presence of "the cause of Jesus" within the lives of his disciples.

Moltmann, Jürgen. *Theology of Hope.* Translated by James Leitch. New York: Harper & Row, 1967; *The Crucified God.* Translated by R. A. Wilson and J. Bowden. New York: Harper & Row, 1974. Together with Pannenberg, Moltmann has restored the resurrection of Jesus to a position of preeminence in Christian theological inquiry. Moltmann has especially explored the theological relationships that exist between the crucified and the risen as central expressions of the Church's Christology.

Nickelsburg, George W. E. *Resurrection, Immortality, and Eternal Life in Intertestamental Judaism.* Harvard Theological Studies 26. Cambridge: Harvard University Press, 1972. One of the foremost academic studies of life after death in Early Judaism, especially in the Apocrypha and Pseudepigrapha. Nickelsburg traces the origins of resurrection hope to Israel's struggle with "the persecuted and vindicated righteous one" — a long-standing theological motif in Israel's prophetic and wisdom writings. On Qumran, see also "Resurrection." Pages 764–67 in vol. 2 of *Encyclopedia of the Dead Sea Scrolls.* Edited by L. Schiffman and J. Vanderkam. 2 vols. Oxford: Oxford University Press, 2000.

O'Collins, Gerald. *What Are They Saying about the Resurrection?* New York: Paulist Press, 1978. An accessible introduction to the current state of theological reflection on the resurrection as of the date of publication, including a fine orientation to the theologies of Pannenberg, Moltmann, and Bultmann, as well as the implications of biblical studies by Marxsen and Fuller. His own approach is more fully stated in *The Resurrection of Jesus Christ: Some Contemporary Issues.* Milwaukee, WI: Marquette University Press, 1993.

Pagels, Elaine. *The Gnostic Gospels*. New York: Random House, 1979. This popular introduction to Gnostic literature and thought opens with a careful survey of controversies over the resurrection in the post-Pauline age, including a detailed survey of how the resurrection was understood in Gnostic Christianity.

Pannenberg, Wolfhart. *Jesus — God and Man*. 2d ed. Translated by L. Wilkins and D. Priebe. Philadelphia: Westminster, 1977. An ambitious exploration of Christology, which asserts the historicity of the resurrection and supports this view with a variety of compelling arguments. Pannenberg's theological reading of the resurrection remains one of the most important approaches to this problem emerging in the twentieth century.

Park, Joseph S. *Conceptions of Afterlife in Jewish Inscriptions: With Special Reference to Pauline Literature*. WUNT 121. Tübingen: Mohr (Siebeck), 2000. An epigraphic study of Jewish burial inscriptions, together with an assessment of how such epigraphic evidence may help us better understand the terminology of Paul.

Perrin, Norman. *The Resurrection Narratives: A New Approach*. London: SCM, 1977. Perrin provides a study of the Gospel resurrection narratives and concludes that the empty-tomb stories are theological interpretations of the resurrection, rather than memories of a historical event.

Polkinghorne, John, Sir. *The God of Hope and the End of the World*. New Haven, CT: Yale University Press, 2003. A theological reading of early Jewish and Christian eschatology, including resurrection of the dead, in light of contemporary challenges facing the human race in the area of science. Polkinghorne's theology indicates how resurrection of the dead remains an important hope in the discussion of theology and science.

Prendergast, R. T. "Resurrection." Pages 680–91 in vol. 5 of *Anchor Bible Dictionary*. Edited by D. Freedman. 6 vols. New York: Doubleday, 1992. A succinct discussion of resurrection beliefs in the Bible and some early Jewish texts. See also the following article under the same title by George W. E. Nickelsburg.

Puech, Émile. "Messianism, Resurrection, and Eschatology." Pages 234–56 in *The Community of the Renewed Covenant: The Notre Dame Symposium on the Dead Sea Scrolls*. Edited by E. Ulrich and J. Vanderkam. Christianity and Judaism in Antiquity 10. Notre Dame, IN: University of Notre Dame Press, 1994. Accessible to the English reader, this essay presents the essence of Puech's theories regarding Essene belief in the future life. He argues that Essenes did believe in the resurrection of the dead. Puech's magisterial study of this question (in French, *La croyance des esséniens en la vie future* [2 vols.; ÉBib, NS, 21; Paris: Gabalda, 1993]) shares the "maximalist" approach to the resurrection in the Hebrew Scriptures and early Jewish literature, including the *Thanksgiving Hymns.*

Schleiermacher, Friedrich. *The Christian Faith.* Edited by H. R. Mackintosh and J. S. Stewart. Philadelphia: Fortress, 1976. Schleiermacher's theology attempted to minimize Christianity's dependence upon supernatural events, such as the resurrection of the dead. Instead, he argued that the essence of Jesus' teachings during his life remains important for Christian theology today. The resurrection is, therefore, not constitutive for Christology.

Schüssler Fiorenza, Francis. *Foundational Theology: Jesus and the Church.* New York: Crossroad, 1984. A critique and revision of the Church's "fundamental theology," which sought to offer apologetic affirmation of the facts of sacred history (such as the resurrection). The author suggests that this theological approach has collapsed and that Christian theology must move toward what he calls "foundational theology," a hermeneutical reconstruction of the meaning of early Christian proclamation from a variety of viewpoints. The resurrection provides the first topic within which this theological proposal is argued.

Segal, Alan. *Life after Death: A History of the Afterlife in Western Religion.* New York: Doubleday, 2004. An ambitious treatment of life after death that begins with the mythological origins of the afterlife in the Ancient Near East and then treats the distinctive development given to the question of the afterlife in Judaism, Christianity, and Islam. The work is distinguished by its wide-ranging survey of materials and by its tendency to view portrayals of the afterlife as projections of existing sociological realities among the religious communities that envisioned the world to come.

Spong, Bishop John Shelby. *The Hebrew Lord.* San Francisco: HarperSanFrancisco, 1993. A popular denial of the resurrection of Jesus.

Tromp, Nicholas J. *Primitive Conceptions of Death and the Nether World in the Old Testament.* Biblica et orientalia 21. Rome: Pontifical Biblical Institute, 1969. An important work for understanding the ancient Near Eastern backgrounds to Israelite beliefs about death and the hereafter. The author employs a careful study of Ugaritic literature, to elucidate biblical views about Sheol and the denizens of that world, the Rephaim (*rĕpā'îm*).

Wright, N. T. *Resurrection of the Son of God.* Christian Origins and the Question of God 3. Minneapolis: Fortress, 2003. A comprehensive historical and theological study of resurrection in Early

Christianity. Through a study of the earliest evidence, the author begins with the assessment that the resurrection is a thoroughly Jewish idea. Then Paul provides the starting point for a thorough exegesis of early Christian beliefs about the resurrection. Wright also endeavors to provide some modest apologetic support for Christian belief in the resurrection of Jesus.

Yarbro Collins, Adela. "The Empty Tomb in the Gospel according to Mark." Pages 107–37 in *Hermes and Athena: Biblical Exegesis and Philosophical Theology*. University of Notre Dame Studies in the Philosophy of Religion 7. Notre Dame, IN: University of Notre Dame Press, 1993. The author has argued that Mark was the first to tell the empty-tomb story and may well have been its original creator.

Index of Ancient Writings

Index of Subjects and Authors